D0930444

MEMORIALS OF THE GREAT WAR IN BRITAIN

THE LEGACY OF THE GREAT WAR

A Series sponsored by the Historial de la Grande Guerre Péronne-Somme

General Editor
JAY WINTER

Previously published titles in the Series

Patrick Fridenson
THE FRENCH HOME FRONT 1914–1918

Stéphane Audoin-Rouzeau
MEN AT WAR 1914–1918

Gerald D. Feldman
ARMY, INDUSTRY, AND LABOR IN GERMANY 1914–1918

Rosa Maria Bracco
MERCHANTS OF HOPE

Adrian Gregory
THE SILENCE OF MEMORY
Armistice Day 1919–1946

Ute Daniel
THE WAR FROM WITHIN
German Working-Class Women in the First World War

Annette Becker
WAR AND FAITH
The Religious Imagination in France, 1914–1930

David W. Lloyd
BATTLEFIELD TOURISM
Pilgrimage and the Commemoration of the Great War in Britain, Australia and Canada, 1919–1939

MEMORIALS OF THE GREAT WAR IN BRITAIN
The Symbolism and Politics of Remembrance

ALEX KING

Oxford • New York

First published in 1998 by
Berg
Editorial offices:
150 Cowley Road, Oxford, OX4 1JJ, UK
70 Washington Square South, New York, NY 10012, USA

Berg is an imprint of Oxford International Publishers Ltd.

Library of Congress Cataloging-in-Publication Data

A catalogue record for this book is available from the Library of Congress.

British Library Cataloguing-in-Publication Data

A catalogue record for this book is available from the British Library.

ISBN 1 85973 983 0 (Cloth)
1 85973 988 1 (Paper)

Typeset by JS Typesetting, Wellingborough, Northants.
Printed in the United Kingdom by WBC Book Manufacturers, Mid Glamorgan.

To the memory of
Anne King
and
Julian Sullivan

Contents

Preface

My interest in war memorials was originally aroused by seeing, in quick succession, two particularly dramatic but contrasting monuments to people killed in the First World War – the memorial to the staff of the Lever Brothers company at Port Sunlight, and the memorial to Edward Horner in the parish church at Mells in Somerset. The first is set in a modern industrial suburb, some of it under construction during the war; the other in a medieval parish church, surrounded by memorials to the dead man's ancestors. The settings complement the monuments in a way which gives them an extraordinary power. In the first, working men in uniform, women and children huddle together, in the midst of the ideal village built for Levers' factory workers, to ward off the attack of an unseen enemy on their homes. In the second, the lonely figure of a young officer rides through the darkness of the church towards eternal light represented by a virgin and child hovering before him in a stained glass window. The emotional impact of these memorials seemed to depend, to a large extent, on the sense of distance which exists between the time and circumstances of their creation and our own time. Trying to penetrate their remoteness involved asking other questions which have always interested me concerning how such things have meaning, and why so much importance is attributed to them. This book is only one step towards answering those questions; but it does, I hope, suggest a fruitful way of approaching them.

I owe two very special debts in the writing of this book. One is to Adrian Forty, who supervised the research on which it is based, and has continued to take a sympathetic interest in what I have done since. The other is to Annabel Gregory, who has read and re-read the text, and given guidance and a great deal of essential encouragement. Both have been excellent advisers and editors, and their clarity of mind has been an indispensable help. It was the Department of History at Birkbeck College that set me on course to writing the book, and its staff played a large part in my qualifying for the British Academy Studentship which provided for the research, and later for a research fellowship at the Institute of Historical Research. I am very grateful to all three institutions for the opportunities they have provided. At Birkbeck, Roy Foster, in particular, gave me early encouragement to undertake something of this sort, and his subsequent support and advice have been very much appreciated. The support and interest of Anne and Walter King have always been of enormous importance to me.

Many people have helped materially in the work, by showing or lending me things, and by talking about the subject. I would particularly like to thank Mark Swennarton, Tom Gretton, John Bourne, Jay Winter, Catherine Moriarty, Angela Gaffney, Nicos Georgiadis, George Yerby, Nick and Wendy Jotcham, Tom Callahan, Richard Glassborow, Alan Dun, Sue Malvern, who introduced me to some important German writing, and Gotthelf Wiedermann, who helped me to understand it. Nick and Anne Raynsford and Pip Phelan kindly lent facilities for the photography. Work on the book involved repeated or extended visits to a number of places which I have very much enjoyed, and I am most grateful for the hospitality of John and Dorothy Millard, Tom Barker of the Scottish National War Memorial, Col. Darmody of the Royal Artillery Charitable Fund, and Tomos Roberts of University College, Bangor. Thanks are also due to the Trustees of the Scottish National War Memorial, the Association of Northumberland Local History Societies and the Royal Artillery Charitable Fund for permission to use their records.

Illustrations

Photographs are by the author.
Dates are those of completion unless otherwise stated.

Introduction

War memorials arouse a variety of emotional responses, ranging from pious devotion to outright hostility. They have also been taken to mean a wide variety of different things, from an exhortation to die for one's country to a warning that war will only be avoided in future if its horror and suffering is not forgotten. These differences, and the controversies to which they give rise, have a long history. John Bright is reported to have told his son, sometime in the 1870s, that the Brigade of Guards' memorial to the Crimean War in Waterloo Place, London, was the commemoration of 'a crime'.[1] In 1992, the unveiling of a memorial to Sir Arthur Harris, chief of RAF Bomber Command in the later part of the Second World War, caused a controversy which reached from London to Dresden. But the power of these memorials to arouse feelings and arguments drains away with the passage of time. All those memorials to the Great War which so often seem lost in the clutter and movement of towns or scattered inconsequentially in parks originally had a resonance which is not readily apparent to us now.

The purpose of this book is to explore the impact of these ubiquitous symbols on the society which created them. It is not essentially a book about works of art and artists, but about a far wider range of commemorative symbols and a wider community of producers. Many memorials were not objects which we would readily recognise as 'symbols'. They could be charitable facilities or services, as well as monuments; and although memorial buildings, of whatever sort, were usually designed by professionals, many ordinary members of the public were involved in their production. Sometimes they exerted a very powerful influence over them.

The majority of war memorials were, indeed, monuments of a conventional type; ranging from familiar abstract symbolic forms, such as the cross or obelisk, to buildings of an equally monumental character, in traditional classical or gothic styles. Occasionally such buildings were large and imposing, like the Scottish National War Memorial in Edinburgh Castle, or Birmingham's Hall of Memory, but most were of a far more intimate character (see Figure 3). On the other hand, there were many memorials which were of quite another nature. Almost all the forms of charitable services which are now familiar to us as the beneficiaries of commemorative funds can be found as war memorials, from inscribed benches in public gardens to hospitals, recreation grounds, and almshouses. A number of memorials have no physical form at all, but only a monetary existence, as funds to provide medical or educational facilities, either for a whole community, or for those in special need.

These un-monumental memorials were also symbols, although their main purpose was to offer a facility, not to evoke an idea. Through their dedication to the dead they were given a distinct meaning. Their helpful functions were chosen as representative of the altruistic ideals which the dead were thought to have embodied. Actions can also be symbols, and we shall need to consider a number of ceremonial and practical actions as being part of the same repertoire of symbols as physical memorials, if we are to discover their full significance. Actions were obviously symbolic when they formed part of a ritual, such as a remembrance ceremony; but practical service also acquired symbolic significance through its dedication to the dead. The service of a district nurse could be made into a symbol in the same way as the provision of a clinic or hospital could be - as an act of homage to the dead and as an example of an ideal.

Commemoration of the First World War is especially interesting as it set a model for the commemoration of most wars subsequently fought by Western nations, both in the pattern of actions it prescribed and in the attitudes it expressed. Moreover, the work of erecting local memorials is remarkably well documented. Although they were not generally erected by local authorities, the memorial committees which did erect them usually handed them over to local authorities for future maintenance, together with the committees' records. These records survive widely in borough and county record offices, and offer a unique body of evidence concerning the creation of public symbols and responses to them.

What Did War Memorials Mean?

The meaning of war memorials was complex and elusive. This may seem surprising at first sight, for such conventional objects, but contemporaries would not have been surprised to hear this said. They knew that memorials could be understood in different ways, and that their capacity to convey a particular meaning was not entirely reliable. The proper understanding of a memorial required a deliberate effort. Commenting on the burial of the Unknown Warrior, the *Manchester Guardian* expressed the conviction that even though the warrior's grave had been completed physically, it still remained necessary to make 'the greatest effort of all - to put into the chosen symbol all the meaning it should have'. A symbol, the writer maintained, can mean anything or nothing. 'All the virtue and energy of its significance come from the heart and mind of him who uses or accepts it.'[2]

In 1925, the *Birmingham Post* said of the city's war memorial, the Hall of Memory:

> Symbols are naturally and inevitably imperfect things even when translated into terms of architecture, and cannot express the deep things of the heart. But within their limits they can go a long way. To a very great extent their success is dependent upon the temper and imagination of the individual. One gets from a poem in marble and granite, as in the case of a book, precisely what one takes to it.[3]

Only the vigilance of right-thinking people would give the commemoration of the dead what the paper believed was its correct meaning. 'Our true task is to make sure the memory is a right memory.'[4] The existence of such doubts about the meaning of memorials suggests that any correspondence between the structures themselves and people's emotional and intellectual responses to war should not be taken for granted. There was a difficulty in connecting the physical forms of memorials with the ideas or feelings which they were intended to articulate, and this raises the question whether or not they were capable of conveying the things which people wished to say about war and death.

Difficulty in representing the experience of war has been noticed in all forms of art, especially where traditional forms of expression were used, although it has been most frequently discussed in connection with literature. Paul Fussell has pointed out that writers who described the war relied on familiar literary conventions to give initial shape to their narratives; but, he argues, the actuality of the war could not be adequately conveyed in any of the available conventions.[5] He sees the creative achievement of their work as lying in the extent to which they managed to overcome this problem.

The most obvious outcome of using a vocabulary which is out of touch with the experience to be described is euphemism. Where euphemism obscures the reality of the thing being described, it may be regarded as dishonest, and charges of dishonesty have often been levelled against official war commemoration. However, there were ways in which the gap between cultural conventions and the desire to articulate an unprecedented experience could be bridged. Familiar forms of expression could be re-worked to accommodate the new experiences which had rendered their previous interpretations hollow. One way of doing this, according to Fussell, is to exploit the ironic possibilities of conventions. He argues that, by invoking the apparently inappropriate literary tradition of the pastoral to describe warfare, writers could distance themselves from what they described, and retain a sense of humanity in the face of an inhuman reality. At the same time, the ironic twists and contrasts which they introduced into their pastoral framework conveyed a sense of the strangeness and brutality of the original experience.[6] As this mode of writing generally had critical and irreverent implications, it was, Fussell acknowledges, unsuitable as a form of consolation, and so not applicable to the commemoration of the dead.[7]

On the other hand, many popular writers of the post-war period had frankly moralistic motives for their work, which gave them much in common with those who organised the commemoration of the dead or designed war memorials. Rosa Maria Bracco has argued that such writers did not resort to irony to portray the war, but attempted to re-define moral and political values of the pre-war period and apply them to the post-war world.[8] Even though they clung to established forms of thought and expression, it seems that they too had to make a deliberate effort to reconcile these with a new awareness of war.

In particular, the moral concepts which had long been central to the commemoration of war, and were frequently alluded to in memorials, were subjected to this process of re-definition. Hugh Quigley's reflections on the well-worn notions of glory and heroism, with which he concluded the diary of his experiences of 1917, is a striking example. Glory, for Quigley, had been present in the war, but he understood it as the persistence of the essential beauty of life through even the most terrible circumstances. This was a view he appears to have adopted at the front. To see 'the beautiful in nature, even in the bleak horror of shell-holes, seemed the essence of life to me, the only thing worth seeking in the misery of this war.'[9] He returned to this thought later, lying wounded in a hospital bed: 'There are other glories in life than a senseless rushing over No Man's Land into an improbable victory', he wrote; 'glory is a silent thing, a chaste thing sent from a great beneficent power to ennoble the spirit; it lives in the air, in the walls, in the pillars, in the beds, and comes through them to perception'.[10]

Heroism, too, had been present in the war, but this he re-interpreted as the affirmation of the human spirit against injury and despair. Opposite him in the hospital ward was 'the only hero I have ever met'. This man had been wounded by shrapnel and a bayonet in the stomach. Yet he had survived, full of humour, injuries which Quigley believed he himself would not have had sufficient will-power to survive.[11]

For many, like Quigley, who reflected on the war in personal reminiscences or in remembrance of the dead, old assumptions about glory and heroism would no longer do. While the words themselves might confer honour on the dead in a way sanctified by tradition, they had now to mean something much larger than their former patriotic, masculine and military connotations. But in making their re-interpretations publicly clear, they issued a challenge to those who did not share them, and who therefore had in some way to reply. As a result, the understanding of symbols took on the character of a public debate. This was a socially creative and individually absorbing part of the commemoration of the dead. Its consequence was that memorials could not, in fact, 'embody in permanent form ideas about war',[12] but offered people the opportunity to give their own interpretations. A great deal of this book is devoted to examining the variety of ways in which people interpreted commemorative symbols.

What commemoration meant to contemporaries was, I contend, a matter which they themselves had to work out, and we must reconstruct their sense of meaning from their own creative process. This process was fundamentally political, because it relied for its organisation on the institutions of local politics, on the press, and on other forms of association whose activities, if not overtly political, had political implications. It required the exercise of official and unofficial power, which is a normal part of the life of such institutions and associations. Personal feelings and needs were deeply involved in the practice of commemoration; but it was the organisation of public action which gave it form. At the same time, commemoration raised political issues which participants had to address, and they exploited it to pursue various purposes which they believed to be valuable. All these factors influenced the meaning they attributed to symbols and ceremonies. I argue, therefore, that the meanings given to commemoration depended to a very large extent on the procedures available to facilitate and control the conduct of it, and on the ulterior aims of those who participated in it.

Public commemoration of those killed in war has been discussed by a number of writers, and their approaches to the subject fall broadly into two groups. Some argue that the principal force was the affirmation and propagation of political ideas about wars and the nations which fight them.[13] Others argue that the need to express and resolve the emotional traumas caused by war[14] was the principal force shaping commemoration. The latter see the erection of memorials as a requirement of the grieving process, given added force by the numbers involved, or as part of the process by which ex-combatants came to terms with their war experiences and established their post-war sense of identity. Both approaches have provided important insights into the meanings of war memorials; but the primacy they have given to a single psychological process or political intention in the formation of commemorative symbols leads, I think, to an incomplete account of both their origins and their social functions.

Samuel Hynes has contrasted official memorials of the Great War with what he sees as an alternative and opposed genre of 'anti-monuments'. The former he sees as 'official acts of closure . . . that bring war to a grand and affirming conclusion'.[15] They affirm, he argues, the grand concepts traditionally associated with an heroic and romantic view of war, and ignore the squalor, the suffering and the waste. There were many who did not accept an heroic and sanitised view of the war, especially amongst those who had directly experienced fighting and killing; but in order to reject this view, Hynes argues, they also had to reject the monumental forms in which it was expressed.

As a result, they produced in their paintings, poetry, novels, journalism and autobiographies, a body of anti-monuments, which were, characteristically, 'monuments of loss: loss of values, loss of a sense of order, loss of belief in the words and images which the past had transmitted as valid'.[16] This disillusioned reflection on the war constituted 'a counter-culture, rooted in rejection of the war and its principles'. It found expression in resolutely non-monumental media which avoided any connection with traditionally heroic accounts of war. In Hynes's view, the monuments themselves were irredeemable.

Although Hynes is right to identify the existence of vehemently opposed opinions about the war, he is mistaken in assuming that 'the rejection of the war and its principles' also required the rejection of traditional forms for commemorating the dead (which, as I have already pointed out, were not necessarily 'monumental' in the artistic sense). One of his chief examples of a maker of anti-monuments is the journalist Philip Gibbs, who wrote a number of books after the war containing vivid and harrowing accounts of the nature of face-to-face combat, and of the brutalising effect which war service had on those who performed it. However, Gibbs was also a great believer in monumental (as against utilitarian) war memorials, as he believed they would remind people in future of the 'slaughter and ruin', and teach them to avoid such stupidity in future.[17] A number of people rejected official commemoration outright, like the journalist Francis Meynell, who condemned the burial of the Unknown Warrior in Westminster Abbey, in 1920, as a 'pageant' organised by those responsible for the war in the first place.[18] A great many, however, of differing shades of opinion, thought it right to join in the public commemorative ceremonies, and in the erection of memorials, although they understood what they were doing in widely differing ways.

Jay Winter has understood the meaning of memorials to be more fluid than Hynes. He sees this as a function of the passage of time, and argues that, initially, their purpose was the expression of grief and the facilitation of mourning. Once grief and a sense of horror had dissipated, they would accommodate quite different meanings, and their primary purpose was replaced by others. Winter bases his argument on an examination of the rituals performed at memorials, especially unveilings.[19]

These ritual events undoubtedly constituted interpretations of memorials, but they were not, in fact, the earliest occasions on which people had the opportunity to express their sense of a memorial's meaning. Before memorials could be the objects of ceremonial attention, they had to be built. Building them involved discussion about their purpose and meaning, which was carried on in public and committee meetings, in newspapers and in pamphlets. These discussions generally centred not on how to express or assuage grief, but how to express moral or political values. Such ideas may be seen as a way in which meaning was attributed to death, and thus as a means of consolation to the bereaved; but they also constituted meanings in their own right. They were regularly referred to in commentaries on memorials, even before they were built, or in reports of ceremonies held at them, as if they were of primary significance. At any time, the memorial would be interpreted from a variety of points of view, each of which gave priority to a different aspect of its character, or to a different matter of concern to the interpreter.

The wider political context of war commemoration is also important in creating differences of practice and interpretation. Ken Inglis and Jock Phillips have identified an important instance of this in Australia, where an unusually high proportion of memorials, by international standards, are dedicated to all who served in the war, not just to the dead. They argue that this is due to the absence of conscription in Australia, and to the political controversy which surrounded the government's unsuccessful attempt to introduce it. The controversy lasted beyond the end of the war, and had an effect on post-war ideas about citizenship.[20] In a number of countries, especially Germany, commemoration of the war dead appears to have been conducted and understood in ways unlike those typical in Britain. These differences provide an important insight into the way in which the social institutions and political circumstances of different societies could affect the making and interpretation of symbols. It will not be possible to undertake a proper international study here, but I shall make comparisons in a few instances, where suitable evidence is available.

Contemporary interpretations, and especially the differences of response which they reveal, should be at the centre of our attempt to understand what war memorials meant, because they provide us with what Timothy Clark has called 'tests of appropriateness'[21] for our reconstructions of the meanings of memorials. Without such tests, our formal or iconographical analyses are liable to be anachronistic and contradictory, as we are merely repeating, out of historical context, the interpretative exercises contemporaries were themselves performing. Clark is also exemplary in his exploration of differences and difficulties of interpretation. Misunderstandings, failures to communicate, breakdowns in the protocols which normally govern the creation and viewing of art provide, in his work, important evidence for elucidating the contemporary impact of works of art. I have taken a similar course in this book. Many of the examples in my argument are significant precisely because they show breakdowns in the normal procedure for commemorating the dead. The subsequent attempts to restore normality make clear how the normal procedure worked, and the intentions and forms of power which lay behind it.

Symbols and Society

It is frequently suggested that symbols, along with rituals, affect people's behaviour or outlook by propagating fundamental ideas about the world. People then use these ideas as reference points for understanding what is happening to them. Writers who adopt this approach do so in order to acknowledge that beliefs and cultural activities have their own autonomous life and power, and cannot simply be understood as by-products of supposedly larger and more potent social forces such as economic change. They wish to assert that the symbolic repertoire of a society is itself a formative influence on social order and change.

The anthropologist Clifford Geertz has exerted a significant influence on recent historical studies of symbols as instruments of social and political stability or change.[22] The basic assumption behind these studies is that symbols and rituals represent the social world as if it was organised according to certain categories. People come to accept these categories as natural, and as necessarily true descriptions of reality, either through acquiring familiarity with them in the normal process of socialisation (in societies where traditional authority remains in force), or through deliberately adopting a new outlook, involving a new set of categories (where a change in the structure of power has occurred).[23] In so far as categories are shared, they provide individuals with a common understanding of the form and processes of the society they inhabit, and with common values through which they can relate to one another.[24] Thus the civic parade in the United States has been seen as 'a public lexicon that organised the diverse population of the city into manageable categories', and performed a 'cultural and social service during times of major transformation'.[25]

According to Geertz, such shared categories, expressed in symbols and entailing a body of social values, are perceived as sacred, revealing what appears to be an ultimate truth about the character of human society and its relation to nature.[26] The 'sacred', in this sense, stands at the centre of the social order, as an explanation of it, and as a guarantee of its stability. When these categories cease to be credible, new ones have to be found and embodied in symbolic expressions. They then provide the basis for new standards of social behaviour and new institutions.[27] If the categories in question cease to be credible only to a section of society, members of that section re-interpret the symbols concerned. They deploy their new system of interpretation in opposition to the prevailing system, to the values associated with it, and to the social structure it sustains, as a political challenge.[28]

I share the conviction that symbols and symbolic action play an important part in creating social stability or change; but I do not share the belief that they do this by communicating ideas and obtaining implicit assent to them. In fact, to see symbols in such terms obscures much of their relation to the behaviour of their creators and audiences. The communication of ideas plays an important part in producing and understanding symbols, but other social processes are crucial influences in shaping symbolic activity and imagery, and in determining their effects on people. In modern Western society the most important of these social processes are, on the one hand, commerce and, on the other, the power of institutions to promote public action, to control public space, and to police behaviour. Political performances of the sort so often discussed in terms derived from Geertz involve policing audiences as much as addressing them, and pageants of state require organisation and money which are supplied by a bureaucracy able to deploy the ultimate sanction of force against its subjects.[29] The part played by institutional power in organising these activities must call into question the extent to which they depend on or are animated by shared values or categories of thought.

An alternative to the theory that symbolic displays embody the fundamental shared values of a society is the idea that they are the expression of deep communal emotions which exist quite independently of beliefs. David Kertzer has gone further than other writers in allowing for variation in the understanding of symbolic acts, maintaining that 'ritual can serve political organisations by producing bonds of solidarity without requiring uniformity of belief'.[30] No consensus on the meaning of a symbolic action is necessary at all, he argues.

Certainly, a variety of interpretations is evident, in pluralist societies, amongst participants in rituals. There must, nevertheless, be consensus on the practical aspects of organising and resourcing symbolic events, and attracting and controlling participants. Flags waved at a jubilee, or chants at a football match, may be emotional acts, but they are parts of larger occasions which offer appropriate moments, formally or informally defined, for them. Organising such occasions requires a great deal of rational choice, calculation of interest, and negotiation of consensus. To Kertzer, these utilitarian considerations are irrelevant;[31] but they are of central importance to the understanding of symbols. In Kertzer's view, symbolic acts are expressive gestures performed by collectivities. I shall treat them, on the contrary, as media of expression produced by collectivities, because this will give a far fuller account of their relation to the social formations in which they occur.

An Alternative Approach

To make adequate sense of memorials to the Great War, we need an approach to symbolism which does not purport to reveal the underlying meaning of symbols, but describes the process by which people came to see meaning in them. The anthropologist Dan Sperber has argued that the interpretation of a symbol does not reveal a meaning which it communicates, nor does it tell us what purpose the symbol serves for its users. It is what he calls a 'development' or 'extension' of the symbol.[32] A symbol, he says, does not contain the kind of logical or referential elements which constitute a proposition, so an interpretation of it cannot be the elucidation of something which has already been said in it. An interpretation is actually an extrapolation from the symbol, not an analysis of its content. Taking its cue from associations which the symbol calls to mind, the interpretation develops those associations further, in a way which relates the symbol to the situation in which the interpretation takes place.

Malcolm Quinn has applied Sperber's work to the modern European use of the swastika as a political symbol. A symbol, he says, acts as a focal point around which people assemble their thoughts, drawing together diverse ideas which may not readily be associated with each other, but which can be associated with the symbol, largely because of the symbol's lack of specific meaning. The symbol 'focuses and channels our construction of sense and meaning without itself being "meaningful"'. Quinn stresses that symbols are objects to be used by people, rather than signs to be understood, but that one important use of them is to elicit interpretations.[33]

Contemporaries clearly thought that war memorials and commemorative ceremonies did and should have explicit meanings, and they devoted a great deal of time and paper to interpretations which provided meanings. But it is useful to follow Sperber in regarding their interpretations as elaborations of the symbols, rather than as revelations of meanings already encoded in them. These elaborations gave the symbols relevance to a particular topic, made them appear important and, indeed, 'meaningful'. In other words: the process of interpretation did not spell out meanings which ceremonies and memorials contained; rather, it attributed meaning to them, making them into valued symbols.

If war memorials do not convey messages, what are they for? The symbols and rituals of commemoration, and the symbolic language commonly attached to them, did not themselves propose how people should make sense of the war, or of social relations in the post-war world. Rather, they were things which required sense to be made of them, offering opportunities for people to express the varied senses they were making of the war and its aftermath.

Memorials functioned chiefly as focal points for collective activity – the activity involved in preparing for or producing them, using and maintaining them. To perform these acts people came together to form organised groups and practical relationships. Knowing they had different views, they needed an etiquette for these activities which allowed for difference. The one they adopted was participatory and, in a sense, democratic, consulting and making decisions accountably. It demanded mutual respect for differing views, and willingness to accept the decisions of the majority. To join in the creative, meaning-giving, processes of commemoration one had to join in the relationships prescribed by this etiquette.

To act thus in co-operation required people to communicate publicly in explicit and literal ways - in speech and writing - about issues which readily came to mind as a result of their feelings about the war and the dead. They might not come to an agreement about what they wanted their memorial to mean, but they had, at least, to establish a working relationship which would accommodate their differences of view. This meant each knowing what the other thought, and stating the terms on which they would participate, by making their interpretations clear to each other. In so doing, they were advertising their sectional views of war and death as far as the etiquette of co-operation allowed; but they were also using the expression of interpretations to form and adjust the relationships required to create the memorial in the first place. Their interpretations had both expressive and practical (that is to say, organisational) purposes. Their practical purposes might well entail modifications of their expressive ones, and we must understand contemporary interpretations in this light.

Furthermore, war commemoration offered potential benefits to participants for purposes which had nothing intrinsically to do with the war or the dead. One of the objects of public commemorations before the Great War, such as Victoria's jubilees, had been to draw together respectable organisations of all creeds and classes to celebrate, in co-operation, aspects of their communal life. They were also opportunities for participants to demonstrate practically their sense of civic responsibility and their importance in the community, and to elicit the recognition and respect of the other participants.[34] Public commemoration entailed assembling resources and creating a large audience. It offered funds which could be put to philanthropic uses, a market for artists, a platform for politicians. These practical benefits were recognised by contemporaries and exploited as much in connection with commemoration of the Great War as in earlier times. Consequently, we must look beyond what was being said about the dead, and consider the range of other things which were being done in the process of erecting a war memorial, as these played a crucial part in determining choices made about memorials, and so affected their meaning.[35]

In order to integrate the expressive and practical dimensions of commemoration into a single account, I propose to consider it chiefly as a process by which the participants formed relationships with each other. I will investigate how relationships were constructed, and what purposes they served, in order to describe the range of purposes which were being served through commemoration. Specifically, I will examine the institutional power applied in forming and managing these relationships, and the conventions which prompted public expectations of how they should work and what they should achieve. In this way, I will try to analyse a cultural activity - commemoration as a means by which the dead, and through them values, were represented - in relation to the exercise of formal and informal political power, without collapsing one into the other, but also without disengaging them from each other.

Where commemoration drew on existing practices it had to be organised, and, when memorials were involved, financed. Where it departed from precedent, new idioms had to be developed and popularised. It required, therefore, a large amount of creative effort. Much of this was the responsibility of professions traditionally thought of as creative, especially artists, architects, and writers; but many of the actions performed and ideas expressed in commemoration were introduced at the prompting of others, such as clergy or government ministers. In addition, as it was normal practice for members of the public to be involved in the choice of a local war memorial, they too had to decide what they wanted to say about the war and how best to say it.

My argument is divided into two parts. The first six chapters examine the erection of memorials, and consider what their purpose was. Chapter 1 introduces the principal actors - local committees - and describes their membership and the conventions which prescribed the way they should work. Chapter 2 looks at the origins of these conventions in the nineteenth century and in the Great War itself. It describes the pre-war precedents which informed the work of memorial committees, and the use which had been made of these precedents during the war to commemorate the dead through remembrance ceremonies and war shrines with both a consolatory and a propagandist purpose.

Chapters 3 and 4 discuss how people thought about the different types of memorial which they might erect, and how a community eventually chose one. One of the main functions of war memorial committees was to give people an opportunity to talk about commemoration, to air their differences of opinion and to work out a form of memorial project which would bring together all the diverse interests within the local community. However, it was not the arguments which people used in favour of one kind of memorial or another which ultimately determined what would be erected. This depended on who was best able to exert the authority needed to direct the memorial project. It depended on who could obtain the money and professional services required, and under what conditions they would allow them to be used. It was essentially a question of the power to allocate and control resources.

Chapters 5 and 6 consider the role of artists in commemoration and the symbolism of war memorial art. The professional authority and experience of artists played an important part in establishing the consensus required for a memorial project to be a success. Artists' methods of dealing with clients, choosing appropriate imagery, and presenting their designs in an accessible way assisted greatly in making public participation coherent and in creating confidence in a proposed memorial. While most monuments took forms which were already widely familiar, some new forms which seemed conspicuously relevant to the experience of war were developed. In either case, memorials were subjected to a constant stream of words, in print or speech, which suggested interpretations of them and connected them with ideas about the war. The opportunity to make interpretations, and to debate differences of interpretation, enabled a wide range of participants to join in the process of giving meaning to their memorials, rather than merely donating resources to be used at the behest of civic leaders and artists.

The last three chapters discuss more broadly the meanings attributed to war commemoration, in order to explain why contemporaries understood memorials as they did, and what they achieved by erecting them. Chapter 7 describes the moral qualities attributed to the dead, and why general assent was given to this extraordinarily elevated view of otherwise ordinary people. They were seen, traditionally enough, as heroic, but as having not so much military as ethical qualities of the highest order, and they were held up as the embodiment of supreme human values. The moral qualities of the dead were also regarded as qualities the living should emulate if they were genuinely to honour them, and Chapter 8 discusses how people tried to put this obligation into practice, making remembrance of the dead as much a political debate as a commemorative ritual.

But in spite of the political differences expressed in it, commemoration of the war dead remained a remarkably united movement. Chapter 9 shows how it was sustained as united action on a nationwide scale. All those who wished, for whatever reason, to join in had to accept the etiquette of commemoration which regulated relations between participants with different aims and views. Acceptance of the etiquette was not merely voluntary. It was physically enforced in a number of ways by civic authorities, employers, crowds or private individuals, who all might act, sometimes violently, to protect the sacred times and places of commemoration. Commemoration of the dead was conducted, in fact, by a disciplined and powerful movement which could impose its authority.

In many respects, commemoration was a religious phenomenon; but even the clergy, who might have had a special interest in its religious interpretation, tended to treat it as, first and foremost, a civic and ethical matter. The distinction between religion and politics was, in fact, far from clear. For many people, disarmament and the League of Nations were not simply political issues but ethical and religious ideals. The Churches played an important part in attaching a concern for world peace to the commemoration of the dead. As the Archbishop of Canterbury told an interdenominational conference in October 1935, 'the principle of collective responsibility for the peace of the world' through the League was 'a practical application of the principles of Christianity'.[36]

I shall only deal with religious aspects of commemoration in so far as they bear on its organisation, and on the significance of its symbolism. Some of the more obviously mystical elements of remembrance had precedents in late Victorian and Edwardian religious movements. Commemoration lent itself to ecumenism, and to a syncretic mixture of Christian and other beliefs which appeared elsewhere in religion and the arts in the inter-war period. There were divisions of opinion over the design of war cemeteries which owed much of their acrimony to a clash of religious and political beliefs, having little specifically to do with the war. These themes are fascinating, but they belong to a study of inter-war culture more generally, much of which was concerned with mortality, time and war, and are too large to be accommodated here.

Notes to Introduction

1. G. M. Trevelyan, *The Life of John Bright*, London, 1925, p. 252.
2. *Manchester Guardian*, 11 Nov. 1920.
3. *Birmingham Post*, 4 July 1925.
4. Ibid.
5. P. Fussell, *The Great War and Modern Memory*, Oxford, 1977, pp. 155–87.
6. Ibid., pp. 235, 238–9, 267–8.
7. Ibid., p. 168; J. M. Winter, *Sites of Memory, Sites of Mourning: The Great War in European Cultural History*, Cambridge, 1995, p. 5.
8. R. M. Bracco, *Merchants of Hope: British Middlebrow Writers and the First World War*, Providence and Oxford, 1993, especially pp. 3, 96–7 and 124–38.
9. H. Quigley, *Passchendaele and the Somme: A Diary of 1917*, London, 1928, p. 174.
10. Ibid., p. 181.
11. Ibid., p. 185.
12. S. Hynes, *A War Imagined: The First World War and English Culture*, London, 1990, p. 270.
13. Hynes, *A War Imagined*; G. L. Mosse, *Fallen Soldiers: Reshaping the Memory of the First World War*, Oxford, 1990; E. Homberger, 'The Story of the Cenotaph', *Times Literary Supplement*, 12 Nov. 1976, pp. 1429–30; B. Anderson, *Imagined Communities: Reflections on the Origin and Spread of Nationalism*, London, 1991, in passing treats war commemoration from this point of view.
14. The most important of these are E. Leed, *No Man's Land: Combat and Identity in World War I*, Cambridge, 1979; D. Cannadine, 'War, Death, Grief and Mourning in Modern Britain', in J. Whaley (ed.), *Mirrors of Mortality: Studies in the Social History of Death*, London, 1981, pp. 187–242; A. Gregory, *The Silence of Memory: Armistice Day 1919–1946*, Oxford, 1994; Winter, *Sites of Memory*.
15. Hynes, *A War Imagined*, p. 270.
16. Ibid., p. 307.
17. See Chapter 3 for a longer discussion of Gibbs's views.
18. *Daily Herald*, 11 Nov. 1920.
19. Winter, *Sites of Memory*, pp. 93–8.
20. K. S. Inglis and J. Phillips, 'War Memorials in Australia and New Zealand:

A Comparative Survey', in J. Rickard and P. Spearritt (eds), *Packaging the Past? Public Histories*, Melbourne, 1991, (*Australian Historical Studies*, special issue, vol. 24, no. 96), pp. 186 and 191.

21. T. J. Clark, 'Preliminaries to a Possible Treatment of "Olympia" in 1865', *Screen*, vol. 21, no. 1, (1980), p. 31. Clark discusses the importance of 'tying' one's analysis back to the terms of original interpretations here and in Clark, 'A Note in Reply to Peter Wollen', *Screen*, vol. 21, no. 3, (1980), pp. 97–100.

22. L. Hunt, *Politics, Culture and Class in the French Revolution*, London, 1984, and A. Ben-Amos, 'The Sacred Centre of Power: Paris and Republican State Funerals', *Journal of Interdisciplinary History*, vol. 22, no. 1, (1991), pp. 27–48 make use of the concept of charisma taken by Geertz from Edward Shils, and ultimately from Max Weber. P. A. Pickering, 'Class Without Words: Symbolic Communication in the Chartist Movement', *Past and Present*, no. 112, (1986), pp. 144-62, and J. Epstein, 'Understanding the Cap of Liberty: Symbolic Practice and Social Conflict in Early Nineteenth-century England', *Past and Present*, no. 122, (1989), pp. 75–118, make some use of Geertz's concepts of personality and charisma, while addressing themselves chiefly to questions raised by Gareth Stedman-Jones about the restrictive effect of language on the political imagination. Cannadine takes the idea of 'thick description' from Geertz, to argue that the meaning of state ritual depends on its political context, and is not simply given by its form. See D. Cannadine, 'The Context, Performance and Meaning of Ritual: The British Monarchy and the "Invention of Tradition", *c.*1820–1977', in E. Hobsbawm and T. Ranger (eds), *The Invention of Tradition*, Cambridge 1984, pp. 101-64.

23. C. Geertz, 'Centers, Kings and Charisma', in J. Ben-David and T. Nichols Clark (eds), *Culture and its Creators, Essays in Honour of Edward Shils*, 1977, pp. 150–71, especially pp. 152-3.

24. C. Geertz, 'Ethos, World View, and the Analysis of Sacred Symbols', in Geertz, *The Interpretation of Cultures, Selected Essays*, New York, 1973, pp. 126–41.

25. M. Ryan , 'The American Parade: Representations of the Nineteenth-century Social Order', in L. Hunt (ed.), *The New Cultural History*, London, 1989, p. 152.

26. C. Geertz, 'Centers, Kings and Charisma', p. 171; see also Geertz, 'Ethos, World View and the Analysis of Sacred Symbols'.

27. L. Hunt, *Politics, Culture and Class*, *passim*.

28. J. Epstein, 'Understanding the Cap of Liberty', *passim*. An argument which also concerns competitive pluralism in interpretation appears in J. Bodnar, *Remaking America: Public Memory, Commemoration, and Patriotism in the Twentieth Century*, Princeton, 1992, but there the process is seen as working the other way, as diverse interpretations gradually giving way to uniformity.

29. Susan G. Davis acknowledges the importance of policing of American parades, see S. G. Davis, *Parades and Power: Street Theatre in Nineteenth Century Philadelphia*, Berkeley and London, 1988, pp. 165 and 167. The importance of organisation and policing in the creation and suppression of symbolic acts is obvious from Epstein's account of the Cap of Liberty as used by early-nineteenth-century radicals, and of the official response to it at the Peterloo Massacre: see Epstein, 'Understanding the Cap of Liberty', *passim*.

30. D. I. Kertzer, *Ritual, Politics and Power*, New Haven and London, 1988, pp. 67, 72 and 75.

31. Ibid., p. 2.

32. D. Sperber, *Rethinking Symbolism*, Cambridge, 1975, pp. 8–16 and 48.

33. M. Quinn, *The Swastika: Constructing the Symbol*, London, 1994, pp. 5 and 10.

34. I have discussed this subject at length in A. King, 'Acts and Monuments: National Celebrations in Britain from the Napoleonic to the Great War', in A. O'Day (ed.), *Government and Institutions in the Post-1832 United Kingdom*, Studies in British History, vol. 34, Lewiston and Lampeter, 1995, pp. 237–68.

35. I am indebted to J. L. Austin's theory of speech acts for the idea that an utterance is not merely a representation, but also the performance of an action, governed by conventions, which entails the formation of social relationships, and often involves the sanction of some sort of power. See J. L. Austin, *How To Do Things With Words*, Oxford, 1976, especially pp. 4–7, 98–9.

36. *Headway: The Journal of the League of Nations Union*, vol. 17, no. 11, Nov. 1935, p. 211.

1

The Composition of a National Cult

The commemoration of the Great War consisted of two principal activities: performing ceremonies and making memorials. Both occurred almost everywhere: in private as well as public places, and in a great variety of communities and institutions. They made up a national observance of intense public interest which persisted for twenty years, until overshadowed by a second world war. Throughout the country, the erection of war memorials and the conduct of Armistice Day ceremonies followed common patterns, suggesting a nationwide uniformity of aims and attitudes, and a desire to conform to national stereotypes. Nonetheless, commemoration focused closely on the part played in the war by local communities, and on the local people who had been killed. It depended for its conduct very largely on local initiative. This chapter offers first an impression of the scope of commemorative activity and of the responses it elicited. It then describes the local organisations which sustained it, and how they were formed by the communities in which they acted.

The Nation's Act of Homage

At 11 a.m. on 11 November, Armistice Day, every year, almost all activity, whether private or public, was interrupted for two minutes to observe the Great Silence in memory of the dead. Formal ceremonies with prayers, the laying of wreaths at memorials, and speeches were held in town squares, on village greens, in shops, offices, factories, schools and other places. Where there was no formal ceremony people went to windows or into the street to form an impromptu congregation. In 1919, the streets of Leeds 'presented a strange and reverent aspect as pedestrians stood still, the male section baring their heads'.[1] It may not have seemed to everyone that 'a sort of mysticism made itself felt',[2] but for many the commemoration of the war dead was an intense emotional experience, and it was expected to be so. In the first Armistice Day silence, 'women sobbed and even men were moved to tears'.[3]

Commemorating the war dead was regarded as a sacred act. The 11th of November became known as 'Armisticetide',[4] giving it the air of an ancient religious tradition. In 1920 *The Times* described the attendance at the newly unveiled Cenotaph in Whitehall and the Grave of the Unknown Warrior in Westminster Abbey (estimated at over half a million people in four days) as a 'Great Pilgrimage', comparing it to Lourdes.[5] In 1930 the Bishop of Ripon called Armistice Day 'a religious anniversary . . . the new Good Friday of the post-war world'.[6] When Randolph Churchill was criticised for holding an election campaign meeting on Armistice Day 1935, he acknowledged that 'the Two Minutes Silence is the most sacred ceremony Britain observes'.[7] On this day the whole country was transformed into a sacred place dedicated to the memory of the dead. Particular local days of remembrance also existed. Stockport held a local military anniversary, Saint Julien Day, on 30 July.[8] At Llandrindod Wells the anniversary of the unveiling of the town war memorial was kept as a remembrance day (partly because, being in July, the weather was likely to be better).[9] In Bethnal Green a service was held every year in mid-June to commemorate 18 local schoolchildren who had been killed in an air raid in 1917.[10] Less regularly placed local events might start with a formal homage to the dead. At Sheffield, in March 1927, the English Junior 10 Mile Road Walking Championship started with the laying of a wreath at the city war memorial.[11]

In many of the places where people held remembrance ceremonies there were war memorials. As well as the significant public locations in towns and villages, they were to be found in civic buildings, in the premises of commercial firms, in clubrooms, churches and schools. The Imperial War Graves Commission put up memorials in the cemeteries where servicemen who had died in the many military hospitals, after being brought home from theatres of war, had been buried.[12] Most memorials were dedicated to the dead of a specific locality or institution, but some commemorated more broadly-defined groups. All the British cyclists who had died in the war are commemorated on Meriden Green, near Birmingham (where annual remembrance ceremonies were also held).[13] Very occasionally a memorial might commemorate people from no clear group. On the memorial which local ex-servicemen erected in Harrogate to 'their fallen comrades', it is not clear whether this meant exclusively Harrogate men, or simply any comrades they had lost during the war. Animals, too, had their memorials. There is a monument to the horses of the Empire in Saint Jude's church, Hampstead Garden Suburb. All service animals are commemorated at the RSPCA memorial clinic in Kilburn and in the Scottish National War Memorial.

The appeal of war commemoration remained strong throughout the 1920s and 1930s. Year after year, tens of thousands turned out on Armistice Day to join in the silence at municipal ceremonies. By the late 1920s there was some sense of change in the public mood. Armistice Day was becoming more formal, less emotionally charged, according to several commentators. *The Times* found it 'a slightly more reasoned, slightly less emotional reverence' in 1926.[14] In 1933 the *Morning Post* found that 'the crowd is no longer tragic with mourning; time, which confirms the Armistice Ceremony, gradually remits its overburdening unhappiness'.[15] Yet any suggestion that the strict etiquette of remembrance should be relaxed aroused fierce opposition. In 1930 the Labour government proposed informally that foreign delegations should no longer, as a matter of protocol, be expected to lay wreaths on war memorials. These acts were not regular formal ceremonies; they were purely occasional, and not significant public events. All the same, Ramsay MacDonald, the Prime Minister, was criticised in Parliament for interfering with the right to lay wreaths. In defence of the proposal, he explained that the point had been 'to obviate any risk of a ceremony which should be simple and spontaneous becoming a mere formality of international courtesy'.[16] The government's proposal had been 'out of touch with public feeling', said the Liberal *News Chronicle*.[17] The British Legion's national executive resolved in October 1930 that it 'adheres to the policy which has inspired the Legion since its inception that no diminution of respect for the memory of our fallen comrades will be tolerated'.[18]

The commissioning and building of memorials continued throughout this period, though at a diminishing rate. Liverpool's city cenotaph was only unveiled in 1930, Bristol's in 1932 and

Gloucester's in 1933.[19] As long after the Armistice as the late 1930s, *The Times* was still reporting the unveiling of memorials. Most of them were military and in Flanders, but some were in Britain. London University unveiled a memorial to members of its Officer Training Corps killed in the Great War in January 1937, having had to wait for the new University building to be sufficiently near completion.[20] In December 1937 a memorial window, donated anonymously and dedicated to all Britons killed in the war, was unveiled at Sherburn-in-Elmet parish church.[21] The very last unveiling of a local war memorial recorded by *The Times* before the outbreak of the next war was to townsmen of Mumbles, a seaside resort near Swansea, erected in July 1939.[22] Male passers-by raised their hats to the Cenotaph in Whitehall, as the centre of the commemorative cult, on ordinary days as much as on ceremonial occasions, and this custom, too, persisted into the 1930s.[23]

Local war memorials were expected to be of interest to travellers and tourists as much as to residents who had some personal connection with them. A booklet for the Holidays on Merseyside Association, published in 1934, contained a photograph of the Liverpool memorial to ship's engineers on the Pier Head. The three-volume guidebook *Wonderful Britain*, published in parts in 1928 and 1929, devoted three out of its over one hundred chapters to 'Our War Memorials', with a considerable number of photographs. This book was intended both for the general reader and for the rising number of leisure motorists, to whom it offered suggestions for excursions along with road maps.[24] Referring to the density and visibility of local memorials, the novelist Ian Hay wrote, 'every English highway is now one continuous memorial avenue. The cumulative effect upon the traveller's mind is almost unendurable in its poignancy.'[25]

The printed word played an extensive part in the commemoration of the war dead. National and local press coverage made Armistice Day a co-ordinated national event, not only by passing on information about its organisation, but also by providing models for others to follow through detailed reports of ceremonies. The two minutes' silence, which was the hub of the national homage to the dead, was instituted by the government, in the King's name, but relied for its implementation on voluntary co-operation from local authorities and others who controlled public spaces or places of work. The government communicated its intentions to those members of the public whose co-operation it hoped for through newspapers. The official press release announcing the arrangements for Armistice Day 1919 stated: 'The Government feel that carrying out the King's wishes [for the ceremony] must be left to the sympathetic good will of the community. No general instructions can ensure the success of a ceremony which can only be truly impressive if it is universal and spontaneous.'[26] The government was simply issuing 'suggestions . . . to afford some guidance to local authorities and the nation generally', it said. The Metropolitan Police were instructed to stop the traffic for two minutes, and it was hoped that other local authorities would do the same. Factory employers and employees were urged to 'make such arrangement as will best carry out the spirit of the scheme', and pedestrians 'can best co-operate by simply standing still when the signal sounds'. This use of unofficial channels to co-ordinate the national observance was deliberate policy, as a letter from a civil servant on the subject to Lord Curzon, who chaired the Cabinet committee, made clear. The writer pointed out that the press had always been used to communicate with local authorities in matters relating to Armistice Day celebrations, rather than official Home Office channels.[27]

National and many local papers reported the ceremony held at the Cenotaph every year, allowing their readers to share in it to some extent, no matter how remote they were from London, and so making it a national focus for the celebration of Armistice Day. Papers carried images of the monument on the day. In later years these were sometimes montaged with other images of the war such as marching soldiers,[28] a device also used in films, from which the newspapers may have borrowed it. Through these reports attention could be directed to one point in London as the centre of the country's united act of remembrance. Radio broadcasting of the ceremony, begun in 1928, continued this already established focus. Some national papers also gave accounts of provincial, even village celebrations of Armistice Day, which extended the sense that every community was sharing in a single commemorative event. Editorials and reports published on 11 November and the immediately following days often included commentaries interpreting the meaning of Armistice

Day and its rituals. An especially intense style of prose was common to Armistice Day reports, regardless of the character of the newspaper. In 1919 the *Daily Mail* described the ceremony in Whitehall thus: 'emotion vibrated from roof to street . . . till you could scarce see the Cenotaph for the *aura*, the halo, the throbbing air that encompassed it . . . All the while the sun shone; and there was mystic meaning in that too.'[29] The importance of print as a means of sharing in commemorative acts, and also of colouring readers' perceptions of them, was apparent to contemporaries. The *Daily Mail* reported two occasions on which clergymen used its own account of the burial of the Unknown Warrior in sermons.[30] They had probably done this in order to exploit the vivid and emotional impression created by the language typical of such reports.

Memorials too were frequently discussed in print, and images of them circulated widely. They were described and their meanings explained in newspapers, appeal leaflets and in the programmes for unveiling ceremonies. The press played an important part in encouraging and giving practical support to the erection of war memorials, as we shall see later. A large number of postcards of local war memorials were published, ranging from crosses in tiny villages to big city monuments.[31] People could come to see the memorial in a place they visited and leave with a souvenir of it. Ceramic reproductions of the Whitehall Cenotaph and of other memorials, suitable for the mantelpiece, were available.[32] In some cases images of memorials had a more personal value, such as the photographs of James Budgett and Company's memorial tablet, which were presented to the next of kin of those commemorated on it.[33]

Memorials could thus be experienced vicariously in the same way as ceremonies. In a book about the Scottish National War Memorial in Edinburgh Castle, Ian Hay explained that he intended his description to be a substitute for an actual visit to the building 'for the benefit of those who are precluded, by conditions of space and circumstances, from visiting the memorial'. For this reason he had gone into detail which 'may prove at once superfluous and inadequate to those who have made the pilgrimage themselves'.[34] He wished to re-create the emotional experience for those who could not actually go, and so extend the sense of participating in a national homage to the dead.

The Organisation of Local War Memorial Committees

The nationwide interweaving of actions, words and objects to commemorate the war dead was composed mainly through local initiative and local organisation. In many places local authorities convened a public ceremony for the two minutes' silence on Armistice Day. They organised the signal for the silence and stopped traffic. Where no civic ceremony was organised others might take the responsibility. In 1924 a leader of Southgate Ratepayers' Association noticed that people gathered spontaneously at a road junction in the town centre. He organised services there in the following three years with local clergy officiating.[35] The erection of memorials was also the result of local initiative and organisation. The institutions involved ranged from the councils of large municipalities to church congregations, commercial enterprises and clubs. The most prominent memorials were usually those of large urban communities, but these were sometimes rivalled by those of private institutions such as regimental associations or large firms. While clubs, churches, firms, and other kinds of association often joined in the erection of town or village memorials, they also erected memorials of their own. A few of these memorials will be discussed in this book, but I will confine the discussion mainly to public memorials, intended to represent entire town or village communities.

There are two reasons for concentrating on memorials of this kind. First, the organisation required to erect them was the most complicated and socially comprehensive, and its social significance was the greatest. Second, the general principles behind the organisation of these public and communal memorials usually applied to the memorials of private institutions as well. However, in the latter they were likely to be implemented through the existing structure for governing the institution concerned, rather than through the specially formed committees which were characteristic of public commemorations. Apart from these public and private memorials, a number were erected in Britain by the Imperial War Graves Commission. The most notable are the memorials to the missing of the Royal and Merchant Navies at Chatham, Portsmouth, Plymouth, and Tower Hill in London. These were paid for out of funds provided by the British, Dominion and Indian governments, and the general public was not involved. Only the services directly concerned were consulted to any significant extent. I shall not discuss them here.

Erecting a memorial was itself a symbolic act; as much so as a remembrance ceremony. It was not merely the practical provision of an object for subsequent use as a ceremonial site. Organising a local memorial committee, and collecting for or giving to the memorial fund, were acts with moral significance: a sacrifice of time and resources, dedicated to the dead, and a coming-together of the community to express sorrow and respect. A fund-raiser in Sheffield saw it as such when she wrote to the Town Clerk, 'do let us endeavour to reach the hearts of the people, that our war memorial may be an outpouring of love and enthusiasm'.[36] Subsequently, the memorial would be honoured in a more ceremonial, but not a more expressive manner. A completed memorial was a sign that the appropriate actions had been performed, and the dead properly appreciated, by the inhabitants of a particular place.[37]

It was generally expected that every civil community (a place with a statutory local authority - parish, district, town) should have a memorial, and the community's official leaders were expected to see to the matter. A Leeds alderman wrote that, quite apart from any national commemorative schemes which might be proposed, 'Leeds ought not to overlook the honour due to its men and the need for an adequate local memorial.'[38] A Southgate councillor said that 'it had always seemed to him a blot on Southgate, its not having a suitable war memorial'.[39] If a community's official leaders did not start an organisation to provide a memorial, someone else usually did. In 1919 the vicar of Hayton in Cumberland asked the parish council if it intended to initiate the erection of a war memorial. On being told that it did not, he called a public meeting for the purpose himself.[40] In Hull, where a substantial relief fund had already been established in memory of the dead, but no monument erected, ex-servicemen began agitating for a city cenotaph in 1922.[41]

War memorials were normally erected by local committees, whose organisation varied according to the kind of community in which they were formed. Nevertheless, their actions generally conformed to a broad pattern characterised by the opportunity for public participation. The large majority of organisations to be studied here were formed from and served the people of cities, boroughs, urban or rural districts, and parishes. Towns usually confined their organisation to the area governed by their corporations or urban district councils. Villages acted as parishes, observing their local authority boundaries too. This was a convenient arrangement. Local communities defined by these administrative boundaries could look to an obvious official leadership - the mayor, or council chairman, and councillors - to take responsibility for starting a war memorial organisation. The local authority could also provide administrative support and experience of commissioning public buildings of many kinds.

Formerly independent villages or parishes which had been incorporated into major conurbations like Leeds and Bradford sometimes had quite costly memorials of their own. The Bradford wards (and parishes in their own right) of Allerton, Eccleshill and Thornton each had a substantial figurative bronze memorial. These cases seem to contradict the principle that the community for whom a memorial was erected conformed to local government boundaries. However, it seems likely that a strong remnant of the former independent institutional life of these localities remained after their incorporation into larger municipalities, with a matching consciousness of communal independence. A sense of local identity, with organisations to sustain it in practice, probably existed in these Bradford suburbs as strongly as it did at Stanwix, a parish not long incorporated into Carlisle. The chairman of Stanwix war memorial committee said many people 'were not very proud of their association with Carlisle' and 'it would be a disgrace if they did not do something' of their own.[42]

In towns, the initiator of the commemorative movement was generally the mayor, or chairman of the council. These leaders would call an inaugural meeting, at which resolutions to start a fund and establish a memorial committee would be passed. It was deemed right ('natural' according to the *Hoylake and West Kirby Advertiser*)[43] for the officially constituted leadership of the town to take the first step. The inaugural meeting could take the form of a 'Town Meeting' open to all citizens,[44] or be called by more specific invitation to people and organisations regarded as representative of 'public and social' life in the town.[45] At these meetings committees were formed to choose the type of memorial a community would have and to organise its production. Motions put to the meeting, and perhaps a list of people who should form the committee, would probably have been composed in a preliminary private or town council meeting.[46] Thus, even though the memorial was intended to be an expression of popular feeling, the controlling committee's composition and agenda were not left to the spontaneous decision of whichever members of the public chose to attend.

Memorial committees normally had a structure which was intended to make them representative of the local community as whole. The purpose of this arrangement was to encourage all sections of the community to contribute to the memorial and to feel that their views were taken into account in deciding what sort of memorial to erect. A letter to a local newspaper in Edmonton explained that, 'in order to be successful all sections of the community should be asked to co-operate and an opportunity given for discussion and suggestions'. The committee should be formed 'from all public organisations. Then, and not until then, will Edmonton succeed in its belated effort to erect a fitting memorial to our fallen brothers.'[47] The *Barnsley Chronicle* believed that Barnsley's 'townspeople will have every reason to be satisfied' because 'at every stage the "vox populi" will be taken fully into account' as a result of the memorial committee's representative nature.[48]

Bethnal Green's executive committee involved representatives of the council, Christian clergy, the synagogue, two benevolent societies, friendly societies, two hospital aid funds, the Union of Boot and Shoe Operatives, the Rifle Club and the Special Constables.[49] The committee at Barnsley (its second) which finally got a memorial project under way included representatives of eleven local clubs, both middle- and working-class, Liberal and Labour clubs, regimental and ex-servicemen's associations and seven local churches ranging from Anglican to Baptist and Primitive Methodist.[50] Hoylake and West Kirby, two resorts on the Wirral coast which formed a single urban district, set up a joint committee containing councillors, the MP, some prominent private citizens, the cinema proprietor, representatives of the local railway company, clergy, doctors, ex-servicemen, and the joint trade union committee of the two towns.[51] Sleaford, a small agricultural town in Lincolnshire, specified 12 councillors, 12 clergy, 15 ratepayers, 18 ladies and 15 ex-servicemen for its committee.[52]

In some towns, war memorial committees were not socially and politically inclusive. The membership of Islington's committee was confined to councillors, MPs, clergy, some charity heads, and the local Hospital Extension Committee. (One of these charities, Highbury Patriotic Platform, was largely working-class.)[53] Here 'representative' was taken to mean local persons of note: 'public representatives of the Borough who would most likely form a powerful and influential committee';[54] yet the importance of public representation in some form was still, thereby, acknowledged.

The basis for organisation of war memorials in villages was the parish, in either its civil or ecclesiastical identity. Parish councils had few powers.[55] Far more administrative power lay with the rural district councils, but the boundaries of the districts did not match geographical loyalties or social networks. It was to the feeble parish councils, rather than district councils, that country communities usually turned to establish war memorials. Village memorial projects were often inaugurated at the annual general parish meeting, open to all voters for the election of new councillors. Alternatively, the parish priest called and chaired a parish meeting. (It was quite common for the parson also to be an active and influential member of the parish council.) A local committee was then formed, normally involving the parson and any local landlords active in parish affairs. Farmers, tradesmen and schoolteachers were also regularly members.

Money

Money was the lifeblood of any memorial project, and the need to get money was an important influence on the form of organisation adopted by committees. Many of the representative bodies included on war memorial committees had experience of raising money for charities, or of donating to charities from their own funds. The collection of money was not just a practical necessity. It was also treated as a means of expression for the citizens at large. For most people, participation in the production of a war memorial took the form of contributions to the memorial fund. The generosity which members of the public could demonstrate by giving had two important symbolic meanings. In the first place, it provided a means by which all members of the public could make a concrete contribution to the production of a war memorial, indicating that it was genuinely a gift from the whole community. As the *Barnsley Chronicle* commented, it was 'in the best sense a popular feature' of a war memorial fund 'that everyone is to be given the chance to contribute'. Its purpose was 'not so much to raise a record amount, as to make the memorial really representative of all classes and sections and creeds in the community'.[56] In the second place, subscriptions willingly made to a memorial fund showed that the citizens were genuinely grateful to the war dead for their self-sacrifice. The dead, in the words of an appeal at Brampton, Cumberland, had been prepared to give 'the greatest, their lives',[57] and this imposed on the living an obligation to give, in turn, what they could in recognition of the generosity of the dead. The appeal continued, 'Surely where much has been given, much is required.' Gifts to Bethnal Green memorial fund were intended, in the words of an appeal leaflet, 'to show our gratitude' to the dead.[58]

It was widely held that voluntary subscription was the only acceptable way to fund a war memorial. Only willing gifts would adequately express recognition of the sacrifice the dead had made. The *Hackney and Kingsland Gazette* argued that recourse to the rates to fund a war memorial would be 'a very doubtful compliment to our gallant fighters' because the money would not then have been raised as a voluntary gift.[59] A letter to the *Islington Daily Gazette*, in favour of extending the local voluntary hospital as the borough war memorial, said 'every brick in the building should have the charm of a voluntary offering, as opposed to the compulsory rate'.[60]

What constituted voluntary giving was open to argument. Many of the parishioners in a Gloucestershire parish felt that to canvass for donations at all was against the voluntary principle.[61] At the dedication of the memorial cross at Brancepeth, County Durham, the officiating clergyman condemned the use of entertainments to raise money, as this did not constitute a 'free gift'.[62] In general, though, people saw little contradiction between providing fund-raising entertainments and regarding the results as a voluntary gift. At the village of Llanymynech on the border of England and Wales, the local committee voted at its first meeting to erect a village hall as their memorial 'by voluntary subscription'. At the second, they resolved that the ladies be invited to arrange a victory ball to raise money if negotiations for a site for the hall were successful.[63] Hoylake and West Kirby District Council chose the proprietor of the Kingsway Picture House as one of their first co-optees to the war memorial committee.[64] This was probably not because he was noted for his piety or patriotic enthusiasm, but because by 1918 cinemas were an important part of local fund-raising networks.[65] A committee member at Stoke Newington praised the contribution made by local cinemas to their war memorial fund.[66] At Barnsley, brass band concerts in the park, charity balls, collections in cinemas and a benefit match by Barnsley Football Club all helped to swell the fund. But here, a local philanthropist who had sponsored a wartime convalescent home to the tune of nearly £4,000 resigned from the war memorial committee because, he said, 'I cannot associate myself with the method which the committee are using to raise funds.'[67]

The only universal agreement was that memorials ought not to be paid for out of a local authority's funds; but there were instances of even that stipulation's being abandoned when sufficient could not be raised voluntarily. The much delayed war memorial rose garden at Broomfield Park, Southgate, opened in 1929, was paid for out of council funds. Some towns had to find extra money from special sources when voluntary fund-raising fell short. Sheffield war memorial committee obtained £1,500 from the Sheffield Trustees,[68] who administered a charity based on property in the city yielding between £6,000 and £7,000 a year.[69]

Although voluntary giving was the approved way to raise funds, the whole armoury of fund-raising gimmicks was usually required to persuade people to part with their money. The response to appeals for funds could be very disappointing. A member of Stoke Newington memorial committee privately criticised local people of means who had given only 'a guinea or so' because they had 'done the fund positive harm and have shown themselves utterly incapable of grasping how a large sum is to be raised'.[70] Appeals used the language of moral exhortation, local patriotism, personal and institutional rivalry, and even self-interest in the evasion of a future sense of guilt. Workington's appeal maintained that 'No one would care to be saddled with a life-long and ever-present regret that he missed the opportunity of doing his share in acknowledging his gratitude to his fellow-townsmen who cheerfully endured unspeakable hardships, and now lie in a soldier's grave.'[71] Subscription lists were published in newspapers, and subscribers encouraged to make sure their names were seen on them. Workington proposed to keep a full list of subscribers in the town hall 'to be handed down from generation to generation'[72] along with, presumably, the odium attached to not being on it. A member of Pudsey war memorial committee confessed to manipulating the publication of subscription lists. The committee had 'followed the policy of only publishing the larger sums at present as a bait for the wait and see what others give people'.[73]

Stoke Newington war memorial committee employed a professional fund-raiser. There and at Deptford public lotteries known as 'silver ballots' were held to augment flagging funds. These were, strictly speaking, illegal, and if an objection was made to the police the responsible individual would be prosecuted. The mayors of both places were summonsed and fined. At Deptford, the complaint against the mayor was made by the local Council of Christian Churches.[74] The possibilities and risks of this form of fund-raising were well known. As chairman of the Scottish National War Memorial, the Duke of Atholl advised the memorial's fund-raiser not to use it, especially as he anticipated great hostility to it from church ministers.[75] Nevertheless, a prize draw was held at Penrith, with a car offered by a motor dealer at cost price as the prize, and there do not appear to have been any repercussions. In spite of its illegality, the running of a ballot did little to tarnish a mayor's reputation. Deptford Borough Council reaffirmed 'its unabated confidence' in its mayor 'with much enthusiasm' after his prosecution.[76]

The efficiency of local fund-raising systems varied from place to place. Glasgow, a city of about one million people at the time, raised nearly £104,000 for its memorial fund. It was loyally supported by a number of extremely rich donors from the region, who had also given large sums to monuments before the war.[77] The patricians of the west of Scotland were a well-disciplined fund-raising body. Leeds, by comparison, a city with almost half that number of inhabitants, raised only some £6,000. Barnsley, with a little over 53,000 people in 1921, raised around £3,000. The district of Hoylake and West Kirby raised nearly £8,000 from a population of 17,000. These figures do not represent the actual expenditure of the communities in question on war memorials. Many people might have contributed to memorials more local than those for the city or town they lived in, especially church or school memorials. They reflect, rather, the effectiveness of civic leaders in rallying support for the project they had initiated.

Leadership and Power in Local Memorial Committees

The roles played by social leaders in a memorial movement differed between urban and rural communities. In a city or borough it was customary for the lord mayor or mayor, who would normally be *ex officio* chairman of the war memorial committee, to change annually. This meant that the leading public figure who made appeals for the memorial fund and opened fund-raising events did not continue for the duration of the memorial-building process. In towns it was common for the administrative co-ordination of a memorial project to be given to the town clerk's department of the local authority. The town clerk would be honorary secretary of the war memorial committee. A local bank manager would probably be honorary treasurer. Town clerks and borough architects or surveyors would put their experience of public building projects at the service of the committee. Urban local authorities frequently provided additional resources for a memorial. They gave sites free of charge to the memorial committee and made up foundations at their own expense, sometimes using the project as an unemployment relief scheme.[78]

The services provided by a mayor as figurehead for the local memorial committee, and the town clerk's department as its administrative agent, were offered as an official duty incumbent upon the occupants of these positions rather than as a personal one. A few mayors did identify themselves very personally with a particular memorial proposal, but this was an old-fashioned and not very popular approach. The mayor of Stockport offered the personal gift of a park for the town's memorial, but it was turned down in favour of an art gallery built by general public subscription. The mayor took no further part in the committee's business after his gift was refused.[79] In general mayors simply gave, at most, a substantial donation, and made themselves responsible for raising adequate funds from the community at large. Their personal contributions were models for their social peers to follow, often published at the head of the subscription list. At Stoke Newington the mayor in office in 1918 led the list with a donation of £105 (one hundred guineas - subscriptions from respectable people were often calculated in guineas), and eight of his colleagues followed suit.

The requirement that a memorial should be a collective

gift from the community, and the practical requirements of organising a voluntary fund-raising campaign, raised the expectation that leaders of a town memorial committee would not dominate the processes of giving and making decisions too conspicuously themselves, but would allow a large opportunity for public participation. The mayor and local administration offered facilities for the members of a community to make their own memorial. They were not supposed to be making it for them, although, as Chapter 4 will show, they could dominate the proceedings in other ways.

In rural war memorial committees, parsons and notable local citizens frequently took the honorary offices more as a personal than as an *ex officio* duty. Their social and business connections made them the most suitable people to hold these places. Estate owners and their managers had experience of building and of the business of buying and selling land. They knew architects, and sometimes had employees of their own with appropriate skills, such as masons. They offered these services as part of their contribution to the war memorial, and might also supply materials or a site free if they could. The manager of Lord Boyne's estate at Brancepeth was secretary of the village war memorial committee and had the memorial cross constructed in the estate yard using stone donated by Boyne himself.[80] Lady Howard, who was a member of Greystoke war memorial committee in Cumberland, provided a mason and offered to supply stone for the parish memorial.[81]

Rural social leaders were offering as a personal duty services which would be available from the public authorities of a town but which a parish could not offer. Several of them personally took responsibility for seeing that a local memorial was erected, and made a financial commitment to match. Lord Derwent, a North Riding landowner, proposed an obelisk 'in some conspicuous place' as the memorial for his parish.[82] His idea was adopted by the parishioners, but during its construction the price rose considerably owing to the rising price of stone. Derwent took personal responsibility for paying the increase.[83] Katherine Grey, another Yorkshire landowner, took the same personal responsibility for Sutton and Huby war memorial. There was a question of revising its design to make it less expensive, but the committee 'decided that we should prefer the Cross as originally designed', wrote Grey, 'only because I promised to pay the increase in price. It is hard on me, but I should not like the Cross to be a failure in any way.'[84]

This sense of responsibility was not peculiar to the erection of memorials. It was a feature of the ordinary work of parish councils where sympathetic landlords took an interest in parish affairs, and it can be considered part of the regular pattern of rural local politics. Brampton parish council, in Cumberland, had depended a great deal in its work on the generosity of Lord and Lady Carlisle. The radical Lady Carlisle had been a member of the parish council, and one of its representatives to the rural district.[85] Over the years she and her husband had given footpaths and recreation land to the parish, and his Lordship's influence had been instrumental in obtaining 'a telephone call office' for the village.[86] Thus, in discharging what they felt was a duty to use their personal wealth and facilities in the service of the community, rural social leaders were, like their urban counterparts in a different way, conforming to the expectations normally held of people in their position.

Civic leaders had the duty of seeing that a proper commemoration of the dead was conducted in their communities. Their conception of their roles, and the problems they faced, differed considerably between predominantly rural and predominantly urban communities. The differences were created by the forms of power available to them in town and country. In towns the power of civic leaders was based on the co-operation they established between important interest groups, facilitated by the institutions of local government. In villages it depended more on the provision or control of resources by social leaders personally. The nature of public participation, and the share of responsibility taken by groups outside the civic leadership, differed accordingly. Nevertheless, in all kinds of communities, the pattern to which the conduct of war memorial committees usually conformed had both symbolic and practical purposes. There were certain principles - the representation of all sections of the community, co-operative effort and voluntary gifts of money - which ought to be enacted in the production of a memorial. Acting in accordance with these principles gave the required meaning and sanctity to the object which was eventually erected.

Notes to Chapter 1

1. *Morning Post*, 12 Nov. 1919.
2. *Daily Mail*, 12 Nov. 1919.
3. *Daily Herald*, 12 Nov. 1919.
4. *Daily Mail*, 8 Nov. 1930; *Manchester Guardian*, 10 Nov. 1930, letter from the Secretary, Haig Fund.
5. *The Times*, 15 Nov. 1920.
6. *Manchester Guardian*, 10 Nov. 1930.
7. Ibid., 11 Nov. 1935.
8. *Stockport Advertiser*, 5 Oct. 1921.
9. Powys Archives, R/UD/LW/234, Llandrindod Wells War Memorial, File 3, letter from A. G. Camp to D. C. Davis, 13 July 1922.
10. Tower Hamlets Local Studies Library, 082.2 contains cuttings from 1920 to 1935 on this event.
11. Sheffield Record Office, CA 653 (19), letter from Chief Constable to Town Clerk, 14 Mar. 1927.
12. In the immediate post-war years many communities were still in the process of commissioning memorials, and other sites were found for official ceremonies and wreath-laying. In Manchester on Armistice Day 1919 wreaths were placed on the memorial in Saint Ann's Square to those killed in the Boer War. In Edinburgh, the old Mercat Cross was used until a city memorial was provided in 1927. A delegation from Southgate UDC regularly took a wreath down the road to lay on Wood Green's war memorial until 1928, before the Southgate memorial garden was opened. At Hoylake and Stockport, ceremonies were held on what were to become the sites of their memorials.
13. *The Times*, 2 May 1937.
14. Quoted in E. Homberger, 'The Story of the Cenotaph', *Times Literary Supplement*, 12 Nov. 1976, p. 1430.
15. *Morning Post*, 13 Nov. 1933.
16. *Parliamentary Debates*, fifth series, vol. 244, p. 35, 29 Oct. 1930.
17. *News Chronicle*, 11 Nov. 1930.
18. Wirral Archives Service, ZWO/16, Hoylake and West Kirby War Memorial Fund, vol. 3, press cutting.
19. See D. Boorman, *At the Going Down of the Sun: British First World War Memorials*, Dunnington Hall, 1988, for an extensive survey of memorials in Britain.
20. *The Times*, 27 Jan. 1937.
21. Ibid., 11 Nov. 1937.
22. Ibid., 31 July 1939.
23. Its continuation was noted by Sir Ian Hamilton in F. C. Inglis, *The Scottish National War Memorial*, Edinburgh, 1932, p. 7.
24. C. Barman, 'Our War Memorials: 1 – The London Area', F. J. Maclean, 'Our War Memorials: 2 – The Great Cities and Some Others', W. F. Aitken, 'Our War Memorials: 3 – In Town and Village', in J. A. Hammerton (ed.), *Wonderful Britain. Its Highways, Byways and Historic Places*, London, vol. 3, no. 22, 1928/29, pp. 1017–36, no. 23, pp. 1083–1102, no. 24, pp. 1137–56.

25. I. Hay, *Their Name Liveth: The Scottish National War Memorial*, London, 1931, p. 4.

26. Public Record Office, HO 45: 11557, File 392664/1.

27. Ibid., File 392664/20.

28. For example: *Daily Mail*, 11 Nov. 1926; *Morning Post*, 11 Nov. 1933.

29. *Daily Mail*, 12 Nov. 1919.

30. Ibid., 15 Nov. 1920.

31. Imperial War Museum Department of Printed Books, album of postcards, class 333.0.

32. B. Jones and B. Howell, *Popular Arts of the First World War*, London, 1972, pp. 162–3.

33. Guildhall Library, 20,374, James Budgett & Son, letters of appreciation for memorial tablet.

34. Hay, *Their Name Liveth*, p. v.

35. *Palmers Green Gazette*, 18 Mar. 1949, obituary.

36. Sheffield, CA 653 (17), War Memorial Sub-committee, letter from L. Rhoden, 14 Feb. 1925.

37. A number of studies of war memorials in specific British localities have been made, see K. S. Inglis, 'The Homecoming: The War Memorial Movement in Cambridge, England', *Journal of Contemporary History*, vol. 27, no. 4, (1992), pp. 583–605; M. Connelly, 'The Commemoration of the Great War in the City and East London', 1995, unpublished Ph.D. thesis, University of London. G. Bell, '"Monuments to the Fallen": Scottish War Memorials of the Great War', unpublished Ph.D. thesis, University of Strathclyde, 1993, is particularly concerned with Glasgow; A. Gaffney, '"Poppies on the Up Platform": Commemoration of the Great War in Wales', unpublished Ph.D. thesis, University College of Cardiff, 1996, gives details of many local projects.

38. *Leeds Weekly Chronicle*, 15 Nov. 1918.

39. *Palmers Green Gazette*, 1 Apr. 1922.

40. Cumbria Record Office, Carlisle, PR/102/81, Hayton War Memorial, Minutes, 15 Dec. 1919.

41. *Eastern Morning News*, 2 Dec. 1922.

42. *Carlisle Journal*, 25 July 1919.

43. *Hoylake and West Kirby Advertiser*, 7 May 1920.

44. Metropolitan Borough of Bethnal Green, Minutes of Proceedings 6 Feb. 1919; Carlisle, S/UD/M/1/2Z/6, Maryport Town War Memorial Committee, Minutes, 29 Jan. 1919.

45. Metropolitan Borough of Islington, Minutes of Proceedings, 7 Feb. 1919; West Yorkshire Archives, Bradford, BBC 1/56/4/6 Bradford Corporation Special Committees Minute Book No.4, 25 July 1919.

46. Strathclyde Regional Archive, G4.1, Glasgow War Memorial Committee, Minutes, 26 May 1919, and circular letter 9 June 1919; Metropolitan Borough of Deptford, Minutes of Proceedings, 28 Jan. 1919.

47. Enfield Archives, Edmonton United Services Club, press cuttings.

48. *Barnsley Chronicle*, 24 July 1920.

49. Tower Hamlets Local Studies Library, Bethnal Green Borough War Memorial Committee, Minutes, 12 Feb. 1919.

50. Barnsley Archives, Town Clerk's In Letters, File 35.

51. Wirral, ZWO/16, Minutes, 20 Dec. 1918.

52. Lincolnshire Archives Office, SLUDC 11/6, Sleaford War Memorial Committee, Minutes, 30 June 1919.

53. *Islington Daily Gazette*, 26 May 1919.

54. Metropolitan Borough of Islington, Minutes of Proceedings, 26 May 1919.

55. B. Keith-Lucas, *The English Local Government Franchise*, Oxford, 1952, p. 42.

56. *Barnsley Chronicle*, 24 July 1920.

57. Carlisle, DX/5/59, Brampton and District War Memorial Cottage Hospital, Interim Report, 18 Apr. 1924.

58. Tower Hamlets Local Studies Library, appeal leaflet, March 1920.

59. *Hackney and Kingsland Gazette*, 28 July 1919.

60. *Islington Daily Gazette*, 30 Sept. 1918.

61. Gloucestershire Record Office, P 348 VE 2/1, All Saints Viney Hill, Church Parochial Council, Minutes, 10 May 1920.

62. *Durham County Advertiser*, 10 June 1921.

63. Shropshire Record Office, 1919/1, Llanymynech War Memorial Committee, Minutes, 16 and 23 Jan. 1919.

64. *Hoylake and West Kirby Advertiser*, 11 Dec. 1918.

65. J. Cox, *The English Churches in a Secular Society*, Oxford, 1982, p. 205.

66. Hackney Archives Department, SN/W/1/13, draft speech.

67. Barnsley, Town Clerk's In Letters, File 35, letter from G. B. Lancaster, 16 Aug. 1922.

68. Sheffield, CA 653 (1), Minutes, 11 Aug. 1925 and CA 653 (14/1).

69. *Kelly's Directory of Sheffield and Rotherham*, London, 1928.

70. Hackney, SN/W/1/13, manuscript notes on reverse of subscription list.

71. Carlisle, S/MB/Wo/1/3/863, Workington War Memorial, papers, leaflet (no date).

72. Ibid.

73. Borthwick Institute of Historical Research, University of York, Atkinson Brierley Papers, Box 56, Pudsey War Memorial, letter from W. Shackleton, 20 Mar. 1920.

74. *Kentish Mercury*, 18 June 1920.

75. Scottish National War Memorial papers, Bundle 14, letter 21 Dec. 1921.

76. *Kentish Mercury*, 18 June 1920.

77. Strathclyde, G4.1, Gladstone, Kelvin and Roberts Memorials.

78. City of Carlisle, *Proceedings of the Council and Committees*, vol. XXXIII, 1921–1922, pp. 172 and 254.

79. Stockport Archive Service, B/AA/4, Minutes, 5 June and 22 July 1919.

80. *Durham County Advertiser*, 10 June 1921.

81. Carlisle, PR/5/186, Greystoke War Memorial Committee, Minutes, 18 Nov. 1919.

82. Atkinson Brierley Papers, Box 105, Hackness War Memorial, letter from Derwent, 20 Mar. 1919.

83. Ibid., 5 Sept. 1920.

84. Ibid., Sutton and Huby War Memorial, letter from Gray to Brierley, 11 June 1920.

85. *Carlisle Journal*, 2 May 1919.

86. Carlisle, DX/5/59, Brampton Parish, Jackson Papers, draft speech, 19 Mar. 1919.

2

A Commemorative Tradition and its Application in War

Although some elements in the commemoration of the First World War were new, the way in which it was organised and the form it took continued a pattern which had developed in the previous century. It also drew on commemorative practices which had become widespread during the war itself, partly for propaganda purposes and partly as an element in the wartime pastoral work of the Church of England. During the nineteenth century a tradition of national commemorative events had grown up. Its organisation was predominantly local, and combined the efforts of private citizens, voluntary organisations and local authorities. It was financed out of funds raised locally by voluntary bodies under the patronage of civic leaders, and as high a level as possible of public participation was encouraged. Coronations, royal jubilees and deaths were its main occasions. By 1918 the familiarity of such events offered well-established conventions for the organisation of festivities and the erection of permanent memorials.

Wars, and the aftermath of wars, had played an important part in the development of the commemorative tradition. In 1809, during the Napoleonic wars, King George III's jubilee was celebrated to raise national morale,[1] and memorials to the King and to military leaders of that period were erected by subscription funds, some of which encouraged the participation of members of the working class.[2] The Boer War of 1899–1902 was commemorated by many monuments to its dead. During the Great War some forms of ceremony and of commemorative objects - shrines and monuments - had come into use in which references to the war dead played an important part. This chapter will explore the precedents thus set for the commemoration of the Great War.

Civic Commemoration before the Great War

By Edward VII's reign the commemoration of events of national importance had become a common feature of civic life in communities of all sizes. The public meeting to launch a fund and decide what should be done with it, a representative committee to manage the use of the fund, the encouragement of communal unity and the participation of all classes, within a framework provided by the local government system, were common.

Victoria's jubilees in 1887 and 1897 were commemorated largely through local organisation, and this procedure was endorsed by the government. When Lord Randolph Churchill, the Chancellor of the Exchequer, was questioned in Parliament about the government's intentions for a national celebration of the Golden Jubilee, he replied that, 'all celebrations of this kind will probably possess greater value in proportion as they arise from the spontaneous action of the people'.[3] Local committees were established, funds were raised for celebrations and memorials, and the participation of all classes was encouraged. Leeds Jubilee Committee went to great lengths to include working-class organisations in the arrangement of the celebrations. It set up a sub-committee 'to consider and consult with the representatives of the working classes as to the best way of carrying out a resolution to organise a general rejoicing suitable to the occasion'.[4] Representatives of various trades and benefit societies met the mayor to discuss the question. At a public meeting in Lewisham, in 1897, held to form a committee for the Diamond Jubilee, the vicar moved 'that all classes of the community be invited to co-operate in this loyal commemoration', which was resolved *nem. con.*[5] It was widely felt that creating a memorial, whether an institution or a monument, on such occasions was a civic duty, and that failure to erect one was a slur on the community. A speaker at a public meeting in Greenwich thought 'the inhabitants of the Borough would be ashamed if some permanent memorial was not established' to commemorate the jubilee, and was supported by cries of 'hear, hear'.[6] In 1901, after Victoria's death, the mayor of South Shields initiated a movement to erect a memorial to her. He had enquired about the intentions of other towns and 'had found that there was a general desire on the part of municipalities throughout the kingdom to have memorials of their own'.[7]

While many such memorials were monuments, they could also be utilitarian buildings intended to provide medical, educational or social facilities. One precedent for commemorative endowments of this sort was the ancient tradition of wealthy individuals' establishing named charitable funds both as gifts to the communities in which they lived, and as monuments to themselves. Another precedent was the continuing practice of entertaining the elderly, the poor, and children to special meals and festivities on commemorative occasions. Victoria's jubilees had been widely celebrated in this way. This charitable element in commemoration had both symbolic and hard-headed practical value. Many people thought that if money was to be disbursed it should serve a constructive rather than a merely sentimental and decorative purpose. If a memorial could be useful as well as impressive, it would be that much more appreciated. In 1818, the then Chancellor of the Exchequer, asked about a monument to victory over the French, told the House of Commons that 'nothing could be more fit than that national monuments should be rendered applicable to purposes of general utility'.[8] On the other hand, a charitable memorial also acted as a gesture of social reconciliation, bringing benefits to the entire community, and so reinforced the theme of communal unity in the celebrations.

Contributions to memorials were understood to serve a symbolic as much as a practical purpose. Giving was the essential commemorative act, showing the community's appreciation of the person commemorated. C. J. Darling, MP for Deptford, noted that the resolution to establish a borough jubilee fund in 1897 did not specify a use for it. 'What was desirable', he said, 'was that the fund should be no mean expression of the feeling of that borough',[9] regardless of its eventual use. It was therefore open to memorial committees to choose as their memorial whatever they thought would best arouse public generosity. The *Kentish Mercury* urged in 1887 that an endowment fund for the local voluntary hospital in Greenwich and for the Royal Kent Dispensary would be an ideal jubilee memorial because they were institutions about whose value all sections of opinion could agree, and to which all classes could be expected to contribute.[10] It would therefore constitute the most effective symbol of the community's appreciation.

Commemoration of those who had died in the Boer War foreshadowed that of the Great War in many ways. The war had involved the civilian population of Britain to an unusual degree. It had been extensively reported in newspapers. It had given rise, especially during a week of catastrophic British defeats in December 1899, to fears not only for the security of the Empire, but even of an attack on Britain herself by the European powers. At the unveiling of the Northumberland Boer War memorial in 1908, the Lord Mayor of Newcastle reminded his audience of 'that terrible time . . . when our hearts were sick with fear, and a black and ominous cloud hung over us, and we dreaded from hour to hour the news which might come'.[11] About two hundred thousand recruits were raised in response to this crisis during January and February 1900.[12] In addition to the regular army, a popular volunteering movement was started. Fifty-four thousand volunteers joined the imperial forces in South Africa in the course of the war to serve in special volunteer units such as London's City Imperial Volunteers, some fourteen hundred men. Around twenty thousand British personnel died, the vast majority of them from disease, and the losses were keenly felt.[13] The *Yorkshire Herald* remarked in 1905, 'It is an unprecedented circumstance in the modern military annals of the country that one county should lose as many as 1459 of its sons in a single campaign'.[14]

The raising of memorials to these casualties generally followed the arrangements for late Victorian and Edwardian festivals of state, although on this occasion the lead was not necessarily taken by the local authority. Memorials in large towns were, frequently, county memorials dedicated to the dead of the county regiment and its associated volunteer units, and the movements to erect them were under the formal leadership of the Lord Lieutenant. They appealed to the county rather than the municipal community, but they were no less concerned to encourage united communal action than strictly municipal memorial projects.

In 1900 the Lords Lieutenant of the three Ridings of Yorkshire had formed a committee with the Commander-in-Chief, North Eastern Command to raise a memorial at York to the dead of the county. They resolved that 'all classes be invited to subscribe in order that the proposed monument should be a fitting testament to the memory of our soldiers and sailors'.[15] When Lord Granby launched the appeal for Leicestershire's Boer War memorial at Leicester, he hoped 'the small subscribers . . . would be numerous, in order that the whole county and borough, rich or poor, may participate'.[16]

There was no annual ceremony of remembrance comparable to Armistice Day to commemorate the Boer War. There were, however, regular anniversary dinners to celebrate the reliefs of Ladysmith and Mafeking.[17] There was sufficient awareness of 'Ladysmith Day' in Leicester for Lord Granby to propose it as an appropriate time for the churches to take a collection in support of the county Boer War memorial at their Sunday services.[18] At Liverpool, an annual ceremony was instituted in 1907; but this was rare if not unique. It was held at the memorial (erected the previous year) in Saint John's Gardens which commemorates not so much the Boer War dead as the entire history of the King's Liverpool Regiment, which had taken part in the defence of Ladysmith. The memorial was decorated for Ladysmith Day by men of the regiment, with the approval of the Lord Mayor. Wreaths were placed there by relatives of soldiers who had died in the war; but on the first occasion there was no formal parade. The *Liverpool Echo* reported: 'The demonstration was the more significant seeing that all present had been drawn together without formal invitation, and with a general desire to honour the memory of men who had gallantly died for their country on far off fields of war.'[19] In subsequent years there was a march past the memorial and a church service for men of the regiment.[20] It is conceivable that this apparently spontaneous development was influenced by knowledge of Memorial Day in the United States, instituted after the Civil War; but there is no clear evidence.

Home Front Morale and the Commemoration of the War Dead 1914–1918

During the First World War, commemorative ceremonies and objects, partly or exclusively concerned with the war dead, became widespread and popular. Mass open-air rallies and church services were held, and ephemeral or permanent memorials of various kinds were erected. References to those who had been killed had a prominent place in them, in prayers, tributes of flowers, inscriptions and images. The commemoration of the dead was often combined with prayers for the safety of the living and with the promotion of patriotic sentiments. Rolls of honour in places of work, churches or public spaces carried the names of local people on active service, and of those killed, and were expected to encourage patriotic devotion generally as well as respect for the individuals named on them. Remembering and honouring the dead was intended to provide some relief for the feelings of the bereaved, and some encouragement to them; but it also made an important contribution to the home front propaganda offensive.

On each anniversary of the outbreak of war, 4 August, large patriotic rallies were held. This day became known as 'Remembrance Day'[21] until it was superseded in 1919 by 11 November. The first anniversary ceremony in Portsmouth was allegedly attended by a hundred thousand people. The crowd declared its 'inflexible determination to continue to a victorious end the struggle in maintenance of those ideals of Liberty and Justice which are the common and sacred cause of the allies'. In 1918 the same ceremony was conducted, including the words 'silently paying tribute to the Empire's sons who have fallen in the fight for freedom on the scattered battlefields of the world war'.[22]

Existing religious or patriotic festivals were given a reference to the war dead. Hackney parish church added a commemorative element to its evening service for Easter 1916. The names of local men who had been killed were read from the altar steps, the Last Post was sounded, a guard of honour presented arms, and a procession was formed carrying a wreath of laurel and lilies along with Allied flags.[23] The Empire Day celebrations that year at Gayhurst Road School, Hackney, included a pageant in which children carried shields inscribed with the names of dead and wounded old pupils.[24] The Navy League organised a service at Saint Martin-in-the-Fields church for Trafalgar Day in October 1916, to be followed by the laying of wreaths at Nelson's Column in memory of officers and men killed in the Battle of Jutland.[25]

Commemorative rolls of honour and, later, religious shrines came increasingly into use. Rolls of honour were lists compiled by communities or institutions naming their members who had joined the forces. They had been used as part of the recruiting campaigns of 1914 and 1915. In September 1914, Walter Long MP, a Wiltshire landowner, held a public meeting in the village of West Ashton at which he exhorted local men to join up rather than 'live at home in ease, a craven at heart'. He told them that 'here in this village, and in other villages where I have influence I mean to have a great placard headed the roll of honour. On that will be inscribed the names of any man who joins the Colours; a copy of it will be sent to every house or cottage in which he has dwelt, and where his family are, and a permanent copy will be given to his family to keep as a lasting record of the fact that he did his duty.'[26] Around February 1915 a County of Bute Roll of Honour was published, saying: 'Some day *you* will want a share in the joy and honour of *victory*. You don't want to be out of it at the end; you can only avoid that by being *in it* now.'[27]

Permanent memorials in stone, not, at this stage, to the dead, were also conceived as aids to recruitment. Stone crosses were awarded in 1915 to the villages of Knowlton, Kent, Dalderby, Lincolnshire, and Barrow-on-Trent, Derbyshire, as prizes for having the highest proportion in their counties of eligible men enlisted. At Knowlton the prize-giver was the local *Weekly Dispatch*,[28] at Barrow Mr F. C. Arkwright, later a deputy lieutenant of the county,[29] and at Dalderby the Lincoln Chamber of Commerce. The sculpted head of the Dalderby cross was donated by A. J. Tuttell, head of a firm of masons, and J. M. Harrison, a builder, donated the base. The rest of the cost was paid by subscription amongst other Chamber of Commerce members. The recruiting competition was announced in mid-April 1915, 'as a stimulus to recruiting during the next few weeks',[30] and the prize cross was finally unveiled in October 1916.

Death intruded increasingly into these memorials and rolls of honour. The London County Council had the first part of its roll of honour of staff killed in the war on sale in April 1915. (The proceeds may have gone to a relief fund.) On 4 August 1916, a stone cross commemorating Lord Kitchener, recently killed at sea, John Cornwell, the Jutland hero, and dead soldiers of Bishopsgate and the Honourable Artillery Company was unveiled at Saint Botolph's church, Bishopsgate, in the City of London.[31] Bermondsey Liberal Association unveiled its roll of honour in April 1917. On this occasion the association instituted a modest act of remembrance – setting aside 'a few moments' at each meeting to concentrate on the war and those serving in it. The assembled members stood in honour of those on active service, and the chairman read a 'rubric holding in reverence the memory of those who have fallen in the war for liberty, sympathising with the wounded and sick, recognising sacrifice, praying for the safety of those who were well and confidently looking forward for [*sic*] a triumphant and final victory which will secure the enduring peace of the whole civilised world'.[32]

The idea of publicly commemorating all local soldiers, either currently serving or now dead, was taken up by town councils. In October 1916, The Borough of Hackney proposed a temporary memorial. Stoke Newington's mayor was discussing a comprehensive roll of honour for the borough in January 1917.[33] Rolls of honour displayed in prominent places were subsequently adapted to record distinctions won by the servicemen whose names appeared on them, and deaths amongst them.

Meanwhile, Anglican clergy had started a movement to erect simple and cheap shrines in streets, dedicated to inhabitants who were in the services, with a special place for the names of any who had been killed. The clergy intended their parishioners to participate in the production and care of the shrines, and subsequently held regular short services of intercession and remembrance at them, processing around the parish to them with their choirs and collecting a congregation as they went. Shrines were first put up in working-class streets in the parish of Saint John of Jerusalem, South Hackney in (probably) April 1916.[34] The idea had occurred to the rector that Easter.[35] At the London diocesan Conference in May, Bishop Winnington-Ingram described the pioneering shrines, and commended the idea to his clergy. 'Don't be satisfied with your roll of honour in church, go into the streets and make them understand', he said.[36]

The movement to erect street shrines was particularly favoured by the more Catholic-inclined members of the Church of England, a group to which the Bishop of London belonged. The idea and its intention followed a pattern of missionary initiatives aimed by high Anglicans at the metropolitan poor through the settlement and other socially engaged movements for several decades past. Clergy from less ritualist sections of the Church were sometimes suspicious of them, believing that they furthered a tendency to adopt Catholic religious practices which was growing in strength amongst Anglicans during the war.[37] A parish priest, dedicating a shrine in Lambeth, hinted at his own reservations when he 'expressed the hope that it would not be regarded in any superstitious sense'.[38] But the movement soon became accepted even amongst Nonconformists, one of whom wrote to a local paper in Hackney to defend street shrines and public intercessionary prayer for soldiers at the front against criticism from extreme Protestants.[39]

The earliest shrines were improvised from cheap materials by clergy and their parishioners. Hackney's first street shrines consisted of lists of all the men from a street who had joined up, written on 'framed parchments' (more likely, pieces of paper or card) 'surmounted by a wooden cross'[40] with a prayer beneath 'which the people were asked to learn and to say daily'.[41] Vases of flowers were placed on either side. In Saint Pancras two contrasting shrines were recorded. One of them consisted of 'a cheap oblong frame of oak' containing two cards which listed 'The Roll of Honour' and 'The Heroic Dead', lettered 'in the vicar's delicate hand'. On one side was a union jack and on the other 'a picture of Christ supporting a soldier pale from the agony of his wounds' (probably a print or magazine illustration). There were finally 'a few chrysanthemums in a couple of cheap tin brackets'. The other shrine stood on the pavement in front of the area-railings of a row of houses. 'The base of the shrine is an old kitchen table, on which there is a cloth of red twill and an apron of decorated plush stuff' with 'God Bless Our King in gilt embroidery'. A frame contained lists of the servicemen and of the dead. 'Two green flags with the Irish harp in yellow, are entwined with Union Jacks, and all about the frames are flowers . . . at the base of the table a score of evergreens in pots, and red, white and blue tissue paper.' There were photographs of Kitchener, Jellicoe and Sir John French. 'Robinson V.C. smiles out of the smother of chrysanthemums. And near these great men, modestly put to the side . . . photographs of the local heroes - laughing Tommies, smoking and in their shirt sleeves.'[42]

By August 1916 a cheap shrine was available commercially, consisting of a tripartite frame to contain lists of names and pictures, with a horizontal board above it to carry flags on short staffs, and flower-holders at each end. The design was patented by Mr T. A. Hand of Longton, Staffordshire, and retailed at 6s 6d each.[43] A leading firm of monumental masons was advertising professionally-made shrines in December 1916.[44] As the war progressed the commercially available products became more elaborate and costly. Examples were offered consisting of ornamental cabinet-work and lettering, sometimes containing cast bronze crucifixes.[45]

Street shrines were promoted by the Church of England in conjunction with other public outdoor activities especially concerned with the war, the high point of these activities being the National Mission of Repentance and Hope, launched officially in the autumn of 1916. The Mission consisted of a drive to reach a wider public, and to arouse interest in religious practice and ideas, in connection with the war. It included speaking tours by well-known preachers, such as the Bishop of London, and intensified parochial activity involving the lay members of local congregations. Alan Wilkinson has described the Mission as:

> an attempt by the Church of England to respond to the spiritual needs of the nation; an attempt to discharge its sense of vocation to act as the Christian conscience of the nation. It was also intended as a powerful reply to those (including Horatio Bottomley [the chauvinistic editor of *John Bull*]) who argued that the Church of England was not rising to the needs of the hour.[46]

The previous nine months had been filled with preparatory work and publicity for the Mission, in which shrine-making played a part. Already, at New Year 1916, the Church had held three days of intercession, in which 'a real effort was made to bring home to people the spiritual issues on which victory or disaster depend', and 'solemn open-air processions . . . were a feature of the devotions in many parishes'. The vicar of South Hackney was one of those who held a procession around his parish. 'In the principal streets the names of those who had gone out from each street were read out and they were commended to God in prayer.' He distributed prayer cards at a subsequent church service to all whose interest had been aroused, with the intention of forming 'a league of prayer' for the parish.[47] Informal organisation of this sort probably mobilised the supporters necessary to get the movement to erect war shrines under way.

The street shrines spread rapidly throughout the country from mid-1916. Although they were obviously popular, they ought not to be seen, as some writers have suggested, as an essentially spontaneous phenomenon.[48] They originated with the Church of England's wartime evangelism and continued to be promoted very largely by the clergy and church workers, with support later from the newspaper press and other commercial organisations. Early reports acknowledged that the beginnings of the shrine movement were not spontaneous. 'All the breezy persuasion of the clergy was needed to bring the parishioners to see shrines as the right thing', said the *Evening News*, because the British were 'a shy and secret race' and the emotionality of the shrines 'came oddly' to them.[49] Nor was their propagation left to spontaneous popular action. At South Hackney, one of the curates had specific responsibility for organising the street shrines. In August 1916, four months after the movement started, he was still charged with 'the principal work of organisation' in connection with the shrines. In October clergy elsewhere were 'encouraging their people to compile lists of the men who have gone out and to erect and maintain shrines of their own'.[50]

The usefulness of the shrines in the programme of the National Mission of Repentance and Hope was described by the vicar of Longton, Staffordshire. He wrote, 'the shrine is made the centre from which our women and girls, divided into groups of eight or ten each, under a leader, ask if they may come and hold a prayer meeting in the cottages whence the lads have gone'. These groups later returned to the parish church 'bringing with them as many "outsiders" as possible' for a service of intercession. 'Such prayer meetings conducted by the laity alone are of immense value, if only to the workers themselves, teaching them their priesthood, and how to make the church a real house of prayer'.[51] The exercise thus served two important goals of the National Mission: to draw in new church members and to renew and enliven the commitment of existing members.

Initially, the emphasis in public services of intercession, and in the words and imagery of the shrines, was on the well-being of soldiers at the front. Deaths, however, inevitably attracted increasing attention, and this offered the clergy another way of communicating Christian ideas. The vicar of Longton explained that when a man from the street already listed on the shrine was reported killed, his name was 'solemnly transferred across the thin black line separating the living from the dead. Still there on the shrine, still in the great family of God, still to be prayed for! What an opportunity for teaching the great doctrine of the Communion of Saints.' This 'simple action' was more comprehensible than sermons on the subject, he thought, and 'you get people there whom you seldom, if ever, get in Church'.[52]

Hackney's war shrines first came to general public notice when Queen Mary made an informal visit to them in August 1916. Their existence was reported in local and national newspapers, and further royal visits attracted attention elsewhere. In October, the *Evening News* decided to raise a fund to provide materials for shrines in poor areas, and rallied influential and wealthy support for the movement.[53] The Lord Mayor of London and the mayors of Battersea, Holborn and Hackney expressed their support for the paper's initiative, and Selfridges offered to pay for all shrines erected within a mile of the shop. Clergy of several denominations asked the paper for assistance with their local shrines.[54]

The *Evening News* proposed to select a few sites 'in conjunction with the clergy and others concerned' for shrines to be erected under its patronage. It commissioned a design from the architects Bodley and Hare for a wooden structure (Figure 1) consisting of a frame containing a cross, with doors which, when opened, revealed the roll of honour inscribed on their inner faces. A low pediment at the top carried Allied flags, and a ledge was

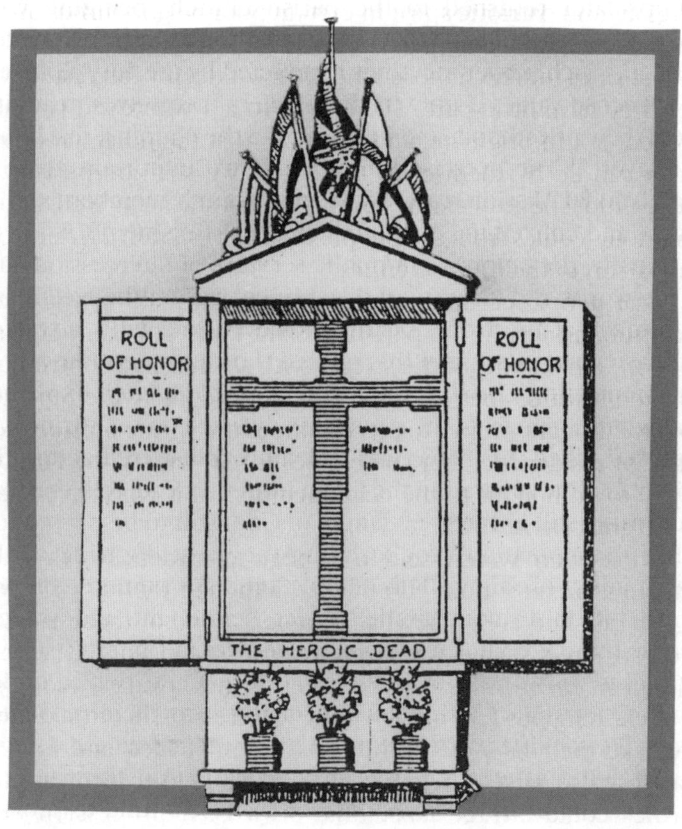

Figure 1.

provided at the bottom for vases of flowers. As inscriptions, 'Greater love hath no man than this, that a man lay down his life for his friends' and 'For God, King and country' were suggested. Other artists and architects submitted designs speculatively, and the paper encouraged more to do so.[55]

However contrived their origin may have been, street shrines were supposed to be an expression of the public's desire to honour and support those of its members who had gone to fight in the war, and great emphasis was laid on the part ordinary residents should play in making and caring for them. When the *Evening News* intervened in the shrine movement it insisted that popular initiative and participation should be in the foreground. The original idea, it claimed, had been 'the outcome of a truly religious and patriotic spirit in certain poor neighbourhoods . . . There is no wish on our part for a scheme which will dot London with shrines in which those who are most deeply interested will feel they have little part. The idea is to aid where aid is really needed, not to originate, and the more that the inhabitants of a street can do by themselves the better we shall be pleased.'[56] Clergy, too, spoke of shrines in this way. A shrine in Well Street, Paignton, 'comes from the people themselves', said a letter from the parson to the *Church Times*.[57]

Local people certainly did participate in making and looking after shrines. In the parish of Saint Peter's, Regent Square, London, inhabitants of the streets with shrines had contributed 2d each towards them.[58] Some Islington people were reported 'to have thought proper to place a miniature shrine outside their place of residence . . . In some cases it may satisfy the family's desire to do honour to the dead members of it who have fallen in the great fight . . .'.[59]

Shrines were widely held in respect. As evidence of this, the *Hackney Gazette* pointed out that 'although thefts of flowers in the East End are somewhat common' none of those used to decorate street shrines had been stolen.[60] The mayor of Hackney told the *Evening News* that the street shrines 'awake a good deal of latent religious feeling. The roughest treat them with respect and take their hats off as they pass them'.[61] Men and boys of Longton also raised their hats.[62] Services held to dedicate the shrines could attract substantial crowds. A procession held in Stoke Newington to dedicate five street shrines attracted several hundred people in Hawksley and Woodlea Roads, small residential streets near the parish church.[63] The dedication of a shrine in Mapledene Road, Dalston, included a contingent of local Volunteers, and attracted nearly a thousand people.[64]

Approval of war shrines was not universal. Opposition to them had religious motives, and was aimed at supposedly Catholic connotations in their imagery and in the religious acts associated with them. Objectors did not necessarily oppose the public display of simple rolls of honour,[65] although one opponent, while religiously motivated in the main, had a more general objection: 'War shrines . . . are no credit to our heroes or our boroughs, with dirty torn flags and empty jars or dead flowers.'[66] The collusion of the press in the shrine movement was attacked by a serving officer, who wrote that there were 'many who view with extreme alarm the seductive effort that is now being made at home by a certain portion of the mammon Press to "spiritualise" the nation into blindness' and out of 'the manly faith of true Protestantism'. This 'octopus of journalism' had revealed itself as 'the friend of superstition and priestcraft'.[67]

In April 1917, the controversial anti-Catholic Revd J. A. Kensit preached a sermon against war shrines at the Raleigh Memorial Church, Stoke Newington, in what had been advertised as 'a real patriotic protest against the memory of our brave soldiers and sailors being insulted by the idolaters of ritualism'.[68] After the meeting he was attacked by a waiting crowd of about fifty women and boys. He was severely bruised, and his hat, coat, umbrella and briefcase were stolen. His attackers also assaulted the conductress of the bus he was trying to catch, and a ticket inspector.[69] The *Hackney Recorder*, whose partiality in the matter is clear from its language, described the perpetrators as 'Angry women, whose loved ones have gone forth to the present awful conflict, many alas! never to return; and lads old enough to appreciate the situation and reverence the monuments at their street corners.'[70]

There is no direct evidence to tell why Kensit was so roughly handled. Sectarian violence of this sort might more normally be expected against Catholics or ritualist Anglicans than against an anti-Catholic like Kensit. While it is improbable that members of the crowd were, in principle, full of zeal for the ritualist wing of the Church of England, it is possible that they were acting out of a sense of personal loyalty to a popular high-church parish priest.[71] Alternatively, their behaviour is not unlike that meted out to many London residents of German origin at critical moments during the war. It may have been motivated by the same kind of nationalist hysteria.

It may also have been motivated by attachment to the war shrines as bringers of luck, in this case to friends and relatives serving in the war. A religious response to uncertainty had not been uncommon around the turn of the century. Jeffrey Cox has described the importance of such religious practices as New Year watchnight services, harvest festivals and 'churching' after childbirth to working-class residents of Lambeth, in the late nineteenth century, as invocations of good luck against the uncertainties of life in a poor community.[72] During the war, the anxiety of families and friends for those at the front, and the anxiety of service personnel themselves, led to an increased interest in religious observances which might contribute to their safety. Rural clergy in Oxfordshire noticed an increase in attendance at church, especially amongst women whose husbands were on active service.[73] The *Hackney Gazette* reported that 'letters written home by the men themselves show how much they personally appreciate [the] acts of thoughtfulness and devotion' which shrines represented.[74] In the context of such attitudes as these, a condemnation of street shrines might have been interpreted as hostility to the safety of the servicemen themselves.

Shrines were intended not only to comfort the anxious or bereaved, but also to support the war effort. A number of supporters of the shrine movement explicitly intended them to promote patriotic enthusiasm, and may have thought them an antidote to war-weariness amongst the working population. The Lord Mayor of London wrote to the *Evening News* that war shrines would, amongst other things 'keep alive the fires of patriotism'.[75] The shrines themselves sometimes contained patriotic images of military leaders, royalty and other war heroes. One of the street shrines in Saint Pancras displayed a union jack with the slogan 'Work for it, Fight for it', and the accompanying picture of Christ supporting a wounded soldier carried the words 'Hit hard, lean hard'.[76] In the closing stages of the war, Alderman Saint of Islington thought that a shrine proposed for Islington Green 'would also serve as a stimulus to the people not to be a party to an inconclusive peace which might mean a repetition of this terrible slaughter in the course of the next generation'.[77]

The religious message of the shrine movement was, for the

most part, the belligerent, crusading message of churchmen like Bishop Winnington-Ingram of London, who cultivated the view that all who died in the sacred cause of the Allies would be assured of their own redemption, sidestepping the orthodox doctrinal insistence on the necessity for Christian faith and repentance.[78] In 1915, Winnington-Ingram had written: 'Christ died on Good Friday for Freedom, Honour and Chivalry, and our boys are dying for the same things . . .. You ask me in a sentence as to what the Church is to do. I answer MOBILISE THE NATION FOR A HOLY WAR.'[79] If the shrines carried the message of a national crusade fought by local heroes, it is not surprising that those who objected to them were seen not simply as anti-Catholic but as enemies of the community and the nation.

The street shrine movement was especially addressed to women. An editorial in the *Evening News* maintained that shrines 'will be the care of the women whose men's names are inscribed thereon'.[80] At Longton it was the women and girls of the parish who held prayer meetings in the homes of mothers or wives of absent servicemen. Although workplaces and public institutions had their rolls of honour honouring employees or members who had joined up, and representing patriotic self-sacrifice as an heroic duty, women fully occupied keeping homes might rarely see such things. Street shrines with their associated activities were an opportunity to present to them the idea that citizens in arms were bearers of special moral worth, and that their sufferings were achievements of public significance. The *Hackney Recorder* had used the presence of women in the attack on J. A. Kensit to give legitimacy to the feelings behind it, emphasising the anger of the anxious or bereaved women. Beyond maintaining the shrines out of sentiment for their men, the women were, apparently, determined to defend them as objects of fervent devotion, and this was seen by the paper as a just and responsible attitude.

Shortly before the end of the war, there was a new development in the commemorative movement. Its aim was to create, under civic sponsorship, sacred commemorative centres for entire towns and cities, at which public ceremonies and private acts of devotion alike could take place. It stemmed from a large rally held in Hyde Park on 4 August 1918 to commemorate the fourth anniversary of the outbreak of war. A shrine was built on the site to act as a centre for floral tributes to the dead. It consisted of 'a large white Maltese cross' forming the base, 'with a spire 24 feet high . . . surmounted by a Union Jack, and around it the flags of the allies'. The spire was a tapering octagonal timber structure draped in purple and white cloth.[81] Purple is the liturgical colour worn by priests for the burial of the dead, especially by high Anglicans or Catholics when communion or mass is to be celebrated with the funeral. It is normally worn as a purple stole over a white surplice. Purple had also been used to drape the streets of London for Queen Victoria's funeral, in preference to black.[82]

Twenty thousand people were reported to have been present at this shrine on 4 August, and up to a hundred thousand to have visited it within a week.[83] By 15 August the organisers were claiming that two hundred thousand had laid flowers on it, and more people had visited it on the second weekend of its existence than on the first.[84] The *Evening News* supported a campaign to prevent the structure's being removed by the park authorities,[85] and it remained there, often needing refurbishment, until some time in September or October 1919.

Construction of the shrine had been arranged by Bishop Winnington-Ingram, with the support of the Lord Mayor of London and the advertising entrepreneur Charles Higham. It had been paid for by Sir Samuel Waring, of the drapery firm Waring and Gillows.[86] Plans existed for other towns to erect 'a great pyre symbolical of the graves' of the dead in parks or market places for the laying of flowers on the same day, 4 August.[87] There was pressure to keep these shrines as well, and 'Mayors throughout the country to whom appeals were made to retain all shrines until the end of the war' sent 'sympathetic replies', according to the *Evening News*.[88] Waring offered to pay for a more substantial structure in Hyde Park, and a design was commissioned from Sir Edwin Lutyens.[89] Sir Alfred Mond, First Commissioner of Works, who had responsibility for the royal parks, supported the scheme, but there was opposition to the design from the King, the Duke of Connaught, and from senior Office of Works officials, as well as controversy in *The Times*. The King later consented to a modified design, but it was never built.[90] At the same time, Charles Higham was promoting the idea of shrines for other large cities which would, apparently, be permanent. In this connection, the *Evening News* reported on 14 August that 'the movement to have a permanent shrine in each town bids fair to become national'. The mayors of Derby, Lancaster and South Shields were considering schemes. Leicester and Wolverhampton had already expressed approval.[91]

On 16 August the *Islington Daily Gazette* reported that the Hyde Park shrine had 'prompted public desire everywhere for local shrines', and that Higham had written to the mayor of Islington requesting 'that I may have the privilege of presenting [a] shrine to South Islington'.[92] Higham had a political interest in this particular locality. By October 1918 he had been adopted as the prospective Conservative candidate for Finsbury and Islington South in the next general election. A week after his offer of the shrine was announced, he began a campaign in the local newspaper promoting himself as 'the best-known advertising man in Europe'. He described how he had started his business from nothing, and subsequently worked for Kitchener's recruiting campaign, war savings, the Treasury, and the Red Cross. He did not mention his political ambitions at this stage.[93]

His offer of the shrine was accepted by Islington council, in spite of doubts expressed by one member as to the disinterestedness of Higham and of the predominantly Conservative committee which had first recommended acceptance.[94] The shrine was made of concrete, but otherwise followed roughly the pattern of the Hyde Park shrine, having a tapering vertical element on a cruciform base, topped by a flagpole, and although it is dedicated to the dead, the only individual referred to by name on it is Charles Higham (Figure 2). It was unveiled in October 1918 on Islington Green, where it still stands.[95]

Interest in shrines of this sort continued beyond the end of the war. The Hyde Park shrine continued to be revered for well over a year. A bereaved mother wrote to the Office of Works in October 1919, when she discovered the shrine had finally gone, complaining that its removal was an 'outrage on this small sacred spot to the memory of our beloved boys' and 'a dastardly disgrace to England. Is this how we poor broken hearted Mothers are to be treated?'[96] At Bradford, the committee set up to organise the local peace celebrations in 1919 seems to have had the Hyde Park precedent in mind when it proposed that a shrine of white painted wood, decorated with purple and white cloth, be erected as a ceremonial focus.[97] The object finally produced was a white, tapering, obelisk-like structure on a tall plinth, surmounted by

Figure 2.

a cross.[98] The inscriptions on it dedicated it comprehensively to the dead, wounded, and bereaved, and to all Bradford men and women who had served in the war.[99] After its unveiling on Peace Day, 19 July 1919, people filed past it to lay flowers, as they had the previous year in Hyde Park.

In many respects, wartime commemoration of the war dead fell into the patterns common to civic commemorations in the pre-war era. It owed its growth to the religious, municipal and business leaders of communities, who had been the principal agents of pre-war commemorations, and who were involved in maintaining local support for the war effort in other ways as well, and especially in the encouragement of recruitment in the period of voluntary enlistment up until 1916. A number of these people thought about the wartime commemorative movement, no matter how ephemeral its expression, as if it were a form of civic commemoration on the pre-war pattern.

In many boroughs, such as Hackney and Stoke Newington, mayors lent their prestige to it. In January 1917, the mayor of Stoke Newington unveiled a street shrine in his borough with a contingent of the local Volunteers and Boy Scouts present.[100] Celebration of the local community's part in the war helped to spread interest in the shrine movement, even in its initial stages. Queen Mary had visited Hackney to see the street shrines, according to the vicar, after 'hearing of the great response to the call for men in this parish'.[101] In other words, her visit was as much a recognition of local recruiting achievement as an expression of sentimental interest in the shrines. It was a fillip at least to communal, if not strictly speaking to civic, pride.

The Victorian idea that public memorials ought to contribute to improving the quality of communal life was applied to street shrines. The writer G. R. Sims described the war shrines in 1916 as part of a 'great Festival of Remembrance', and praised them for enhancing the street environment and life in it. 'In many a mean street these War Shrines will be as a green oasis in the desert. They will bring beauty and fragrance into many a grey life and many an unlovely street.'[102] When Selfridges held an exhibition of war shrines, the *Church Times* reviewed it unfavourably, on the grounds that the works exhibited would not contribute to the improvement of daily life. The reviewer judged that the exhibits did 'not give any great encouragement to those who look for a revival of art in daily life' and suggested that clergy should consult architects for designs of a higher quality.[103]

Stress on participation by the community at large was a feature equally of civic commemorations and of the production of war shrines. Shrines were portrayed as an expression of popular feeling through the contributions local people made towards them. They were also seen as a source of increased communal solidarity. The *Church Family Newspaper* stated that 'a deep sense of corporate fellowship has been engendered by the street shrines, uniting the families of those who have been commemorated in a bond of sympathy and comradeship'.[104] Moreover, the interest shown by Queen Mary in the shrines in working-class districts offered an opportunity for the expression of class harmony and of the idea that the burden of anxiety and loss was shared equally by families of high and low social status.[105] No matter how well war shrines fitted the public mood of wartime, they were clearly products of the earlier civic commemorative tradition.

Commemoration of the war dead was not simply a retrospective activity which began with a release of feeling made possible by the end of hostilities. It had been part of the wartime effort to keep up home-front morale and to focus attention on servicemen at the front in a personal way.[106] It was a way which did not depend on stories about a selection of exemplary heroes, but on concern for the vulnerability of the ordinary citizen-soldier. Personal acquaintance and attachment were transformed through commemorative acts into a public affirmation of support for those engaged in the fighting. Through the street shrine movement, ordinary members of the public who were concerned about their friends and relatives in the forces were given an active role in expressing anxiety or a sense of loss, and in taking action to assuage them, so far as that was possible. At the larger wartime public ceremonies of remembrance, homage to servicemen was expressed in massive attendances to lay flowers on shrines. These could also to some degree be 'tended' by mourners through frequent visits to renew their floral tributes.

Fear and danger and the experience of bereavement could not be ignored, either by private individuals or by the public authorities. Commemorative ceremonies and shrines provided vehicles through which ordinary people could participate in making a response to these feelings, and the emotion was channelled into maintaining commitment to the war effort. The celebratory intention of earlier civic commemorations was present, as was the promotion of communal unity regardless of class, but these were adapted to the circumstances of war: widespread emotional stress and the political exigencies of national mobilisation. After the war, a similar mixture of political and emotional purposes continued to inform the commemoration of the dead, as subsequent chapters will show.

Notes to Chapter 2

1. L. Colley, 'The Apotheosis of George III', *Past and Present*, no. 102, (1984), pp. 94–129.
2. A. Yarrington, *The Commemoration of the Hero, 1800–1864: Monuments to the British Victors of the Napoleonic Wars*, London, 1988.
3. *Parliamentary Debates*, third series, vol. 309, p. 1354, 25 Sept. 1886, reply to Mr Lawson.
4. *The Times*, 12 Feb. 1887.
5. *Kentish Mercury*, 23 Apr. 1897.
6. Ibid., 30 Apr. 1897.
7. *Shields Daily Gazette*, 17 May 1901.
8. *Parliamentary Debates*, first series, vol. 37, p. 1116, 27 Jan. 1818.
9. *Kentish Mercury*, 2 Apr. 1897.
10. Ibid., 1 July 1887.
11. Newcastle City Libraries, press cuttings, no title or date.
12. E. Halévy, *Halévy's History of the English People in the Nineteenth Century, Vol. 5, Imperialism and the Rise of Labour (1895–1905)*, London, 1961, p. 93.
13. R. Price, *An Imperial War and the British Working Class, Working Class Reactions to the Boer War, 1899–1902*, London, 1972.
14. *Yorkshire Herald*, 4 Aug. 1905.
15. Ibid.
16. *Leicester Mercury*, 12 Jan. 1903.
17. *Liverpool Echo*, 1 Mar. 1906, 28 Feb. 1908; *Daily Mail*, 18 May 1909.
18. *Leicester Mercury*, 12 Jan. 1903.
19. *Liverpool Echo*, 28 Feb. 1907.
20. Ibid., 28 Feb. 1910.
21. *The Times*, 5 Aug. 1918.
22. W. G. Gates (ed.) *Portsmouth in the Great War*, Portsmouth, 1919, p. 124.
23. *Hackney and Kingsland Gazette*, 28 Apr. 1916.

24. Ibid., 29 May 1916.
25. *Evening News*, 3 Oct. 1916.
26. *Wiltshire Gazette*, 3 Sept. 1914, quoted in P. Horn, *Rural Life in England in the First World War*, New York, 1984, p. 29.
27. Imperial War Museum, Department of Printed Books, box of recruiting leaflets.
28. D. Boorman, *At the Going Down of the Sun*, Dunnington Hall, 1988, p. 55.
29. *Church Times*, 12 Nov. 1920.
30. *Lincolnshire Chronicle*, 17 Oct. 1916; Lincoln Incorporated Chamber of Commerce, *Annual Report*, 1915, p. 13; Lincolnshire, Scrivelsby with Dalderby: par. 8/1, circular 13 Apr. 1915.
31. *City Press*, 5 Aug. 1916.
32. Southwark Local Studies Library, untitled press cutting, 6 Apr. 1917.
33. *Hackney and Kingsland Gazette*, 20 Oct. 1916 and 5 Jan. 1917.
34. *Hackney and Stoke Newington Recorder*, 11 Aug. 1916.
35. *Church Family Newspaper*, 18 Aug. 1916.
36. *Church Times*, 19 May 1916.
37. A. Wilkinson, *The Church of England and the First World War*, London, 1978, pp. 176–8.
38. Southwark, untitled press cutting, 29 Dec. 1916.
39. *Hackney and Stoke Newington Recorder*, 4 May 1917, letter from 'Highbury New Park Resident'.
40. *Hackney and Kingsland Gazette*, 11 Aug. 1916.
41. *Church Times*, 19 May 1916.
42. *Evening News*, 4 Oct. 1916.
43. *The Challenge*, 28 July 1916.
44. *Church Family Newspaper*, 22 Dec. 1916, advertisement for G. Maile and Son.
45. Durham County Record Office, D/Br/E 45(9), Brancepeth Ecclesiastical Parish, Correspondence and Papers Relating to Parish War Memorial, Catalogue from G. Maile and Son, 1917; Clwyd Record Office, Hawarden, P/45/1/379, Northop Parish Church, War Memorial Tablet, Catalogue from J. Wippell and Co.
46. Wilkinson, *The Church of England*, p. 70.
47. *Church Times*, 7 Jan. 1916.
48. Wilkinson, *The Church of England*, p. 67; E. S. Turner, *Dear Old Blighty*, London, 1980, p. 135.
49. *Evening News*, 4 Oct. 1916.
50. Ibid.
51. 'War Shrines and the National Mission', *The Challenge*, 28 July 1916.
52. Ibid.
53. *Evening News*, 4 Oct. 1916.
54. Ibid., 6 and 7 Oct. 1916.
55. Ibid., 9 Oct. 1916.
56. Ibid., 6 Oct. 1916.
57. *Church Times*, 10 Nov. 1916.
58. *Daily Mail*, 4 Oct. 1916.
59. *Islington Daily Gazette*, 1 Nov. 1918.

60. *Hackney and Kingsland Gazette*, 11 Aug. 1916.
61. *Evening News*, 7 Oct. 1916.
62. *The Challenge*, 28 July 1916.
63. *Hackney and Stoke Newington Recorder*, 18 Aug. 1916.
64. Ibid., 15 Dec. 1916.
65. Ibid., 27 Apr. 1917.
66. Ibid., 11 May 1917.
67. *Church Family Newspaper*, 10 Nov. 1916. Even after the Great War, the use of the crucifix as a war memorial, though common, was still opposed by some Church of England administrators and congregations, and court cases were fought over it; see *Builder*, vol. 120, 15 April 1921, p. 485; *Birmingham Mail*, 10 Jan. 1922.
68. *Hackney and Stoke Newington Recorder*, 27 Apr. 1917.
69. Ibid., 11 May 1917.
70. Ibid., 4 May 1917.
71. I am grateful to Dr Gerald Parsons for a discussion on this point.
72. J. Cox, *The English Churches in a Secular Society*, Oxford, 1982, p. 103.
73. Diocese of Oxford, Clergy Visitation Returns, 1918, MS Oxf. Dioc Pp.c. 378, 379, quoted in P. Horn, *Rural Life*, p. 45.
74. *Hackney and Kingsland Gazette*, 11 Aug. 1916.
75. *Evening News*, 6 Oct. 1916.
76. Ibid., 4 Oct. 1916.
77. *Islington Daily Gazette*, 29 Aug. 1918.
78. Wilkinson, *The Church of England*, p. 180.
79. *The Guardian*, 10 June 1915, quoted in Wilkinson, *The Church of England*, p. 253, emphasis in the original.
80. *Evening News*, 6 Oct. 1916.
81. Ibid., 3 and 5 Aug. 1918; *Illustrated London News*, 10 Aug. 1918; *Church Times*, 9 Aug. 1918.
82. E. Longford, *Victoria R.I.*, London, 1964, p. 563.
83. *The Times*, 5 Aug. 1918; *Evening News*, 12 Aug. 1918.
84. *Islington Daily Gazette*, 15 Aug. 1918.
85. *Evening News*, 6 Aug. 1918.
86. Public Record Office, WORK 16/26 (8), letter from C. Higham, no date (but before 24 July 1918); *Evening News*, 6 Aug. 1918.
87. Ibid., untitled and undated press cutting.
88. *Evening News*, 10 Aug. 1918.
89. Public Record Office, WORK 16/26 (8), letter from Sir Samuel Waring, 8 Aug. 1918.
90. Ibid., letter from Lord Stamfordham, 26 Sept. 1918; letter from Captain Ashworth, 24 Oct. 1918; letter to Lutyens from L. Earle 5 Sept. 1918 (also letters between 3 Oct. and 16 Nov. 1918 in part 2 of this file); *The Times*, 4 Sept. 1918, letter from S. Paget, 6 Sept. 1918, letter from A. Leveson-Gower.
91. *Evening News*, 10 Aug. 1918.
92. *Islington Daily Gazette*, 22 Oct. 1918.
93. Ibid., 23 and 30 Aug. 1918.
94. Metropolitan Borough of Islington, Minutes of Proceedings, 24 Sept. 1918; *Islington Daily Gazette*, 24 Aug. 1918.
95. *Islington Daily Gazette*, 28 Oct. 1918.

96. Public Record Office, WORK 16/26 (8), letter from Mrs A. Whitford, 28 Oct. 1919.

97. Bradford, BBC 1/57/25, City of Bradford, Special Committee re. Peace Celebrations, Minutes, 10 May 1919.

98. *Bradford Daily Telegraph*, 21 July 1919.

99. Bradford, BBC 1/57/25, Minutes, 7 July 1919.

100. *Hackney and Stoke Newington Recorder*, 5 Jan. 1917.

101. *Hackney and Kingsland Gazette*, 4 Sept. 1916.

102. *Evening News*, 6 Oct. 1916.

103. *Church Times*, 3 Nov. 1916.

104. *Church Family Newspaper*, 10 Nov. 1916.

105. *Hackney and Kingsland Gazette*, 11 Aug. 1916.

106. This explains to a considerable extent the paradox, noticed by Geoff Dyer, that the form which post-war memory of the dead would take seems to have been anticipated in images from the war itself: see G. Dyer, *The Missing of the Somme*, Harmondsworth, 1995, p. 7.

3

Talking About War Memorials

The first stage in organising the erection of a memorial was a public discussion of what form the memorial should take. There was a wide range of alternative types offered by past practice to choose from. The local memorial committee would invite suggestions and then conduct a debate on the proposals in open or committee meetings. In spite of the availability of precedents to refer to, these debates show that there was considerable uncertainty about what was a suitable memorial. The fact that precedents existed did not mean that it was easy for committees to decide which to adopt.

There were many disagreements on the subject. 'Civis et miles' wrote to the *Carlisle Journal* in May 1919 admitting that 'considerable dissatisfaction and discontent' existed below 'the apparent unanimity' of 'parochial meetings'.[1] The *Journal* itself noted that a 'fundamental difficulty' of war memorial schemes was finding 'a suitable means of expression' which would reconcile all views, and many places were 'finding great difficulty in discovering a satisfactory solution to the problem'.[2] Not only private individuals, but also professional organisations and voluntary pressure groups, who saw memorial projects as opportunities to advance the causes they stood for, contributed to the discussions. Newspapers, books, pamphlets, lectures and exhibitions were all used as vehicles for discussing and disseminating ideas about memorials.

The possible types of memorial divided broadly into two categories: works of public art, and socially useful facilities. Some people believed that the only really suitable memorial was something devoted entirely to the dead, such as a beautiful and morally elevating work of public art. Philip Gibbs, a well-known war correspondent, argued that 'our war memorials should be for . . . Remembrance and not for Utility, first of all, or for Philanthropy before all else',[3] and the sculptor W. Reynolds-Stephens claimed that a utilitarian memorial 'evinces no real desire to keep green the memory of the great heroism of the fallen'.[4]

Others regarded monumental art as worthless because it was expensive and did no practical good. They believed that whatever resources were available should be devoted to producing some social improvement if the result was to have any lasting value. A press cutting sent to the war memorial committee at Llandrindod Wells said that the 'mania' for monuments 'is one of the most wasteful and foolish that now plague the world. Let our monument . . . be the memory of our dead – as well as to do the best we can for those who survive them.'[5] At Wigton, Cumberland, a committee member defended the choice of a recreation ground as the urban district's memorial on the grounds that it was intended to commemorate not only the dead, but those who had received military honours and all who had served. He insisted that 'to talk of putting the whole collection into a glorified tombstone was ridiculous . . .. in these days it would be absurd and a tremendous folly to spend a large sum on a stone which would be of no use except as a memorial'.[6]

This chapter looks at ideas about the purpose of memorials expressed by members of the public and various identifiable groups. The proposals made for war memorials, and the arguments advanced in favour of them, illustrate the issues people thought their memorials should address, and, consequently, the interests they had in helping to erect them. They also show that ideas about the purpose of memorials, and consequently about the kind of memorial to erect, were thoroughly permeated by secular political and social values.

The Alternatives

Monuments pure and simple could be conventional forms of fine or decorative art, such as figurative statues, wall tablets, or stained glass windows, or of a more architectural type: crosses, obelisks or cenotaphs on the model of the one in Whitehall. Monumental arches, a form of monument associated with war since Roman times, were occasionally considered. One was built at Leicester, and another was proposed for the centre of Carlisle.[7] A building could be chosen whose purpose was solely to be a monument or secular shrine (Figure 3), or a monumental

Figure 3.

embellishment could be added to a more functional building. Stockport Art Gallery includes a shrine of striking religiosity, with an apsidal end containing a statue lit dramatically from above. The walls are marble panels carved with the names of the dead (Figure 4).

A number of social service buildings with no pretensions to monumentality were also frequently chosen as war memorials. Small cottage hospitals in urban and rural areas, or new wards or departments for large hospitals, were not uncommon. Entire new general hospitals were built at Watford and Woolwich. Village halls, bus shelters and park benches also made acceptable memorials. Provision for a district nursing service, with a cottage, was made in some places. Menston in Yorkshire, Burwell in Cambridgeshire, and the Cumbrian parishes of Patterdale and Ravenstonedale all chose nursing schemes to be their memorials. At Patterdale the plan was to include a shrine in the nurse's cottage, and at Burwell the cottage has a tablet on one end wall carrying local soldiers' names. Inscriptions or dedicatory plaques on buildings of this kind were often extremely plain and unlikely to attract a great deal of attention. The buildings themselves were not expected to create an impact by their appearance. Their value lay in the life-enhancing service they provided.

Parks, recreation grounds and bowling greens were chosen as war memorials in a number of places. Scholarships were provided for children of the dead, and relief funds for their dependants, or for disabled survivors of the war and ex-servicemen in other difficulties. Hull's war memorial, proposed in 1918, was a large fund, The Great War Trust, for disabled ex-servicemen and merchant seamen, and for the dependants of the dead.[8]

Some more unexpected suggestions were made, such as the proposals at Kirkoswald, Ravenstonedale and Allhallows for the installation of electric light in the villages.[9] At Kirkoswald the electricity was to be generated by water power. At Kirkhaugh in Northumberland one proposal was to lay on water to the village school.[10] At Leeds, someone even suggested donating the city's memorial fund to the Chancellor of the Exchequer to help pay off the national debt.[11]

Many of the suggestions people made for war memorials were based on familiar precedents. The dead of the Boer War were frequently commemorated by monuments in honour of all ranks, especially in those large industrial towns which sent volunteer

Figure 4.

units to South Africa, and in the garrison towns of county regiments. Parish or township memorials can also be found, as at Hawarden, Flintshire, where the monument is a crucifix, or at Low Fell in Gateshead, where it is a small stone figure of a soldier. Some utilitarian memorials were founded in memory of the Boer War dead. The Union Jack Club in London was opened in 1907 as 'a national memorial to the men who died in the South African War and a continual benefit to soldiers and sailors'.[12] A village hall was built at Attleborough in Norfolk as a Boer War memorial.[13]

Socially useful institutions were built to commemorate royal jubilees, deaths and coronations in the late Victorian and Edwardian eras. Bootle's memorial to Queen Victoria had been a nursing fund, supporting two nurses, established in 1901.[14] When South Shields chose to erect a statue to the dead Queen in 1901, other contenders had been a 'memorial temple' (in fact an assembly room or concert hall), a convalescent home for patients from the local voluntary hospital, a fund in aid of the hospital itself, a fund to provide trained nurses, and scholarships 'to encourage special branches of education'.[15] The Welsh National Memorial to Edward VII was a national subscription fund for the prevention and treatment of tuberculosis.[16]

Publicity

By 1918 discussions about war memorials were common in art and architecture periodicals and in the daily press. Many memorial projects were already under way. National and local papers carried a mass of reports of decisions about memorials, commissions for them, and unveilings. *The Times* regularly mentioned the unveiling of memorials in places of all sizes in its brief news items during and after the war. The *Carlisle Journal* had regular reports of the meetings of memorial committees in towns and villages in the north-west, and of the decisions they made. Articles by regular critics and notable figures, like Philip Gibbs, or Sir Alfred Mond,[17] the First Commissioner of Works, appeared in the press, discussing what kind of objects were appropriate, how to judge good design, the best procedures to adopt to ensure it, and what feelings and ideas should be expressed in memorials.

A number of voluntary and official bodies were set up to exploit the interest shown by the general public in commemorating the dead. The arts, religion, education, and philanthropy were all promoted through contributions to the public discussion of memorials, frequently showing an unrealistically high expectation of the changes which could be achieved in the public's aesthetic or religious outlook through the erection of memorials. Many of these campaigns were failures; but they illustrate the range of causes which people hoped to serve by their involvement in memorial projects, and the importance of pressure groups in stimulating discussion about the design and purpose of memorials.

Late in 1915 the Civic Arts Association was formed to promote good design in all aspects of the physical reconstruction of the country which was expected to follow the war, but first and foremost in the production of war memorials. It was led by a prestigious committee including well-known artists and architects, with the Lord Mayor of London as president, and supported by the Arts and Crafts Exhibition Society and the Art Workers' Guild.[18] A press release issued to announce its inaugural meeting warned that,'unless steps are taken to provide direction and advice' war memorials 'will be of the usual trivial and commonplace type'. The Association was 'prepared to offer the guidance of an expert advisory committee to public bodies or private persons desiring such assistance, in all questions of design'.[19]

In March 1918 the Royal Academy of Art announced that they were forming an advisory committee on war memorials 'in response to requests for advice from various quarters'.[20] They issued a leaflet called *Suggestions for the Treatment of War Memorials*, which they circulated to public bodies they thought likely to commission memorials.[21] The Royal Society of British Sculptors also circulated advice to local authorities.[22] Local civic societies and other bodies offered advice, Leeds Civic Society holding an exhibition of war memorial designs in 1920.[23]

The Church issued advice from Deans and Chapters and from Bishops' Conferences at Lambeth Palace. Several dioceses set up advisory committees to which their parishes could refer. Diocesan Chancellors had final authority over what was put up in or near churches, and this gave them a large measure of control on both artistic and doctrinal grounds. Church authorities took this action as a conservation measure, hoping to discourage the erection of a mass of new memorials to individuals in their historic buildings.[24]

These bodies offered advice which was intended to meet the needs of all who wanted to erect a war memorial. There were others who attempted more narrowly to promote particular kinds of memorials. Architects with a special interest in town planning and urban improvement made commemoration of the war dead into a platform to promote their own professional concerns. Stanley Adshead, professor of planning at University College, London, gave a number of lectures on war memorials in 1916 and 1917, proposing that memorials should consist of comprehensive urban improvement schemes. The funds collected for a memorial would, in effect, be used as capital for a high-quality building project in which some monumental item, statue, arch, obelisk, etc., referring to the dead would have pride of place.[25]

Britain's town planning legislation provided by the Town Planning Acts of 1909 and 1919 did not offer an opportunity to implement the kind of comprehensive urban design which Adshead and many of his colleagues were committed to. They hoped that, in the absence of a statutory requirement for such co-ordinated design, opportunities could be created by arousing influential public support. Adshead and the planning pioneer Patrick Abercrombie both stated publicly that comprehensive planning could only be implemented if it won public support.[26] Abercrombie in particular attempted to evangelise the cause of town planning through local civic societies in the 1920s and 1930s. War memorial projects provided a popular forum through which public interest in large-scale redevelopment plans might have been aroused.

Two major redevelopment schemes were advocated for central London. One was a national memorial on the site of Charing Cross station, to contain a great domed memorial building surrounded by terraces and new river bridges, and to be made a sound commercial proposition by taking advantage of the improvement in land values which would be involved.[27] The second, promoted by the Empire War Memorial League, envisaged rebuilding central Westminster to a design by Charles Pawley which included a new university, theatres, art galleries, a 'Hall of Nations', monumental buildings for science and the arts, and a new bridge over the Thames.[28] Lord Leverhulme, Lord Duveen, Arthur Stanley MP, and the steel manufacturer Sir Robert Hadfield were amongst the League's members.[29]

Other civic redevelopment schemes which included a profit-making element were proposed for Leeds, Carlisle and Islington,[30] but none of them received adequate public support. They would have been very expensive, and the Westminster plan very soon came into conflict with the chapter of Westminster Abbey.[31] Even so, the Empire War Memorial League was still active in some capacity in 1923.[32]

In June 1919 a Roads of Remembrance Association was formed, dedicated to 'the adornment of suitable highways and the precincts of schools and institutions with trees in memory of those who gave their lives in the war', recommending especially 'that these trees should be given and planted by relatives, friends, brigade lads, Boy Scouts and school children on or about Peace Day' (19 July 1919).[33] In October 1919 the Women's Institute at the coastal village of Solva, Pembrokeshire took up the idea.[34] By 1929 the association had become the Roads of Remembrance Committee of the Roads Beautifying Association, concerned particularly with beautifying new arterial roads; and although no longer exclusively concerned with the war dead, most of the trees planted in this scheme commemorated people killed during the war.[35]

As early as 1916, when the war shrines campaign was getting under way, a Society for Raising Wayside Crosses was formed, in the hope that the desire emerging 'in almost every village' for memorials to the war dead would offer an opportunity for the spread of crosses.[36] Its president, the Earl of Shaftesbury, sought permission from the Bishop of Salisbury to restore ancient crosses in Dorset as war memorials.[37] In 1917, the society published a pamphlet describing its aims and giving advice about the commissioning and design of wayside crosses. It thought a feeling existed that 'the present time is singularly opportune' for the restoration in Britain of 'Wayside Crosses and Calvaries which in foreign lands are such an appealing reminder to the wayfarer of the great fact of our Redemption'.[38] The purpose of the crosses would be to 'remind all those who pass along the highways and through the villages of the Great Sacrifice [meaning, in this instance, Christ's sacrifice], and of those who in their degree have followed in its steps,' and 'to claim the country-side, if only in an outward and visible way, for the Christian faith'.[39]

The society claimed to be 'working in cordial agreement with the Civic Arts Association', suggesting that its interest lay primarily in promoting the applied arts; but there can be little doubt that its programme was essentially religious. Several clergymen in the council of the society had contributed to the Church's missionary movement in east London parishes. One of its vice-presidents was the Bishop of Stepney, who had taken a prominent part in the war shrines movement there. Another was Lord Hugh Cecil, who was an outspoken high-churchman.[40] By 1919, the society judged its own activities a failure. It announced its winding-up in December, having found the public's response disappointing.[41] This must mean that it had been unsuccessful in its religious aims, for, if its sights were set, as it claimed, principally on the 'outward and visible', the problem it really faced was that its efforts were unnecessary. The cross was widely adopted without the society's encouragement.

Utilitarian memorials also had well-organised advocates. Support for medical facilities as memorials did not need a national campaign, as strong organisations for this purpose already existed throughout the country. A considerable number of voluntary hospitals advanced their claims to attention in local discussions about war memorials. When Bradford Corporation invited local people and institutions to send in their suggestions for a city memorial, the Bradford division of the British Medical Association, the Bradford Council of Public Welfare, the Royal Infirmary, the Royal Eye and Ear Hospital, the Children's Hospital and the Children's Convalescent fund all expressed support for a new general hospital.[42] The working men members of the committee of Workington Infirmary urged a public meeting about the town war memorial to include a 30-bed extension to the Infirmary in their plans.[43] At Islington, on the day before a public meeting was to be held to discuss a memorial for the borough, the Royal Northern Hospital advertised in the local newspaper, presenting its case that an extension of the hospital buildings 'would form a fitting war memorial'.[44]

The Village Clubs Association promoted village halls as suitable war memorials,[45] and the architect W. R. Lethaby, who was contributing a regular column to the magazine *The Builder* at the time, suggested that 'a hall or something socially useful [is] probably the best form a memorial could take, for the living are starved for lack of the means of civilisation'.[46] The Local War Museums Association, with a very well-connected committee, including a number of peers, was founded some time before the end of the war to arouse public interest in museums as memorials. Civic war museums were proposed for Brighton and Glasgow as war memorials.[47]

The architect and town planner Thomas Mawson started a movement, for both personal and professional reasons, to create a commemorative garden city to accommodate disabled servicemen.[48] His idea was based on a suggestion made to him by his son, who was later killed in action. Mawson envisaged raising a large part of the necessary finance through subscriptions in memory of individuals who had been killed, a form of fund-raising also advocated by the theatre impresario Oswald Stoll for housing disabled veterans.[49] Mawson's proposed garden city would initially provide housing and work facilities for the disabled; but he intended it to expand around this core to include the able-bodied members of their families, and to attract other residents as it grew. He came a little way towards realising this dream in his design for Westfield Memorial Village at Lancaster, built between 1919 and 1924, though it contained fewer facilities than he had originally hoped. Garden villages were also proposed to Glasgow war memorial committee by the Scottish Veterans Garden City Association, and at Leeds.[50]

Preferences for Memorial Types

The primary purpose of erecting a war memorial was to honour the dead; but the purpose itself did not prescribe the kind of structure which should be erected or the function which it should serve. While people talked about a sense of loss, about admiration for and gratitude to the dead, and sympathy with the bereaved, when discussing what form a memorial should take, they talked far more about its practical function. They could all agree that it was necessary to honour and mourn the dead, but they frequently disagreed about the form of memorial which would best express these feelings. They introduced into their discussions social, ethical and political ideas which had nothing intrinsically to do with either grief or honour, but which did enable them to develop a preference for one type of memorial or another, and to defend it in a debate.

While people often advanced political arguments for their preferences, there was no simple correlation between someone's political outlook and the type of memorial which he or she advocated. There was no automatic reason for people with left-inclined political views to favour, for example, utilitarian memorials, or for those inclining to the right to prefer monuments. We can find Conservative politicians supporting the idea of a hospital extension as the local memorial as strongly as their opponents on the left, and Labour politicians advocating monuments. There was probably a tendency for the left to be less enthusiastic about monuments than the right; but people's preferences were often powerfully influenced by purely local circumstances, and local political and religious differences, with the result that their views about a memorial cut across party lines. Besides, many of the concerns which affected their preferences, such as the moral or physical welfare of the community, or the prevention of future wars, were shared equally on all sides of the political spectrum.

Some believed that memorials should communicate political messages, and thus were inclined to prefer a monumental memorial. Philip Gibbs was a Liberal whose experience as a war correspondent had deeply affected his attitude to international peace and disarmament. Gibbs wanted memorials to convey an emotive political and moral message, unobscured by any other consideration. War memorials, he wrote,

> should be not only reminders of the great death that killed the flower of our race but warnings of what war means in slaughter and ruin, in broken hearts and agony . . . The Memorial of the dead must be the safeguard of the living by teaching those who follow to learn wisdom by our stupidity, and to cherish the gift of peace with more than idle thanksgiving . . .. Unless our war memorials speak those things they will condemn us of very dreadful callousness, of most shameful selfishness . . . if their is any art in us now it has its chance.[51]

The Conservative councillor George King of Stoke Newington suggested that the local memorial 'should take a Sculptural and Horticultural form' and should represent 'the great cause for which our gallant men laid down their lives – the cause of justice and freedom'.[52] Both men, from their different points of view, saw monuments as active means of expressing political ideas and preserving the values to which they were committed.

Many people judged proposals for war memorials by whether or not they would make a useful contribution to the community's everyday life. In effect, criteria of this sort subjected the choice of war memorial to considerations of welfare policy or to local administrative needs. Proposals for war memorials were frequently presented as supplying a long-felt requirement. At Silloth, Cumberland, the memorial committee secretary said that 'a large public hall' was 'very much needed in the town'.[53] A Leeds resident argued: 'Neither the present art gallery nor the free library is consonant with the pretensions of the city, and a worthy public building . . . would supply a "long felt want" . . .'.[54]

Village halls were seen as an opportunity for the reform of leisure activity and for promoting social harmony in small communities. Nonconformist congregations often favoured village or school halls for wholesome leisure and educational activities, and at Helmsley,[55] in Yorkshire, local Nonconformists, who wanted some form of institute as a memorial, appear to have held out so strongly against a monumental memorial connected with the parish church that the united town war memorial committee collapsed. But Anglicans too might support the choice of a hall. At Steep, in Hampshire, a village hall and a memorial in the parish church were both unanimously approved by a public meeting which the vicar had called, and both were executed. A number of wealthy and titled residents, including the headmaster of Bedales school, provided funds or offered sites. The hall was to be non-denominational, and was intended, in particular, for use by the working people of the village. A village association was formed by the war memorial committee, drawing its members from all classes, to organise the social activities which the hall would accommodate.[56]

British charity hospitals – the large number of hospitals funded by public subscription or endowment – were in particular need of support by the end of the First World War. The rise in wages and costs which the war had brought, and competition for lucrative, if only temporary, business catering for military needs, had left them in serious financial difficulties. There were conflicting views on what should be done about the crisis. The Dawson Report of 1920 recommended an extensive hospital-building programme by the government, and the establishment of local health centres; but later in the same year Ministry of Health expenditure cuts ruled this out.[57] A Royal Commission on Voluntary Hospitals concluded in 1921 that the voluntary system of funding must remain, and that the hospitals could only expect limited and occasional government help.[58] War memorial funds offered an alternative to state aid which the charity hospitals grasped. This was particularly welcome to those who opposed an extension of government responsibility in the medical field. The Conservative Alderman Vorley of Islington saw the use of a war memorial fund as a way of preserving the Royal Northern Hospital as a voluntary charity, maintaining that 'few of us would like to see our hospital rate funded or rate controlled'.[59]

On the other hand, people who believed that an increase in state provision for medical care, housing or education was imminent and desirable after the war might form their preferences with this in mind. In 1918, Alderman Wilson of Leeds argued against providing housing for ex-servicemen and scholarships for their children on the grounds that the corporation, as part of the government's housing programme, was 'tackling the housing question', and 'under Mr Fisher's Education Act so much would be done for the children that if Leeds did its duty there would be no need for them to ask for public subscriptions for education'.[60] Another Leeds citizen thought that hospitals would soon become a state responsibility and that rather than contributing to a new children's hospital, as someone had suggested, it would be better to provide a convalescent home.[61]

Popular self-improvement, temperance, and the repression of prostitution and illicit sexual relations, all traditional objects of philanthropic interest before the Great War, continued to preoccupy people after it. Those concerned with these matters saw commemoration of the dead as offering valuable opportunities. Clubs, institutes, even winter gardens offered facilities for salubrious entertainment and recreation, and for voluntary educational activity. Suggestions for buildings of these sorts came from all sides of the political spectrum. The Conservative Alderman Dod of Stoke Newington wanted the local memorial to be an institute for boys, equipped for physical exercise and games such as chess and draughts, as an alternative to the 'kinema' and music hall. This, he said, would be 'a lasting benefit to those on whom we rely for so much. Our hopes for the future are centred on them.'[62] Another suggestion made at Stoke Newington was a club for 'the Wives, Sisters, Mothers and Sweethearts' of the dead, to 'act as an institution to promote the mingling of the sexes on a high level, affording opportunity for freedom from those snares that are ever to be found in our streets',[63] presumably meaning venereal disease (increasingly discussed in the post-war years) and the perennial issue of prostitution.

Stoke Newington Labour Party proposed a social and educational centre 'to contain one large Hall or Winter Garden' for lectures, concerts and dancing, serving meals and offering non-vocational classes. It should be managed by a committee which would 'safeguard the Institute from any Political bias'.[64] The Liberal shipbuilder Sir George Hunter had something similar in mind when he proposed a winter garden to Wallsend war memorial committee, and 'referred to the great need in the town for a large public hall and a recreational and educational centre'.[65] He himself would present a site for the building and a substantial donation (perhaps as much as £10,000). Sir George had promoted temperance reform and wider educational opportunities on Tyneside for many years before the war, and had established The Wallsend Café in 1883 as a centre for technical education, recreation and temperance.[66]

Ex-service organisations showed a variety of preferences in their contributions to discussions about memorials. The identity of local organisations is sometimes not clear, but most were affiliated to one of the three large ex-service organisations formed during the war,[67] or, from 1921, to the British Legion. The National Association of Discharged Sailors and Soldiers, formed in 1916, had links to the Labour movement. In 1919 it changed its political complexion to an anti-socialist nationalism. The National Federation of Discharged and Demobilised Sailors and Soldiers was founded in 1917, under Liberal leadership, in response to the tightening up of conscription regulations, especially where they applied to men who had already served in the forces and completed their term of enlistment. The Federation was an aggressively other-rank body until 1919, when officers were finally admitted.[68] Many of the members of the Federation appear to have been supporters of the Labour Party, to judge from the considerable number of them who defected to the explicitly socialist National Union of Ex-servicemen when it was formed, also in 1919.[69] The third wartime organisation was the Comrades of the Great War, sponsored by the Conservative Party as a rival to the Federation, with the support of Lord Derby, who encouraged Lords Lieutenant and Chairmen of Territorial Associations to endorse it. Over a period of some months in 1920–21 the three wartime organisations negotiated a union to form the British Legion. The National Union of Ex-servicemen stood out.

The preferences of local branches may up to a point have reflected their political allegiances, but no very clear pattern is visible. At Stoke Newington the local ex-service organisation, a branch of the Federation, proposed a building which would be a self-financing public recreation and education centre with an entrance which would contain tablets commemorating the dead.[70] Later, however, some branch members appear to have supported a monumental entrance to the library and others a granite monument, although the reports are confused and conflicting.[71] (Support for the granite memorial in this case entailed the wish to see a larger proportion of the fund go to charity.) The Enfield Branch proposed a temperance hostel, branch headquarters and memorial hall as a local memorial, and began to collect for it on its own initiative.[72] The Federation Branch at Bethnal Green proposed a maternity home attached to the London Hospital.[73] At Sleaford the local branch simply proposed an ex-servicemen's institute.[74]

Branches of the Association may have taken a greater interest in independent monuments. One campaigned for a monument at Wigton, Cumberland.[75] At Harrogate the Harrogate Ex-servicemen's Association, which may or may not have been a branch of the National Association, erected a crucifix as its own memorial.[76] But a representative of ex-servicemen on Maryport memorial committee, who was probably a member of the local Association branch, proposed a public hall with a wing reserved for the use of ex-servicemen.[77] The Comrades of the Great War do not appear to have made great efforts to put their preferences about war memorials before the public. It is possible that they tended to work through the leading citizens who often patronised their branches, and who were better placed to exert influence on their behalf.

Amongst community leaders, whether they were officially appointed, like mayors, or were simply private citizens with personal prestige, many seem to have been more concerned to ensure that whatever was chosen as a memorial would command wide public support than to pursue a particular preference of their own. In this they were moved by a sense of the responsibility placed on them by their civic status to ensure that the local commemoration of the dead was properly conducted.

Father Crow of Maryport based his opposition to a monumental memorial for the town on the belief that his 'flock' would not approve of one. A hall or a park were his preferences. 'If they gave the workers something that appealed to them', he said, 'the workers would back them up.'[78]

Apparent inconsistencies in the preferences of influential figures may be explained by their sense of what was right in different circumstances. Lord Leverhulme contributed to urban reform movements through membership of concerned bodies such as the Civic Arts Association and the London Society. He endowed the chair of Civic Design at Liverpool University, and commissioned a plan for the redevelopment of Bolton from Thomas Mawson. These interests were reflected in his appearance as chairman of the founding meeting of the Empire War Memorial League, in October 1918, dedicated to raising money for the grandiose civic development scheme for Westminster. Yet he strongly approved of the decision by Port Sunlight war memorial committee 'that the memorial should be an artistic rather than a utilitarian one'.[79]

Likewise, Sir John Stirling-Maxwell, former Conservative MP for a Glasgow constituency and chairman of the Ancient Monuments Board for Scotland, served on the committee which considered the detailed designs for the Scottish National War Memorial, the most flamboyantly monumental of British memorials, and donated £100 of his own money.[80] Earlier, he had expressed a preference for an inexpensive rather than a 'very ambitious' monument for Glasgow. He insisted that the public should be made fully aware that the greater part of Glasgow's war memorial fund would go to helping those who had suffered as a result of the war, and only a small proportion on the proposed cenotaph.[81] It may have been a sense that their duty and loyalties differed in different circumstances, rather than their personal inclinations, which led these two men to adopt what seem to be contradictory positions.

We should be careful, then, not to assume that the views expressed by committee members must have been consistent with their ulterior interests or affiliations beyond the confines of the committees on which they served. Their first priority may have been to act properly as leaders in the memorial movement. They might also be motivated by loyalty to local institutions for which they felt a particular responsibility. Lord Northampton, for example, was a patron and benefactor of the Royal Northern Hospital in Islington, as well as a very large local landowner, and argued strongly in favour of making the borough memorial a contribution to the hospital.[82]

In general, talking about war memorials was intended to resolve uncertainty about what, from amongst all the possibilities offered by past practice, was appropriate. But it is clear that much of what was said was less concerned with the memory of the dead than with the needs of the living. Sometimes, it was about promoting moral or political values through visual art, sometimes about improving the physical or moral quality of life in practical ways. It often suggested a variety of non-commemorative requirements which might be satisfied by a memorial, either to serve the special interests of those already involved in the project, or to encourage others to join in. However, the choice of a memorial involved a great deal more than simply discussing the matter and discovering what members of the public thought, as the next chapter will show.

Notes to Chapter 3

1. *Carlisle Journal*, 13 May 1919.
2. Ibid., 27 May 1919.
3. Carlisle, Ca/C10/12/1, undated and untitled press cutting included in Carlisle Citizens' League Minute Book No.2, 12 May 1915 - 23 Aug 1923, and most probably collected in 1919 or 1920 when the type of memorial for the locality was under discussion.
4. Undated reprint included in Wirral, ZWO/16, with a letter dated 13 Oct. 1918.
5. Powys, R/UD/LW/234, File 2, cutting endorsed 'received 2 Apr. 1919'.
6. *Carlisle Journal*, 20 June 1919.
7. Ibid., letter from F. Telford, 15 Nov. 1918.
8. Hull City Record Office, City of Hull Great War Trust, Charter, 28 Mar. 1923, p. 2.
9. *Carlisle Journal*, 11 Mar. 1919, 1 Apr. 1919, 8 Apr. 1919.
10. Ibid., 27 June 1919.
11. *Yorkshire Post*, 8 June 1920, letter from F. H. Mohun. This suggestion was probably prompted by Stanley Baldwin's anonymous but well-publicised donation of £120,000 for the same purpose, as 'a thank offering', a year previously. See K. Middlemas and J. Barnes, *Baldwin*, London 1969, p. 73.

12. *The Times*, 23 Aug. 1915.

13. I owe this information to Dr Judith Rowbotham. The hall has since been rebuilt.

14. *Liverpool Echo*, 28 Feb. 1906.

15. *Shields Daily Gazette*, 22 May 1901.

16. National Library of Wales, Minor Lists and Summaries 1052, Edward VII Welsh National Memorial Association.

17. *Pall Mall Gazette*, 26 Aug. 1918, quoted in *Journal of the Royal Institute of British Architects*, series 3, vol. 25, Sept 1918, p. 247.

18. *Journal of the Royal Institute of British Architects*, series 3, vol. 22, Oct. 1915, p. 527.

19. Ibid., vol. 25, 5 Feb. 1916, p. 125.

20. Royal Academy, *Annual Report*, 1918, p. 65.

21. Wakefield Borough Council, General Purposes Committee, min. 22 April 1918.

22. Powys, R/UD/LW/234, circular received 25 Feb. 1920.

23. *Yorkshire Post*, 17 Apr. 1920.

24. 'The Origin and Growth of the System of Advisory Committees for the Protection of Churches', in Central Committee for the Protection of Churches, *The Protection of Our English Churches: Report for 1923*, Oxford, 1923, p. 8.

25. *Builder*, vol. 112, 16 Feb. 1917, p. 121.

26. S. Adshead, *Centres of Cities*, Burnley, 1918, p. 18; P. Abercrombie, 'The Place in General Education of Civic Survey and Town Planning', *Town Planning Review*, vol. 9, no. 2, (1921), p. 109.

27. G. Swinton, 'Castles in the Air at Charing Cross', *Nineteenth Century and After*, vol. 80, Nov. 1916, pp. 966–80.

28. *Builder*, vol. 115, 8 Nov. 1918, p. 278.

29. Ibid., vol. 116, 7 Feb. 1919, p. 151.

30. *Yorkshire Post*, 5 June 1919; *Carlisle Journal*, 25 Apr. 1919; *Islington Daily Gazette*, 26 Aug. 1918.

31. *Builder*, vol. 116, 7 Feb. 1919, p. 151.

32. Ibid., vol. 124, 18 May 1923, p. 801.

33. *The Times*, 7 June 1919.

34. *Pembroke County Guardian*, 7 Nov. 1919; National Library of Wales, Ms.10295B, Solva Roads of Remembrance Accounts, Oct. 1919 - Dec. 1956, undated leaflet.

35. *London Society Journal*, no. 148, June 1930, p. 86.

36. The Wayside Cross Society, *Wayside Crosses*, London, 1917, p. 5.

37. *Builder*, 18 Aug. 1916, p. 95.

38. Wayside Cross Society, *Wayside Crosses*, p. 5.

39. Ibid.

40. Ibid., p. 7.

41. *Church Times*, 12 Dec. 1919.

42. Bradford, BBC 1/56/4/6, Minutes, 22 Sept. 1919.

43. *Carlisle Journal*, 21 Feb. 1919.

44. *Islington Daily Gazette*, 1 Apr. 1919. At that time the hospital was called the Great Northern Central Hospital.

45. *The Times*, 5 Apr. 1919.

46. *Builder*, vol. 116, 7 Feb. 1919, p. 128.

47. Ibid., vol. 113, 12 Oct. 1917, p. 215; Strathclyde, G1/3/1, Lord Provost's file on establishment of war memorials in Glasgow, letter, 30 Nov. 1918.

48. T. H. Mawson, *An Imperial Obligation*, London, 1917.

49. An appeal of this nature, supported by Stoll, was launched for disabled veterans' flats in Hackney in 1916 (*Hackney and Kingsland Gazette*, 16 Oct. 1916).

50. Strathclyde, G4.1, Glasgow War Memorial, Minutes, 18 Sept. 1919; *Yorkshire Post*, 15 Nov. 1918.

51. Carlisle, Ca/C10/12/1, untitled and undated press cutting.

52. Hackney, SN/W/1/11, list of suggestions received by the Borough Council up to 18 Mar. 1919.

53. *Carlisle Journal*, 1 July 1919.

54. *Yorkshire Observer*, 11 Nov. 1918.

55. Atkinson Brierley Papers, Box 105, letter from H. E. Newton 4 Oct. 1919, and Brierley's notes on compilation of Helmsley war memorial account.

56. Hampshire Record Office, 31 M 71/Z1, Steep War Memorial, Minutes, 28 Apr., 7 Nov. and 22 Dec. 1919.

57. B. Able-Smith, *The Hospitals 1800–1948: A Study in Social Administration in England and Wales*, London, 1964, 262–82, 291–2, 298.

58. *Reports from Commissioners*, 1921, vol. 6, Cmd.1335, Voluntary Hospitals Committee, Final Report, 13 Mar. 1921.

59. *Islington Daily Gazette*, 10 Sept. 1918.

60. *Yorkshire Observer*, 23 Nov. 1918.

61. *Yorkshire Post*, 24 Dec. 1918.

62. Hackney, SN/W/1/25, untitled press cutting, 28 Feb. 1919.

63. Hackney, SN/W/1/11, suggestion from Mr A. Hutton.

64. Ibid., suggestion 10.

65. *Newcastle Evening Chronicle*, 26 Jan. 1921.

66. W. Richardson, *History of the Parish of Wallsend*, Newcastle-upon-Tyne, 1923, p. 447.

67. A short account of these organisations is given in G. Wootton, *The Official History of the British Legion*, London, 1956, pp. 2–12.

68. At both Hull and Stoke Newington there were ex-service organisations referred to as the National Federation of Discharged and Disabled Sailors and Soldiers (Hackney, SN/W/1/11, and Hull, City of Hull Great War Trust Scrapbook, press cutting, 16 Mar. 1921). I am assuming that these were branches of the National Federation discussed above, but this is not entirely certain.

69. D. Englander, 'The National Union of Ex-Servicemen and the Labour Movement, 1918–1920', *History*, vol. 76, no. 246 (1991), pp. 24–42.

70. Hackney, SN/W/1/11, suggestion 9.

71. Hackney, SN/W/1/25, cuttings dated 18 June 1919 and 20 June 1919.

72. *Enfield Gazette*, 6 Dec. 1918 and 3 Jan. 1919.

73. Tower Hamlets, 082.3 Bethnal Green War Memorial Fund, Minutes, 22 May 1919.

74. Lincolnshire, SLUDC 11/6, Minutes, 30 June 1919 and 9 Mar. 1920 together make this clear.

75. *Carlisle Journal*, 30 May 1919.

76. Harrogate Corporation Minutes, December 1920, p. 9, petition received for site.

77. Carlisle, S/UD/M/1/2Z/6, Minutes, 29 Jan. 1919; *Carlisle Journal*, 31 Jan. 1919.
78. *Carlisle Journal*, 21 Mar. 1919.
79. *The Builder*, vol. 115, 8 Nov. 1918, p. 298; *Progress*, July 1918, p. 79.
80. Scottish National War Memorial, Bundle 45, subscription list, 5 Mar. 1923.
81. Strathclyde, G4.1, Glasgow War Memorial, Minutes, 18 Sept. 1919.
82. *Islington Daily Gazette*, 2 Apr. 1919.

4

The Choice of a Memorial

Choosing the type of war memorial a community should have was an important diplomatic task for local committees. They had to consider the needs, desires and resources of members of the community, and the susceptibilities of groups whose favourable opinion or support was required. A memorial had to be acceptable on two grounds. There must be no serious objection to it from any significant section of local opinion, and, more constructively, it must be of a kind which would arouse the support of the public from whom the funds for it had to be collected. To make sure that a memorial was acceptable, the memorial committee usually consulted the public about what the memorial should be, and obtained ratification of its choice from a public meeting or from a delegate committee of some kind. Public discussion invited the expression of different opinions, and while these might be amicably reconciled, they might also lead to factional divisions within the local commemorative movement.

In some places differences of opinion turned into serious public rows. These instances are of considerable interest, as they illustrate the tension which might exist within a community about a memorial, the resources available for overcoming it, and the process by which a consensus was formed. Where agreement proved difficult to reach, a decision might be imposed through the practical exercise of financial or organisational power. Some participants exploited the possibilities offered for pursuing partisan ends through the management of committees or of the fund-raising system; others denounced this kind of manipulation and impugned the motives of those who practised it.

Consensus and Conflict

Although they needed to take account of differing views, memorial committees tried to avoid public controversy. 'Bearing in mind,' said the mayor of Carlisle, 'that we are engaged in devising the best manner of perpetuating the memory of the honoured dead, it would be fitting that as far as practicable the voice of controversy should be hushed'.[1] In many cases an acceptable choice was made without apparent difficulty. The existence of a variety of rival proposals need not of itself have led to a struggle between members of a committee over which should be adopted.

In some cases it appears that proposals for memorials were made not because the makers preferred them to any other type of memorial, but rather to stimulate a discussion. The matter could then be settled without conflict in an expression of unanimity. At Burwell, Cambridgeshire, the discussion opened with a motion proposing a nursing scheme for the village. It seems likely that this was planned beforehand between the proposer and seconder, perhaps after talking to other people. A number of alternatives or amendments were put to the meeting - almshouses, a recreation room, and a monument of unspecified form. There was a long discussion, but no proposal apart from the nursing scheme was seconded, and it was unanimously adopted.[2] In other words, none of those who proposed other types of memorial felt strongly enough to stand out. At Scaleby, Cumberland, the vote was unanimously for the cross suggested by the chairman after several other proposals had been discussed.[3] It seems that the people who attended were quite willing to accept the feeling of these meetings and join in a unanimous expression of opinion.

For conflict to occur, it was necessary that lobbies should form around proposals, and that each should work for the triumph of its own preference. There had to be a number of people who, for some reason, were prepared neither to leave a committee to get on with the business on their behalf, nor, if they did not like what was being done, simply to take no part. Where the formation of lobbies can be traced, they very often appear to have been connected with other conflicts which originated outside the business of choosing a memorial.

Stoke Newington borough council was split over its organisation of a war memorial by a dispute which a newspaper traced to internal divisions in the local Conservative party about who should stand as Coalition candidate in the 1918 general election.[4] The then mayor, Herbert Ormond, though a Conservative, had stood as a non-party supporter of Lloyd George's coalition government against the officially selected Conservative candidate. There was considerable criticism of this behaviour from Ormond's fellow Conservatives. As mayor, Ormond was *ex officio* originator of the borough war memorial fund, and identified himself firmly with a proposal to build a monumental entrance to the borough library, a project favoured by the borough council's own subcommittee on the subject.

Alderman Francis Dod, also a Conservative, had been a particularly severe critic of Ormond's behaviour in the election, and was tipped to replace Ormond as mayor in September 1918 if Ormond's party decided he was no longer acceptable.[5] The majority of Conservative councillors had forgiven Ormond, but Dod was not reconciled. The clash between them became personal, as Dod had gone so far as to accuse Ormond of telling lies.[6]

Dod was, according to a newspaper commentator, 'a man of outstanding ability',[7] but he aroused the hostility of many councillors by his failure to respect certain proprieties of council business procedure. He insisted that the discussion of Ormond's re-election as mayor should not, as usual, be held behind closed doors, but that the press should be admitted, in order to prevent journalists receiving garbled accounts privately;[8] and his subsequent attack on the mayor's character caused resentment. He nonetheless had considerable support. He was to be elected mayor twice in future, and he took up popular causes such as defence of the interests of local allotment holders.[9] He was in some respects an incautious populist whose words and actions offended more strait-laced leaders of the borough. Throughout the three years it took to complete plans for Stoke Newington memorial, Dod remained the most uncompromising critic of the scheme, although other councillors also opposed it for various reasons at various times. The struggle was conducted first in the council chamber and then in public. It involved the creation of a new war memorial committee, and the manipulation of public meetings and of fund-raising initiatives, as well as protests by ex-servicemen and bereaved relatives. How the battle was fought out will be examined in detail later in this chapter.

Rivalries between religious denominations could also upset the production of war memorials. Many people felt that a war memorial should be on consecrated ground, and so liked the idea of siting it within the precincts of a church. The Bishop of

London had proposed to a meeting of Convocation in 1918 that all denominations should be invited to have the names of their dead relatives inscribed on the parish roll of honour 'so that rich and poor who had died together might be enshrined in it for ever'.[10] Non-Anglicans, in areas where they had large congregations, might also offer to represent the community as a whole. The war memorial hall with three Sunday School classrooms at East Vale Wesleyan church, Longton, was intended to 'commemorate the men of the district, irrespective of denomination, who have fallen'.[11]

In a good many cases, the claim by one denomination to represent all others proved unacceptable. At Brompton, near Northallerton, Yorkshire, local co-operation broke down over differences of view between Anglicans and Nonconformists about the form and siting of memorials. The war memorial committee was led by J. P. Yeoman, wealthy resident, prominent local Anglican, Conservative member of North Riding County Council, and magistrate. He was determined that the memorial should be associated with the parish church, and his committee chose a lich-gate, largely, it seems, on his insistence.[12] Objections were raised to the site by people he referred to, in a letter to Walter Brierley, his architect, as 'a few rabid dissenters'. They had asked him how he would feel if they had proposed to improve the chapel entrance 'by means of a war memorial'. 'The meeting was evidently organised and partly packed against the Church,' he claimed.[13] The committee was deadlocked, and the idea of a memorial to represent all denominations was abandoned. There may well have been a political component to this quarrel. Religious Nonconformity had a strong association with the Liberal Party, and so the people who objected to Yeoman's proposal for the memorial may also have been his political opponents, adding party to sectarian disagreement, even though the issue was essentially a religious one.

A letter to the press from the mining village of Monk Bretton, near Barnsley, objected to the local memorial committee's decision to put up a monument at the parish church, unless all other places of worship were given equal treatment, because, it was claimed, 90 per cent of the local men who had served in the forces were Nonconformists.[14] This was exactly the solution found to sectarian differences at Kirkoswald, Cumberland. The local Wesleyan superintendent 'took exception' to the community's memorial tablet being placed in the parish church, so the vicar proposed a tablet in both the church and the chapel.[15]

The war created two new groups of people whose interests were deeply involved in the commemoration of the dead: ex-servicemen and the bereaved. Ex-servicemen, as the former comrades of the dead, felt they had a special duty to see them properly commemorated. They felt a responsibility to participate in decisions and insisted on their right to do so. Memorial committees normally acknowledged their claims to consideration and were obliged to take particular notice of their views. They not only had prestige in the matter of commemorating the dead; they also had many local branch organisations through which they could exercise their influence in local affairs. The bereaved had a claim to special consideration too, as they had a personal emotional interest in commemorating the dead, and required consolation and recognition of their losses; but they were in a far weaker position than ex-servicemen, and depended on public sympathy rather than on self-assertion. Ex-servicemen and the bereaved were often linked locally through the opportunity offered by ex-servicemen's organisations for widows and dependants of the dead to become associate members, and these organisations were probably the most effective supporters of the bereaved.

The importance accorded to these two groups by memorial committees, and their ability to exert organised influence, meant that their preferences could seriously affect the production of a memorial, and their support could be decisive in conflicts. At Appleby the Federation branch insisted on changing the memorial's site from the churchyard to a more public and visible place, arguing that 'We have done our bit for you and our pals who have died are entitled to the best and most public place you can give them.'[16] At Wigton, Cumberland, the type of memorial chosen - a recreation ground - was condemned by the local branch of the Association as a self-serving manoeuvre on the part of the urban district council to pay for a facility it had promised in the past but had been unable to deliver. As a result of the protest a monument was provided as well.[17] After the formation of the British Legion, service veterans continued to act as guardians of propriety in the commemoration of the dead, and might intervene over the design of memorials. The Swansea branch persuaded the town council to remove bronze tablets which carried the names of civic dignitaries from the Court of Memory at the local cenotaph.[18]

Ex-servicemen would fight for their right to participate where they felt it had been denied. Stoke Newington's British Legion members believed they had been unfairly excluded from a crucial public meeting held to make a final decision on the form of the local memorial. Attendance was by ticket only, and only people who had given over ten shillings to the memorial fund were invited. The secretary of the Legion branch wrote to the secretary of the memorial committee asking him to receive a deputation. 'My members are viewing with alarm the method of calling a meeting of subscribers, and are watching very closely this action of your committee,' he said. 'I may conclude that my members will hold you responsible if we are not given a hearing.' In a second letter he wrote that the branch members, 'feel that they have a right to attend and give the views of our Members, who include many widows and dependants of the fallen, who have subscribed, but not to the amount of 10/-'.[19] On the day of the meeting 'over 200 ex-servicemen, subscribers and widows were outside the hall protesting', according to a letter to the press.[20]

In some small communities, members of the public might be willing to leave important decisions entirely to the bereaved. At Brancepeth, Durham, the choice of site for the memorial was left to the bereaved,[21] and at Hesket, Cumberland, the bereaved were asked to choose a design for the granite cross, which was the type of monument recommended by the committee.[22] However, they were not always given the consideration they desired. A number of them in Cockermouth signed a petition that the memorial should be in the cemetery; but a public meeting, by a large majority, chose Station Road as the site.[23]

In the sectarian conflict about the lich-gate at Brompton church, J. P. Yeoman out-manoeuvred his Nonconformist opponents by winning over the bereaved to his scheme through a personal approach to them. He thus gained greater legitimacy for his own preference, and made what would otherwise have been a purely Anglican memorial into something which represented, in effect, at least the principal mourners in the community. 'I now propose to proceed with the original scheme,' he told Walter Brierley, 'that is for the Vicar and Churchwardens to erect the lich gate on their own, and I have personally called on all the next of kin and obtained their permission to have the names of the young men inscribed on the walls.' The vicar and churchwardens were to take subscriptions, but would 'make nothing in the nature of a public collection'.[24] Yeoman finally thought he could raise up to £600, which argues no lack of support for his actions.[25]

The Management of Choice

Ostensibly, the means by which a memorial was chosen were discussion and argument in public meetings, representative committees and newspapers. However, the arguments people put forward to support their preference for a particular kind of memorial were not very effective in determining what memorial a community would erect, as they were thoroughly ambiguous and could be applied equally well to competing proposals.

Various standards of judgement were suggested by which to make choices. Many argued that the primary purpose of a memorial was to express feeling - grief, admiration, gratitude or sympathy - and claimed that a monument would do this best. F. Richards of Islington argued that, 'a noble piece of sculpture would be the best anodyne and inspiration'.[26] Other people implied that utilities were no less effective as expressions of feeling or as stimuli to appropriate ideas. The Royal Northern Hospital's advertisement, commending itself as the most appropriate memorial for Islington, claimed that an extension of its buildings would be 'a direct and tangible expression of sympathy' for the bereaved, and a constant reminder to them of the borough's gratitude to those they had lost.[27]

The public was often encouraged to choose a memorial according to criteria the dead themselves would have applied. The mayor of Carlisle wanted the first public meeting called to discuss a town memorial to consider the dead and 'try to think what their wishes would have been if they could have been consulted'. He thought they would not have wanted large sums spent on 'comparatively useless' things, by which he meant monuments.[28] However, the same argument could be used in support of the opposite view. A writer to The *Carlisle Journal* thought that to couple a tribute to the dead with a town improvement which would benefit the public at large would not show 'the same unselfish spirit' as the dead.[29]

It was also argued that a memorial ought to stimulate those who saw it to follow the example of service and self-sacrifice set by the dead. Again, either a monument or a utility might serve this purpose. Lord Leverhulme maintained that responsible citizenship and the continuation of the work of the dead would be fulfilled by the monument proposed for his company village at Port Sunlight. He told a general meeting of Lever Brothers staff, 'The most certain way of carrying on the great work for freedom undertaken in the present war was fittingly and impressively to record in letters of bronze on an imperishable monument the name of everyone connected with us who had gone out to this war.'[30] By contrast, an article in *The Times* in 1917 argued that 'our gratitude will show itself best in some effort to preserve for after times the things which our soldiers' sacrifices have saved for us', but a monument rarely 'stimulates us to further their work'.[31] The writer proposed the institution at public schools of memorial prizes for essays on current affairs to encourage a sense of political responsibility.

Arguments about the purpose of a memorial were too ambiguous to rule any type in or out, and so were of limited use in resolving the difficulty of agreeing upon the form a memorial should take. The most they could do was to demonstrate that any given proposal was appropriate, and that it would fulfil whatever requirement a memorial might be expected to satisfy. Arguments could not prove that one type would fulfil the requirement better than another. The public debates which frequently took place about the form of a local war memorial merely began the process of choice; they could not conclude it. They prompted people to think about the memorial project and showed what sorts of memorial were of interest to local people; but a mere show of opinion was not enough to fix the choice. Other, practical, considerations, especially the ability to raise money and obtain a site, would be crucial in deciding which amongst the competing suggestions was finally adopted.

The need to make awkward choices could be reduced by devoting the memorial fund to a variety of purposes, providing something to satisfy everyone. Many communities divided their funds between a monumental and a charitable project, and also allowed subscribers to the fund to earmark their donations for one or other of the chosen objects if they so wished. The Lord Provost of Glasgow recommended 'that the fund . . . should be devoted in the first place to the erection of a Cenotaph and then to the Prince Albert workshops [an institution for disabled ex-servicemen], any surplus to such causes as the committee determined'.[32] Over £103,700 was eventually raised, of which £60,362 was earmarked for the workshops only. Of the remainder, £22,115 was spent on the cenotaph, the balance going largely to military charities.[33] A similar system was adopted in a number of other places where the raising of a substantial fund could expected.[34]

Where no such compromise between opposing claims on the memorial fund could be achieved, a means of arbitration was required which all interested parties would respect. The most obvious and usual was a committee or public meeting recognised as representative of the whole community, making decisions by majority vote. This was an important benefit of the public participation which memorial committees normally encouraged. Other ways of consulting the public were sometimes proposed, such as a ballot of ratepayers.[35]

But public consultation was not simply a way of ascertaining the will of the community. Where a factional struggle occurred, it also offered committee organisers an opportunity for manipulating the decision-making process to get the result they wanted. A second target for manipulation was the memorial fund, as money had such an important place in a memorial committee's work. In the factional rivalry at Stoke Newington, committee members resorted to both these manoeuvres. Stoke Newington council did not, at first, encourage public participation in the choice of their memorial, and subsequently there were serious difficulties in raising a sufficiently large fund. The council had set up a sub-committee of its own to choose a memorial for the borough, and so had tried to keep the final decision in its own hands. The *Hackney and Kingsland Gazette* believed this procedure would be approved 'by all who desire to avoid friction and to rally the wholehearted support of residents in aid of any scheme decided by a majority of the council, whatever this may be'.[36]

Unfortunately, the absence of formal public involvement left councillors vulnerable to the criticism that they were trying to foist their own preference on the citizens without consulting them. When the sub-committee recommended that a new monumental entrance for the borough library be built as the war memorial, Alderman Dod and a number of other councillors opposed the scheme. Dod went so far as to write to the press to suggest that a boys' club would be a preferable alternative, and asked members of the public to make their views known. It was, he said, in the public's interest to do so, as it would have to pay for what was done, either through the rates or by subscription to a memorial fund.[37] The *Gazette* expressed surprise that a councillor should break ranks in this way, and warned that if alternative schemes were promoted many people would take the differences of opinion as an excuse not to subscribe.[38] Two debates, in March and May 1919, revealed acrimonious divisions within the council on the issue. At the first of these, Dod had a long altercation with Herbert Ormond, the mayor, and was himself accused of trying to get a special hearing for his own project to found a boys' institute.[39]

Several councillors appealed for unity, insisted that 'any memorial should have the stamp of public approval on it', and proposed that 'persons outside the council' should be invited to join the committee.[40] In the second debate two proposals - the library entrance and 'a simple form of Monument' proposed by Councillor King[41] - drew equal numbers of votes.[42] One councillor protested at the 'mental atmosphere' of the meeting and said that 'petty jealousy' had intruded into it.[43] The *Gazette* thought the atmosphere had been 'anything but in keeping with the dignity of the subject under discussion'.[44] As a result, the council had to reconstitute the memorial committee so that half its members were from outside the council, and put the disputed proposals to a town meeting. The paper thought this manoeuvre 'one of the most abject confessions of incompetence and lack of discrimination on the part of a public body' that it had seen for some time.[45] At the town meeting Dod kept up his attack, insisting that the 'unsaid message of the dead' was to commemorate them by doing something useful;[46] but the library entrance received the approval of a majority.

The struggle was continued in attempts to control the use of the memorial fund. In November 1919 the fund was not yet adequate for the library entrance. One of the committee members suggested that the scheme was receiving little financial support because it was unpopular, and proposed that it should be reconsidered.[47] Francis Dod was now mayor, and hence *ex officio* chairman of the memorial committee. He suggested that 'a more popular appeal should be made which would attract the general Public'.[48] He proposed to hold a lottery, with tickets for sale to the public and prizes donated by local residents. None of the other committee members approved. Councillor King thought a simple monument would be better than 'an elaborate building raised by such means', and another that 'instead of obtaining from the Borough an expression of its gratitude, we would be appealing to the cupidity of mankind'.[49] Nonetheless, by the end of January 1920 the financial situation was no better, and the majority had come round to Dod's idea,[50] so the lottery was held.

In February 1921 there was still not enough money. Dod, no longer mayor, suggested the choice of memorial should be reconsidered by a public meeting, and he had the support of the town clerk. In response, the supporters of the library entrance proposed a revised and cheaper version of their project.[51] The town clerk thought the reduced library scheme was now insufficiently imposing to have any value as a memorial. Dod thought it would be better to do something for the war widows.[52]

As Dod had raised a large proportion of the available money himself, through the lottery, it remained up to him and his allies to decide what could be done with it. He had obtained the prizes for the lottery on condition, he said, that he did his best to prevent the library scheme from going ahead.[53] He had an obligation to the donors, and could not commit himself without consulting them. He wanted the committee to hold a public meeting of subscribers and prize-givers; but no other members would support the idea. In an attempt to get round the difficulty which Dod presented, the committee expressed its appreciation of his efforts in a resolution 'that he has used his best efforts to have the memorial take the shape of some form other than the Memorial Entrance'.[54] A private meeting of subscribers and prize-givers was then proposed, and Dod agreed to be bound by its decision. The committee later decided to limit the meeting to people who had subscribed over ten shillings, a move which Dod and Councillor King, who was in favour of a cheaper monument, unsuccessfully opposed.[55]

The public knew that the subscribers' meeting was part of a power struggle. We have already seen how the local British Legion branch expressed its concern that the committee was trying to manipulate the outcome. Another resident wrote to the mayor the day before the meeting to warn that 'a small section of the Council will make a determined attempt . . . to capture the war memorial fund'. He urged the committee to make a determined defence of its position 'or the whole thing will be upset. It was upon the Committee's *original* proposal that the subscriptions were given.' He hoped to attend the meeting 'to support *that* proposal'.[56]

When the meeting was convened, early in October 1921, Dod opened the argument by moving that the whole matter be referred to an open public meeting. He was defeated, and two memorial proposals were put to the meeting: the library entrance and Councillor King's 'simple but impressive unsculptured monument', which would leave the lottery money and any surplus to go to charity. A third was moved from the floor: that the memorial should 'take the form of some material assistance to local charities'. An amended motion carried the day: that the library entrance be the memorial, with any surplus going to charity. Thus the principle of giving to charity was included to pacify critics, although the amount available would not be large.[57]

Not everyone was satisfied with the decision. Giving such privilege in the decision-making process to those donors who had the most money to give was very much against the egalitarian spirit of the commemoration of the dead. A member of the British Legion branch, who was also a vocal allotment holder,[58] and so perhaps an active ally of Francis Dod, wrote to the press to complain about the restrictions which had been placed on admission to the subscribers' meeting. 'A more un-Britishlike action, by holding a packed meeting, one would fail to discover',[59] he said. He challenged the moral right of certain people at the meeting to take part in it: 'If my remembrance serves me correct, at least two of the privileged subscribers, who left at the close of the meeting, were, to my knowledge, exempted from service, and if they had given all their worldly possessions, it would have been little sacrifice to the toll many paid, or the broken health of many who returned.' But at least it was a decision, and it was finally accepted. As the Legion's principal object had been to ensure that a memorial was built at all, the branch did not challenge the outcome. The same correspondent added, 'I hope the final settlement will be carried out faithfully to the letter.'[60]

This was not quite the end of the dispute. Councillor King made one last attempt to overturn the decision of the subscribers' meeting and to substitute a cheaper monument; but no-one seconded it. Neither Dod nor the town clerk, who had both opposed the library project, and both of whom were present at this meeting, supported King.[61] In January 1922, Councillor Sheffield, who was the committee's main contact with the honorary architect of the library entrance, moved that, if finances permitted, more stone decoration should be included in the building. Dod tried to convince the committee that there had been a cash limit on how much could be spent on it. There was then an argument about the minutes, during which the secretary threatened to resign, and then withdrew the threat, and all sides protested vigorously at each other's behaviour. But the decision had now been firmly made, and it stood.[62] Once a decision which carried public authority had been taken, dissidents had little alternative but to acquiesce in it. Otherwise they could be accused of preventing the community from properly honouring its dead.

In some other places, too, it is possible to find battles for control of the resources for a memorial. At Enfield, in 1919, a dispute arose over whether money raised during the war by the Enfield Patriotic Committee to support local men at the front and their dependants, and afterwards to commemorate those who had been killed, should be put towards the construction of a cenotaph or the re-endowment of Enfield Cottage Hospital. The latter was the official choice as the district war memorial. The dispute turned on interpretations of minutes and of the wishes of the original subscribers to the fund. The Patriotic Committee's former chairman went so far as to threaten its current officers with an injunction.[63]

Personal animosity, probably with a political origin, was present here. John McEwan, a leading local Liberal, whose wife stood as Liberal candidate in the 1919 general election,[64] was outgoing chairman of the Patriotic Committee. He wanted the balance of its funds passed on to the hospital. The treasurer of this committee, who wanted the money put towards a cenotaph, was H. F. Bowles, Conservative MP for the constituency. His opinion of McEwan may be gathered from his remark in a meeting of the management committee of the cottage hospital that, knowing McEwan's determination, he probably would serve his threatened injunction and see all the fund's money used up in legal fees.[65]

There was also a more general political division. A trade union representative, who was a member of the hospital management committee, was in favour of giving the money to the hospital. Dr Ridge, leader of the hospital's medical staff,[66] who also argued that the money should go to the hospital, was a Liberal.[67] Those who, with Bowles, were in favour of a cenotaph seem to have been predominantly from the political right. They included two Conservative councillors,[68] the chairman of the town Constitutional Club,[69] and an organiser of the local Discharged Sailors and Soldiers Association branch,[70] all of whom were Patriotic Committee members. However, the representative of the local tradesmen's associations, who could well have been a Conservative, said he had always understood the money was intended for the hospital.[71] In the end, supporters of a cenotaph got the better of the dispute, largely because, as officers of the Patriotic Committee, they were already in possession of the money.

Stoke Newington was in some respects an unusual case, but only to the extent that an initial miscalculation on the part of the borough council - the decision to keep the choice of memorial to itself, without public consultation - had to be rectified later. The bitter quarrel developed as the civic leaders tried to adopt the more usual system by which choice was legitimated through public participation. As we have seen,[72] the predominant part played by civic leaders in providing a memorial for the community was normally obscured by the offer of participation to the public, by encouraging discussion of what should be done, and by referring important decisions to widely representative committees or directly to public meetings. Local leaders were then left to get on with the business undisturbed in sub-committees, so long as they were seen to be acting in the community's interests. The breakdown of this system at Stoke Newington shows how thoroughly the usual method of producing a war memorial was part of the local political process. Choosing the memorial there had become too open to manage in a way that would give the conventional impression of unanimity and responsible leadership. In order to regain control of it, all the weapons of political faction-fighting had to be employed.

The Local Politics of Commemoration

Committees made a point of trying to interest the local public in their work. How did the public respond? Many memorial committees had difficulty raising a fund adequate to their plans.[73] They had to use all the normal devices of charity campaigns, which ranged from playing on the sense of guilt to holding lotteries with attractive prizes, to extract what they needed from the public. A number of committees even had difficulty collecting the names of people who should be listed on the memorial. After putting up notices in Post Offices and elsewhere, and advertising for names in local papers, the committee organisers at Llandrindod Wells, Hoylake and Stoke Newington still had to go to considerable trouble to get names which had not been voluntarily submitted.[74] The level of interest in public meetings might also be disappointing. At Leeds only twenty people went to hear Sir Reginald Blomfield present details of the design he had been asked to prepare.[75] The *Barnsley Chronicle* judged the attendance for the public meeting to form a town memorial committee to be 'extremely disappointing'.[76] There was disappointment, too, at the turn-out for similar meetings at Carlisle, where only sixty attended, and Blennerhasset, Cumberland.[77] Although many members of the public were interested in the ceremonies held in remembrance of the dead, it does not seem that a high proportion wished to be involved in the actual business of erecting memorials to them. In villages, where it was easier to approach people personally,[78] and decisions could be taken at parish meetings which were a regular part of local political activity, a higher proportion of the population may have been involved.

Who made the important decisions about war memorials? War memorial committees were formed from representatives of the local interest groups which normally featured in the political and institutional lives of communities, and members of the local political and cultural élites took the leading roles. These were people who had experience of running institutions, held positions which gave them command of suitable resources, led the religious denominations, and patronised philanthropic and educational causes. Special sub-committees charged with choosing a memorial or with choosing options to be put before the public were staffed by them. Even where the final choice of a memorial, and other important decisions about it, had to be ratified by an open public meeting, rather than by a general committee composed of local politicians and pressure groups, it was the committee members who set the agenda and presented the evidence on which the public decision was made. It seems likely, too, from the relatively small attendances, that a large proportion of the people who attended public meetings were committee members and their allies. There can be little doubt that the decision-making process was in the hands of a relatively small number of people, and that those were the local civic leaders and leaders of voluntary associations and of local churches. In this, the process was not very different from any other local political activity.

Just like the procedures they resorted to, the motives which moved civic leaders in the commemoration of the dead were typical of contemporary local politics. In urban memorial committees, community leaders expressed their devotion to local concerns, and to the adequate performance of their social roles in the locality, through the importance they attached to local patriotism and civic pride. They urged the public to see that their community did not fall behind others in honouring their dead. They also insisted that the community should produce a memorial which matched its sense of its own dignity. The special committee on a war memorial set up by Bradford city council was instructed 'to find the basis of an agreed proposal for making the object of a War memorial worthy of the City'.[79] In the small country town of Sleaford, too, the committee expressed concern that the memorial should be 'worthy of the town'.[80]

In the early twentieth century, the idea of civic pride had quite specific political implications. It was connected with an ideal of non-party activism in the cause of urban improvement, and the preservation of social unity through administration which pursued rational policies, derived from concern for the common good, rather than those of partisan politicians. To promote these causes, civic societies were formed in many large towns, in the years just before and after the First World War. Their prime movers were business leaders, local professionals and academics. They relied strongly on ideas developed by the growing movement of professional town planners, and regarded the aesthetic improvement of the town environment, which extended from anti-litter campaigns to the promotion of high-quality architecture, as an important contribution to the improvement of social conditions and the consolidation of social harmony.[81]

The political ideals of the civic societies in this period were expressed by the town planning pioneer Patrick Abercrombie in 1920, when he complained that 'National and Imperial Politics still enter far too largely into the choice of our councillors', and as a result, 'a non-party and non-sectarian society can exercise a useful function' in local politics.[82] Civic pride was regarded as an important weapon in the work of these societies. Pride in one's town would encourage loyalty to it and the desire to serve it and promote its well-being. Neville Chamberlain told Birmingham Civic Society that it should stimulate pride in the city and encourage 'citizens to make some personal contribution to public service'.[83]

Appeals to civic pride, therefore, should not be seen simply as a way of encouraging public interest in a memorial scheme. They formed part of a collection of linked ideas which involved social unity, loyalty to one's locality, and disinterested service to the community and were part of a distinctively urban political strategy intended to cope with the problems of urban society outside the party political system. They were used particularly by those who favoured a combination of political interests, probably against the threat of socialism in the post-war world, but also out of a feeling that the old system of party politics was disastrously corrupt and that war had provided an opportunity to clear it away. In national politics this could be expressed as patriotism, and in local politics as local patriotism or civic pride. In connection with war memorials, this kind of exhortation was confined, on the whole, to towns, which suggests further that it was part of the repertoire of a characteristically urban political rhetoric.

Nonetheless, rural war memorial committees shared a number of the concerns shown in towns, especially the concern for the promotion of social harmony. Many wanted to improve communal welfare facilities by providing village halls or nursing care. But in contrast to the towns, where the political expression of class division was the primary concern, rural communities showed stronger concern with their religious divisions, whether these were manifested in a desire to preserve the distinctive values and interests of the different denominations or to keep the peace between them. The stress on interdenominational co-operation over a memorial, or on the provision of non-denominational social facilities, may have served in rural communities the same purpose as appeals to civic pride and loyalty in towns.

Notes to Chapter 4

1. *Carlisle Journal*, 30 June 1919.
2. Cambridgeshire Record Office, R88/110, Burwell Parish Minutes, 12 May 1919.
3. Carlisle, S/PC/38/43, Scaleby War Memorial Minute Book, 26 Apr. 1919.
4. *Hackney and Kingsland Gazette*, 23 May 1919.
5. Ibid., 20 Sept. 1918.
6. *Hackney and Stoke Newington Recorder*, 24 Jan. 1919.
7. Ibid., 20 Sept. 1918.
8. Ibid., 18 Oct. 1918.
9. Ibid., 7 Feb. 1919.
10. Chronicle of Convocation, 1918, 9 July, pp. 430–1.
11. *Staffordshire Sentinel*, 19 July 1920.
12. Atkinson and Brierley Papers, Box 109, Brompton War Memorial, letters 2 Jan. 1920 and 14 Apr. 1920.
13. Ibid., letter 3 Feb. 1919.
14. *Barnsley Chronicle*, 8 Mar. 1919.
15. Ibid., 6 May 1919.
16. Ibid., 4 July 1919.
17. Ibid., 20 June 1919.
18. *British Legion Journal*, vol. 3, no. 4, Oct. 1923, p. 161. Angela Gaffney confirms that the names were those of civic dignitaries: see A. Gaffney, '"Poppies on the up platform": Commemoration of the Great War in Wales', unpublished Ph.D. thesis, University College of Cardiff, p. 151.
19. Hackney, SN/W/1/9, Spratling Correspondence, letters from B. Mercado to G. King, 29 Sept. and 1 Oct. 1921.
20. *Hackney and Stoke Newington Recorder*, 14 Oct. 1921, letter from J. S. May.
21. Durham, D/Br/E 447 1-4, Brancepeth War Memorial Committee Minute Book, 29 Jan. 1920.
22. *Carlisle Journal*, 3 June 1919.
23. Ibid., 27 May 1919.
24. Atkinson and Brierley Papers, Box 109, Brompton War Memorial, letter from Yeoman, 2 Jan. 1920.
25. Ibid., letter, 14 Apr. 1920.

26. *Islington Daily Gazette*, 30 Aug. 1918.
27. Ibid., 1 Apr. 1919.
28. *Carlisle Journal*, 28 Mar. 1919.
29. Ibid., 25 Apr. 1919, letter from T. W. Winthrop.
30. *Progress*, July 1918, p. 78.
31. *The Times*, 12 Sept. 1917.
32. Strathclyde, G4.1, Glasgow War Memorial, Minutes, 20 Feb. 1920.
33. Ibid., Minutes, 14 Jan. 1926, final account of the fund.
34. *Kentish Mercury*, 16 May 1920; Metropolitan Borough of Deptford, Minutes of Proceedings, vol. 21, p. 65, 11 Jan. 1921; Greater London Record Office, PC/CHA/3-5, London County Council War Charities Act Register, 788, Borough of Camberwell War Memorial (registered 19 Dec. 1918).
35. Hackney, SN/W/1/25, untitled press cutting, 20 June 1919.
36. *Hackney and Kingsland Gazette*, 17 Mar. 1919.
37. Hackney, SN/W/1/25, untitled press cutting, 28 Feb. 1919
38. *Hackney and Kingsland Gazette*, 5 Mar. 1919.
39. *Hackney and Stoke Newington Recorder*, 21 Mar. 1919.
40. *Hackney and Kingsland Gazette*, 19 Mar. 1919.
41. Hackney, SN/W1/11, suggestion 6.
42. Hackney, SN/W1/25, untitled press cutting, 23 May 1919.
43. *Hackney and Stoke Newington Recorder*, 23 May 1919.
44. *Hackney and Kingsland Gazette*, 23 May 1919.
45. Ibid.
46. *Hackney and Stoke Newington Recorder*, 20 June 1919.
47. Hackney, SN/W/1/1, Minutes, 13 Nov. 1919.
48. Ibid., Minutes, 24 Nov. 1919.
49. Ibid.
50. Ibid., Minutes, 30 Jan. 1920.
51. Ibid., Minutes, 4 Feb. 1921.
52. Ibid., Minutes, 23 Feb 1921.
53. Ibid., Minutes, 28 Feb. 1921.
54. Ibid., Minutes, 23 Feb. 1921.
55. Ibid., Minutes, 23 Feb. and 22 June 1921.
56. Hackney, SN/W/1/9, letter from A. Chalmers, 3 Oct. 1921, (emphasis in the original).
57. Hackney, SN/W/1/1, Minutes, 4 Oct. 1921.
58. *Hackney and Stoke Newington Recorder*, 4 Jan 1918, letter from J. S. May.
59. Ibid., 14 Oct. 1921, letter from J. S. May.
60. Ibid.
61. Hackney, SN/W/1/1, Minutes, 17 Oct. 1921.
62. Ibid., Minutes, 30 Jan. 1922 and 17 July 1922.
63. *Enfield Gazette*, 26 Dec. 1919.
64. Ibid., 22 Nov. 1918.
65. Ibid., 26 Dec. 1919.
66. Ibid.
67. I owe much of the information about local personalities to Mr Graham Dalling, Enfield Local History Librarian.
68. *Enfield Gazette*, 12 Dec. 1919.
69. Ibid., 26 Dec. 1919.

70. Ibid., 5 Dec. 1919.
71. Ibid., 26 Dec. 1919.
72. See Chapter 1.
73. See Chapter 1.
74. Powys, R/UD/LW/234, file 3, letter 16 Jan. 1922; Wirral, ZWO/16, min. 11 Mar. 1922; Hackney, SN/W/1/7, Additions and Corrections. Memorial organisers frequently asked for lists from local churches when the response to a public appeal for names was poor.
75. *Yorkshire Observer*, 2 July 1920.
76. *Barnsley Chronicle*, 31 July 1920.
77. *Carlisle Journal*, 11 Mar. 1919 and 28 Mar. 1919.
78. See p. 91.
79. Bradford, Bradford Corporation Finance and General Purposes Committee Minute Book 54, 6 Mar. 1919.
80. Lincolnshire, SLUDC 11/6, Minutes, 21 Feb. 1920.
81. An extended discussion of civic societies in this period can be found in A. King, 'Urban Improvement and Public Pressure: The Civic Society Movement *c.*1902–1930', unpublished dissertation for M.Sc. in History of Modern Architecture, University College, London, 1987.
82. P. Abercrombie, 'A Civic Society, an Outline of its Scope, Formation and Functions', *Town Planning Review*, vol. 8, no. 2, (1920), p. 80.
83. *Birmingham Post*, 10 Jan. 1922.

5

The War Memorial Business

Almost any kind of memorial project included some aesthetic elements, even if only a dedicatory plaque, and therefore required the application of artistic skill. In towns, where commissioning civic monuments was an established practice, and the memorial fund might run to several thousand pounds, the memorial committee usually employed an architect or sculptor to produce an original design. But a committee did not have to employ an artist, and where money was short it might think twice before doing so. An alternative was offered by the range of monuments, shrines, tablets and so on, which could be obtained off the shelf from church furniture firms and monumental masons. Artists were aware of this competition and attempted to persuade potential clients that they could more effectively offer what was needed for a memorial: a distinctive object, of assured artistic quality and propriety, within the budget available.

This chapter argues that the professionalism of artists, both in the techniques of their arts and in business affairs, was an important asset to clients, and that artists' professional institutions and rules offered a system by which the interests of clients could be protected. At the same time, their organisation, training and prestige gave them considerable power in their dealings with clients. In general, they retained control of their working process without compromising their aesthetic standards to satisfy clients' prejudices. Artists determined the aesthetic treatment and quality of war memorials very largely themselves.

Business Opportunities

Artists recognised the professional benefits to be reaped from the large demand for memorials, and attempted to make the most of them through professional organisation and propaganda.

Discussing the matter at the 1917 Annual Meeting of the Royal Institute of British Architects (RIBA), one speaker said,

> We must prepare for the time after the war, making our War Memorial [presumably he meant a general national commemorative effort] the helping of the position and interests of our profession, both for the present and the future, and doing all we can for the young men who are spared to us and who retain sufficient enthusiasm for the profession to return to it.[1]

There were reputations to be made as well. General Du Cane reported to the Royal Artillery's war memorial committee that Charles Jagger saw the commission for the regiment's memorial 'as an opportunity to make his name and he wishes to put in his best work'.[2] Professor Beresford Pite, of the Royal College of Art, believed the reputation of the architectural profession as a whole was at stake. 'The world judges us,' he said, 'employs us and uses us as it thinks best; and its wisdom in that matter is arrived at by our own efforts, our own promises and performances . . .. in memorial art the world will look to us for inspiration and guidance.' If this was not forthcoming, 'the world may cease to look upon us as a great profession'.[3]

Architects were best equipped to exploit the opportunities offered by the market for memorials, and they appear to have received the bulk of war memorial business, whether the commissions were small or large. Sculptors were a less coherently organised group. There was a large body of masons who worked to the designs of architects, and who executed much of the smaller-scale decorative work on memorials. Walter Brierley, who was a prominent architect in York, and County Architect to the North Riding, regularly used the same firm of Yorkshire masons for his commissions. Sculptors with independent practices and reputations gained through public exhibitions saw themselves as a group apart from these provincial firms. Occasionally architects would invite well-known sculptors to work on their commissions, as Brierley invited first Francis Derwent Wood, then Henry Poole to co-operate with him at Pudsey. However, much of the time independent sculptors found themselves in competition with architects, to, they felt, their disadvantage. The Royal Society of British Sculptors (RBS) reported that it

> cannot but recognise the very strong influence of the architect amongst all public bodies, owing no doubt to the fact that the main-

> tenance of townships necessitates an architect being appointed a permanent official of all municipal bodies. It is only natural that in cases of memorials the committees should turn to their architect for preliminary advice, and his thoughts would obviously lay [*sic*] in the medium to which he is accustomed. Your council have made, and continue to make strenuous efforts to counteract these influences . . .[4]

The RBS also saw a conflict between those it represented and the firms of masons who served architects. It blamed architects for undermining the interests of sculptors and, by implication, of fine art itself, by not employing sculptors of an equal professional standing to themselves. Architects, it noted, 'desiring to enrich their buildings with sculptural ornament [were] employing trade sculptors instead of members of the sculpture profession'.[5] The council of the society wrote to the RIBA to ask that 'first-rate sculptors' be consulted for sculptural work, rather than 'trade sculptors who at best must employ or contract with practical sculptors of possibly second or third rate abilities'.[6]

In spite of these differences, architects and sculptors adopted, so far as they could, the same approaches when dealing with clients. They promoted their services by offering aesthetic advice, defended their professional monopolies through disciplined solidarity, and were strict about the legal and commercial aspects of their business dealings. It makes sense, therefore, to treat artists as a homogeneous group in relation to members of the public who commissioned their work. A number of other groups - museum curators, critics, patrons of art, educationists - were aware of the professional concerns and practices of artists, and used a similar language to express aesthetic ideas. Through the press and voluntary bodies interested in art, they assisted artists in upholding professional standards in the production of memorials.

Professional Knowledge

Artists, critics and pressure groups concerned with the arts strongly encouraged memorial committees to seek professional advice when commissioning a design, no matter how modest. They set up advisory bodies to give it, and to help committees conduct their commissions. The most respected sources of advice were well-known members of the artistic professions, and their colleagues in museums, or in newspaper and magazine criticism. Artists' professional organisations such as the RIBA, the RBS, and the Royal Academy of Art, as well as bodies concerned with improving and beautifying towns, or preserving ancient buildings, offered access to experts of this sort. They formed special committees to provide the information and professional contacts which memorial committees required.

The advice from all these sources insisted on the necessity of 'calling in a competent artist'.[7] Professional artists could tell their clients which types of memorial were deemed suitable to different kinds of communities. The architect Edward Warren wrote that small communities should confine themselves to the simplest memorials, such as a cross or simple building. Figurative sculpture, he said, was more suitable for towns.[8] When the village of Dunholme chose a cross for its memorial, the architect W. H. Wood, who had designed it, said, 'I feel it is the correct form for such a memorial to take'.[9]

Professional artists also had the skills necessary to apply these types in a way which was suited to the surroundings in which they would appear, and promised treatments of each commission which were both appropriate and distinctive. The RBS recommended that a qualified artist should be employed on every project to meet 'the wishes of all those who rightly think that these memorials should have an individual character suitable to the particular conditions and surroundings'.[10] Walter Brierley pointed out to one client for a village cross that he had given his design 'a strong Yorkshire character' to 'harmonize well with the quaint and irregular character of the village'.[11]

Artists and critics advised clients to adopt the aesthetic outlook of professionals. They wrote a good deal on the subject in order to introduce clients to professional terms and standards of judgement. The different approaches proposed in this advice each had their origin in the working practices and business needs of artists. They were not formed by the artists in response to demands from clients for memorials, but were derived from the traditions and past practices of the various arts. The market for memorials gave artists and critics the opportunity to offer these artistic options to clients as products or services which they might buy. This was, in effect, a way in which artists could advertise the skills and services they offered. By promoting the idea that their particular style or branch of art was the most suitable for war memorials, artists could encourage business for their own practices, and professional commentators could encourage business for the kinds of practice they preferred.

Arthur Clutton-Brock, art critic of *The Times*, put forward an apparently common-sense argument which maintained that beauty in design was the result of the fitness of an object for its intended purpose. An inscription, he said, 'should be good as an inscription, just as a motor car should be good as a car'. A good inscription 'says what is meant simply and finely', and 'the lettering is also simple, fine, clear and permanent . . . good lettering performs its function well, like a good motor car'.[12] This was, in fact, the central idea of a design tradition derived ultimately from Ruskin and William Morris, and a standard of judgement already adopted by a wide variety of artists and architects by the early twentieth century.

More conservative practices also had their defenders. Aymer Valance, the author of *Old Crosses and Lychgates*, intended to offer 'the most appropriate forms of monument for reproduction or adaptation to the needs of the present'. He wrote: 'Too many of the manifestations of modern so-called art betray its utter bankruptcy, because having broken with tradition, it has no resource left but to express itself in wayward eccentricity and sensationalism, the very antitheses of the dignified beauty which the following of time-hallowed precedent alone can impart'.[13] When P. A. Robson reviewed two of the Civic Arts Association's pamphlets on memorials and inscriptions in 1916, he objected to the 'vulgar criticism [such as Clutton-Brock's] which carps at Gothic . . . The fetish of legibility' should not be imposed on small memorials, he said. 'Is there not a certain sense of delicacy which would guide us into designing such a memorial with some reticence, even obscurity, without losing any sense of art?'[14]

To a large extent memorial committees adopted the attitudes artists and critics hoped they would, although some artists held exaggerated expectations of the impact they could have on public taste through their work on memorials, and were duly disappointed. The RBS hoped that enquiries from the public would allow it 'to diffuse broadcast a greater knowledge of the true intent and purposes of sculpture, and a higher appreciation of the value and importance of taste in selection'.[15] It found, however, that usually, 'the insufficiency of funds, and the reluctance of local committees to surrender their personal judgement . . . has proved a bar to progress'.[16] Nevertheless, the actual conduct of memorial committees suggests that, although they may have been recalcitrant in some ways, and insisted on taking what they believed to be a responsible interest in their commissions, they valued the professional services of artists and deferred to their expertise in their specialist fields. The give-and-take required in dealing with memorial committees was perhaps more familiar and acceptable to provincial artists, especially architects used to the commercial aspects of the building world, than it was to the metropolitan sculptors gathered in the RBS.

Committees took up the offer of advice from professional organisations in their search for suitable artists. The committee at Hoylake and West Kirby wrote for advice to the Royal Academy and was given an appointment with Sir George Frampton, 'than whom no more competent authority could be found', in the words of the *Hoylake and West Kirby Advertiser*.[17] Frampton recommended Charles Jagger.[18] By 1922 the Civic Arts Association claimed to have 'given free advice in hundreds of cases'.[19]

Private contacts with artists, critics or connoisseurs were equally useful in obtaining recommendations. A letter from Sir Reginald Blomfield to Sir Lionel Earle, Permanent Secretary at the Office of Works, giving the names of several sculptors recommended by Blomfield, is amongst the Great Western Railway's company papers, and was presumably passed on to a member of the war memorial committee by a personal acquaintance.[20] At Llanbadern Fawr, near Aberystwyth, John Ballinger, the Librarian of the National Library of Wales, used his private connections with connoisseurs and artists to acquire detailed recommendations on Celtic strapwork for their cross, as well as getting the prominent Welsh sculptor Sir William Goscombe John to provide a layout for the inscription.[21]

Walter Brierley's clients came to him through both formal and informal channels. He was recommended to the Vicar of Horbling, Lincolnshire, through the Royal Academy, to the Parish Clerk of Duckmanton, near Chesterfield, by the Arts and Crafts Exhibition Society, and to the Vicar of Wragley, Yorkshire, by the Dean of York. Elland war memorial committee picked him out from the work shown at Leeds Civic Society's exhibition of war memorial designs. But a great deal of Brierley's memorial work came from personal contacts, especially former domestic and church clients who already knew and relied on him.[22]

Professional advice could frequently be obtained from within memorial committees themselves. Many already included members who understood and valued professional artistic work, and who could encourage their colleagues to have confidence in artists' judgement and methods. Some councillors and council officials had experience of public commissions, and borough or district surveyors and engineers were on hand to give advice. Town clerks, who often serviced war memorial committees as honorary secretaries, were used to handling the legal aspects of local government building. Wealthy mayors sometimes marked their time in office by donating an item of public improvement to their towns. A former Lord Mayor of Leeds, Colonel T. W. Harding, who had privately commissioned plans for the new City Square in 1896, and presented statuary for it,[23] was entrusted with the chairmanship of Leeds war memorial committee in 1921. Leaders of county society like J. P. Yeoman of Brompton and Lord Derwent, both in Yorkshire, knew a good deal about architecture, having commissioned work from Walter Brierley (in Yeoman's case a large house).[24] Both these men appear to have involved themselves in the politics of their parishes, led the movements for war memorials there, and formed the artistic requirements for the memorials very largely themselves in consultation with Brierley. Artists and architects who took an interest in local affairs, perhaps as councillors, members of voluntary organisations, or officers of public institutions, also joined memorial committees and contributed to discussions from their own specialist knowledge. The painter Muirhead Bone was invited to join the memorial committee for Steep, Hampshire, and accompanied several of its members to an exhibition of war memorial designs held at the Victoria and Albert Museum in 1919.[25]

Professional Power

The desire of memorial committees to get the best possible artistic work for their memorials gave artists considerable power in relation their clients, and this power was enhanced not only by the structures and rules of their profession, but also by their more informal relationships. Committees could go further than merely seeking advice on a suitable artist. They could actually leave the choice of both artist and design in the hands of professionals by holding a competition. Indeed, if they wished to consider the work of more than one reputable artist, a competition held according to professional rules, with a respected architect or sculptor as assessor, was hard to avoid. Competitions might be open, or limited to artists invited by the assessor, as was the competition run by Walter Brierley for Ilkley war memorial.[26] In such a case, an assessor's knowledge and connections could be used to encourage suitable practitioners to compete. One architectural firm which Brierley invited to enter the Ilkley competition specifically said it was doing so because it respected Brierley's judgement.[27]

As competition rules were set by the artist's professional bodies, artists themselves generally made sure that the rules were upheld. When the memorial committee for Leominster rejected the RBS's conditions for holding a competition, the Society urged its members 'not to enter into any competition which may be advertised in connection with that town, without ascertaining from your Secretary whether the conditions are fair and reasonable'.[28] The committee of the North Wales Heroes' Memorial at University College, Bangor, decided to hold a competition in order to avoid having to work with Henry Hare, who had designed new buildings for the college before the war, when several senior members of the college had found him difficult to get on with. Sir Aston Webb, the President of the RIBA, was asked to act as assessor. He refused, pointing out that the College could find nothing in Hare's work to complain of, and only 'serious dissatisfaction' could justify giving the job of extending Hare's building to another architect.[29] Webb also said to the College's President, Lord Kenyon, face to face, that he doubted 'any architect of reputation would compete . . . in the circumstances of [this] case'.[30] Walter Brierley stood strongly by the rules when clients infringed them. He objected on several occasions when he discovered that a design he had specifically made at the request of a committee was in competition with other designs although no competition had been announced. He usually received apologies, explaining that the committee had not been aware that such rules existed.

After the appointment of an artist, a less formal kind of professional solidarity could continue. The artist who, as assessor or adviser, had been responsible for the appointment, often gave practical support to the appointee in executing the commission. Walter Brierley acted thus in support of the winner he chose for the war memorial competition at Ilkley, J. J. Joass. The committee complained to Brierley that estimates for building Joass's design were far too high, and Brierley then corresponded with Joass, who was based in London, suggesting local suppliers and contractors who could offer cheaper materials and labour. He also proposed several alterations in the design which Joass gratefully accepted. He wrote to Brierley, 'I am very much obliged to you for taking the matter up in this way and if you have any further suggestions to make I shall be glad to fall in with them.'[31] After seeing Charles Jagger's unconventional figure of a soldier for Hoylake and West Kirby war memorial, Sir George Frampton, who had recommended Jagger to the memorial committee, wrote reassuringly to congratulate them on obtaining 'certainly one of the best, if not the best, statue I have seen in recent years'.[32]

The support of an assessor did not always enhance an individual artist's personal authority with a client. Sir Reginald Blomfield, who was co-assessor with Sir Thomas Brock of the Guards Division memorial competition, took a very close interest in the execution of the winning design by Gilbert Ledward and Harold Bradshaw. He suggested many modifications, and strongly defended what he liked in it against criticism from members of the memorial committee and the Office of Works.[33] Lord Crawford, First Commissioner of Works, believed that Blomfield had taken over the design, to the detriment of its sculptural side, and that the unassertive Ledward was being pushed into decisions he did not really like.[34] Blomfield's intervention may have made things worse rather than better for Ledward; but whatever aesthetic authority the younger man seemed to lack in facing the committee, Blomfield did his best to make up for.

The presence of other artists as members of memorial committees also offered a form of professional solidarity which assisted executant artists in their relations with clients. The architect W. Shackleton was a member of Pudsey war memorial committee, which had commissioned Walter Brierley to design the town memorial. The committee left Shackleton to deal with Brierley more or less as he saw fit. 'I have a pretty free hand given me by the committee in deciding the design finally adopted', he told Brierley.[35] An element of professional conspiracy crept into their relationship. The Mayor of Pudsey asked Shackleton to oversee the work of erecting the memorial personally. Shackleton thought this neither necessary nor appropriate, but did not tell the Mayor so. He wrote to Brierley, 'I think you will quite understand what I mean, and that there is no necessity for the Mayor being told how I have expressed myself in connection with this . . .'.[36]

Although the professional solidarity of artists gave them considerable authority over their clients, the authority was not absolute. While a committee had little option but to employ a professional assessor if it held an architectural competition, it could avoid accepting the results. Brierley's conditions for the Ilkley competition defined his own role as 'to select the Architects . . . who are to be invited, to advise the Committee on the relative merits of the designs submitted and to recommend the design to be carried out, his decision thereon to be final and binding on all parties'.[37] However, the committee's responsibility was qualified. The conditions continued: 'It is the intention of the Committee to accept the Award of the Assessor, and to entrust the carrying out of the work to the author of the design selected by him', with the proviso that if it should prove too expensive, another may be selected with the assessor's advice. But the committee did not 'bind itself to carry out any one of the designs submitted'.[38] The competition conditions for Sheffield war memorial specified that the committee was not committed to executing the winning design, but would do so unless there were 'valid reasons to the contrary'.[39]

Once appointed, artists' relations with clients became subject to the regulations of contract; but this only subjected them to the control of their clients to a limited extent. The contract was likely to include stipulations about the extent to which the artist must get the client's approval of any changes made in the original design. The contract which the Guards Division memorial committee made with Ledward and Bradshaw reserved to the clients the right to request changes, and included arrangements whereby any changes the artists wanted to make were subject to approval by the committee or its officers. It was very precise in its grading of changes and the authority required for them. It stated that 'the dimensions . . . shall correspond in all general particulars' to the drawings and specifications of the approved design, and 'no appreciable change' in form from the model could be made without the written consent of the committee. But 'in the event of the sculptor from time to time considering it desirable from an artistic point of view to make variations in the Sculptural work whether by way of artistic addition or omission such as slight alterations in the position and attitude of the figures or in the pattern of mouldings [etc.] not involving any substantial alteration in the general design', then Ledward should inform the committee, and if no objection was made in seven days, he could go ahead.[40]

In practice, the need to refer new developments in a design to the client committee did not usually result in the artist's being forced to conform to the aesthetic preferences of the committee. That would have defeated the point of employing a reputable artist in the first place. Contractual stipulations appear, rather, to have functioned as a way of preserving consensus about the design in the memorial committee, and to maintain public support for it. In choosing a design, a war memorial committee's first task was to consider the possibilities on offer for memorials and build up a consensus around one of them. Once it was entrusted with donations from the public, and a choice of memorial had been made by or on behalf of the subscribers, the committee had to be seen to conduct its business appropriately, and provide the memorial for which the subscriptions had been given. Maintaining the consensus built up around the chosen design was thus important to the success and public acceptability of the memorial project. Changes which the artist made to the original proposal might threaten the consensus once it was formed, and committees had to guard against this possibility.

The sculptor John Tweed suggested to Barnsley war memorial committee that he should omit a bronze panel representing victory, as a way of cutting the cost of the memorial, which was exceeding the money available (Figure 5). The committee refused to accept the idea on the grounds that the panel had been part of the design mentioned in the appeal for funds. People had subscribed on the strength of that design, and if it was omitted 'adverse comment might arise'.[41] The committee's worry was probably aggravated by political sensitivity over whether or not celebration of victory should be part of the commemoration of the dead, though no one said so. For the North Wales Heroes' Memorial, a proposal was made to replace an oratory containing the names of the dead in the original design by a sculpture as

Figure 5.

the monumental component of the project. The college's building committee was prepared to consider the idea, because it thought there were too many names (eight or ten thousand) to be accommodated on the oratory walls; but the change was rejected by the memorial executive committee because a promise had been made to subscribers to record the names of the dead 'in a building dedicated to memorial purposes'.[42]

Some clients did have strong ideas of their own about how to deal with aspects of a design which they felt fell within their own experience. As we have seen, the possibility of discussing questions of this sort was important in adding a genuine element of public participation to the choice of a design. Artists had to listen sympathetically to such discussions, but they also had to defend their authority as experts against encroachment. Members of the Royal Artillery memorial committee made many suggestions for details to Charles Jagger, which Jagger welcomed when they were concerned with the accurate representation of artillery equipment and practices. He told the committee 'I am most anxious to conform to these criticisms . . . except beyond the point where to do so would seriously affect the design as a work of art.'[43] He had to justify his use of bulky clothing in the figures to members who felt that the costume was unrepresentative (Figure 6). He argued that a large bronze form 'holds its own better against a large mass of masonry'.[44] By saying this, he made the question of costume one which properly belonged in his field of expertise as a plastic artist, rather than a question of accuracy in the representation of military details, which was the expertise of his clients.

The artist's last line of defence against interference was refusal to co-operate. Jagger wrote a letter of resignation to the war memorial committee of the Great Western Railway as a result of its persistent attempts to find an alternative to the one design he was really pleased with. The company's chief engineer called personally within a few days, and the company secretary then wrote that the directors 'have every desire that you should carry it through'.[45]

Although contractual controls existed they did not usually interfere drastically with an artist's intentions. A far more frequent inhibition was shortage of funds. Costs rose considerably in the early 1920s. In July 1918 Messrs Hedley, architectural sculptors of Newcastle-upon-Tyne, were paying 1s 8d per hour to their

Figure 6.

carvers. By October 1919 it was 2s 0d, and in May 1920 2s 3d. In 1923 the rate settled, subsequently varying only between 1s 7d and 1s 8d.[46] Increased costs raised the price of Hackness memorial, designed by Brierley, from £85 to £118 between February and September 1920.[47] At Barnsley, the committee revised its estimate of the donations it could raise from £8,000 down to £5,000. The whole original design was dropped, and a new one, with a different character, adopted, it being agreed 'the new design should be more in the nature of a memorial to those who fell in the Great War rather than symbolical of victory over the enemy'.[48] At the first meeting between Ledward and Bradshaw and the Guards Division memorial committee, the committee immediately ruled out two stone figure groups, intended to go at either side, as too costly.[49] Charles Carus-Wilson's design for Sheffield had a sculpted bronze base incorporating eight different figures. These were eventually reduced to four, all identical, to cut costs (Figure 7). In this case, both the architect and a leading committee member regarded the change as an improvement.[50] Financial problems were a more likely reason for a committee to overrule its artist than differences of taste.

The Importance of Professionalism in Art

Why did committee members give so much respect to the views of artists and critics? It was always important that a memorial, whatever its type, should be a worthy thank-offering to the dead. In the case of a utilitarian memorial, a generous or caring intention, backed by an adequate fund, would suffice. If the memorial was to be a work of art, it was its artistic quality which made it worthy. For the most part, members of war memorial committees would not have seen themselves, or have been seen by the local community, as expert judges of art. They had been appointed to organise, raise money and rally support for the memorial project; for their standing in the community rather than their knowledge of art. To ensure that the memorials they commissioned were of a kind to reflect well both on the people they intended to commemorate, and on themselves as responsible for the commemoration, they welcomed opportunities to take professional artistic advice. The uncertainty of committee members was expressed by General Horne of the Royal Artillery. He did not have, he said, the 'ability to express any strong opinion'. In his

Figure 7.

view, 'we should take the opinion of those who are better able to judge and take advantage in every possible way of their view, for we do want [the memorial] to represent the acme of art as well as the regiment'.[51]

The authority which artists established through their professional organisations was also of great use to memorial committees as a means of arbitrating local differences of opinion. The competition procedure proved useful at Sheffield, where relations between the city council and members of the public over the question of a local memorial became strained.[52] A memorial had been designed at the request of a council sub-committee, but when the design was published there was an outcry against it, largely because no effective public discussion had taken place. After four months of argument in committees and in the local newspapers, no public consensus about a design had emerged, and the council decided that a competition should be held. The assessor, E. V. Harris, who had designed the original memorial, chose Charles Carus-Wilson's unconventional proposal, consisting of a massive flagpole on a bronze base ornamented with figures (Figure 7). He expected opposition to his choice,[53] but the Council approved it 'with very little adverse criticism',[54] and the controversy was closed.

The Vicar of South Kirkby, near Wakefield, who was a personal acquaintance of Walter Brierley, had a dispute over the parish memorial, and appealed to Brierley to back his case before the committee. He explained his ideas to Brierley and then said, 'On hearing from you I shall try to force my committee to collect more money and carry out your suggestions. But I need your advice and to be able to lay your thoughts before the meeting.'[55] At Pudsey, W. Shackleton enlisted Brierley's authority as designer to persuade the committee that it was improper to name the current mayor on the memorial, and that only the names of the dead should appear.[56]

As I have stressed, for a memorial project to be a success, it was necessary to establish a consensus amongst local organisations and individuals who could help to undertake its production, and the employment of a reputable artist could contribute a great deal towards this consensus. A local committee, on whom responsibility for the memorial's production ultimately fell, had to be able to rely on its artist to provide an appropriate product and to satisfy public expectations. If artists justified the confidence which committees placed in them, then committees could, at the same time, justify the confidence of the public in their own leadership.

Not all committees saw the need to consult or employ a professional designer. They bought a standard product from a catalogue or used a local mason instead. To judge from available correspondence, clubs, small firms and local authority schools tended not to consult professional artists for their memorials, perhaps thinking they could not afford it. The records of the war memorial committees at Brancepeth, Durham, and Northop, Flintshire, contain several catalogues of standard memorial designs from monumental masons, collected by their vicars.[57] The variety of products offered in them suggests that these firms expected a brisk trade in memorials. Professional artists' organisations were worried about the competition from manufacturers of this sort. A circular from the RBS 'noted with regret that in many cases stereotyped designs supplied by trade firms are being used'.[58]

Condemnation of such firms was not entirely fair. Several were prepared to undertake original designs, as well as their range of standard products. The Memorials Department of the Army and Navy Auxiliary Co-operative Supply, Ltd, London, sent the Vicar of Northop a hand-drawn design for a brass tablet, endorsed in pencil at the bottom 'original design'.[59] A wall tablet in the firm's catalogue was attributed to M. C. Oliver, ARCA, indicating that the designer was professionally qualified. The distinction between trade and professional art was, to some extent, an artificial one, benefiting professionals with established reputations.

The service offered by artists and required by clients was, above all, professional competence. An artist's personal vision of the subject of a memorial was not considered particularly relevant to this kind of commission, whether by clients, critics or artists themselves. Most clients showed little interest in artists' capacity for individual expression, although a distinctive rather than a merely conventional work of art might increase their satisfaction. Artists did not usually offer their own personal expression or their personal responses to the subject of commemoration. They did not claim to have any special personal insight into the meaning of war and death. On the contrary, they offered the technical skill and experience required to express the feelings of others, a sense of propriety, and an understanding of the goals local committees set for themselves.

There were some exceptions. Michael Sadler, the vice-chancellor of Leeds University, commissioned Eric Gill to produce the university war memorial precisely because he believed that the value of the sculptor's work lay in his personal vision. Sadler expected an idiosyncratic interpretation of the war based on Gill's religious and political ideas, which Sadler himself, to some extent, shared. Sadler had exclusive control of the fund from which the memorial would be provided (a legacy to the university to be used at his personal discretion), and thus many of the problems normally presented by the formation of a consensus around the design did not arise. The resulting sculpture, 'The Money Changers', did, however, cause controversy when it was unveiled, partly for the anti-Semitism of the image. If the commission had been placed in the more public fashion normal for war memorials, this might have been avoided.[60]

Others who might have claimed that their work was informed by special personal insight did not do so. Although Charles Jagger maintained to a newspaper that his depiction of soldiers in his memorial designs was based on the personal knowledge of them gained from his own war service,[61] he did not press this point with his clients. Neither Gilbert Ledward nor Charles Carus-Wilson, who both also served in the war (Carus-Wilson receiving, like Jagger, the Military Cross) appear to have claimed any special authority as a result of their personal experience.

Artists provided their clients with the expertise they wanted, and in return, exacted a price in more than money. The price was recognition of their professional authority. This recognition gave artists a prominent place in determining how the commemoration of the war dead should be given material form. Ultimately, the intervention of clients did not have a strong effect on the aesthetic quality or visual symbolism of memorials. Both were principally the result of the professional judgement and practices of artists. It was very much what Professor Beresford Pite had hoped for in 1917, when he had said that the public would expect 'inspiration and guidance' from the architectural profession.[62] Artists used the authority their clients gave them to ensure that war memorials were executed according to practices and canons of taste which were favoured by their professional leaders, and by the majority of ordinary practitioners. This undoubtedly satisfied the tastes of their clients as well; but it was not principally a response to pressure from clients.

Notes to Chapter 5

1. *Journal of the Royal Institute of British Architects*, series 3, vol. 25, Nov. 1917, p. 6.
2. Royal Artillery War Commemoration Fund, Executive Committee Minutes, 28 Feb. 1921.
3. *Journal of the Royal Institute of British Architects*, series 3, vol. 25, Nov. 1917, p. 7.
4. Royal Society of British Sculptors, *Annual Report of Council and Accounts*, 1921, p. 9.
5. Ibid., p. 8.
6. Ibid.
7. Royal Academy of Art, *Annual Report*, 1918, p. 65.
8. E. Warren, *War Memorials*, London, 1919, p. 3.
9. Tyne and Wear, TWAS 52/80, Records of Messrs Wood & Oakley, Letter Books, W. H. Wood to Mr Wilde, 5 Aug. 1919.
10. Powys, R/UD/LW/234.
11. Atkinson Brierley Papers, Box 105, Whixley War Memorial, letter to A. Taylor, 24 July 1919.
12. A. Clutton-Brock, *On War Memorials*, London, 1917, pp. 9–10.
13. A. Valance, *Old Crosses and Lych Gates*, London, 1920, p. vii.
14. *Journal of the Royal Institute of British Architects*, series 3, vol. 23, July 1916, p. 288.
15. Royal Society of British Sculptors, *Annual Report of Council and Accounts*, 1920, p. 7.
16. Ibid., *Annual Report*, 1921, p. 6.
17. Wirral, ZWO/16, untitled press cutting, 7 May 1920.
18. Ibid.
19. L. Pomeroy, 'The Making of a War Memorial', *Town Planning Review*, vol. 9, no. 4, (1921), p. 215.
20. Public Record Office, RAIL 258/447, letter 10 Jan. 1921.
21. National Library of Wales, Minor Deposit, 321 B, Llanbadern Fawr Parish War Memorial papers, letter from J. Ballinger to R. T. Greer, 28 May 1919.
22. Atkinson Brierley Papers, Boxes 105, 108 and 109, *passim*.
23. E. P. Hennock, *Fit and Proper Persons: Ideal and Reality in Nineteenth Century Local Government*, London, 1973, p. 282.
24. C. Carus, 'Walter Henry Brierley, 1862–1926, York Architect', unpublished dissertation for Diploma in Conservation Studies, University of York, 1973, p. 66.
25. Hampshire, 31 M 71/Z1, mins. 7 July 1919 and 17 Oct. 1919.

26. Atkinson Brierley Papers, Box 104, Ilkley War Memorial, W. Brierley, 'Conditions and Instructions Relative to the Submission of Competitive Designs'.

27. Ibid., Ilkley War Memorial, letter from R. S. Weir, 23 May 1919.

28. Royal Society of British Sculptors, *Annual Report of Council and Accounts*, 1920, p. 8.

29. University College of North Wales, Bangor, Department of Manuscripts, papers relating to the North Wales Heroes' Memorial, letter from Webb to Kenyon, 25 Feb. 1919.

30. Ibid., letter from Kenyon to Lloyd, 25 Feb. 1919.

31. Atkinson Brierley Papers, Box 104, Ilkley War Memorial, letter from Joass to Brierley, 31 Aug. 1920.

32. Wirral, ZWO/16, letter from Frampton to Sir A. V. Paton, 2 Mar. 1921.

33. The Office of Works was concerned in the project because its site was in a royal park. The First Commissioner was supposed to approve the design, and the views of the King had to be taken into account.

34. Public Record Office, WORK 20/142, memorandum, 25 Feb. 1922.

35. Atkinson Brierley Papers, Box 56, Pudsey War Memorial, letter from W. Shackleton 20 Mar. 1920.

36. Ibid., 29 July 1921.

37. Ibid., Box 104, Ilkley War Memorial, 'Conditions and Instructions', clause 2.

38. Ibid., clause 6.

39. Sheffield, CA 653 (2), 'Conditions and Instructions for Competition Designs', Oct. 1923.

40. Public Record Office, WORK 20/142, schedules to contract June 1925.

41. Barnsley, Town Clerk's In Letters, File 35, letter to Tweed, 4 Dec. 1924.

42. Bangor, Heroes' Memorial, Building Committee, Minutes, 12 Feb. 1921; Executive Committee, Minutes, 27 Apr. 1921.

43. Royal Artillery, letter from Jagger to Sclater, 7 Apr. 1923.

44. Ibid., Annual General Meeting, 17 Apr. 1923.

45. Public Record Office, RAIL 258/447, letters from Jagger to Bolter, 4 July 1921 and from Bolter to Jagger, 12 July 1921.

46. Tyne & Wear Archives, TWAS 142/17, Messrs Hedley, order book.

47. Atkinson Brierley Papers, Box 105, Hackness War Memorial, letters from Aneley to Brierley, 23 Feb. 1920, and 31 Aug. 1920.

48. Barnsley, Town Clerk's In Letters, File 35, letters 12 and 19 Dec. 1921.

49. Public Record Office, WORK 20/142, letter from Blomfield to Earle (enclosing committee minutes), 22 Jan. 1922.

50. Sheffield, CA 653 (17), report of meeting 24 Sept. 1924; letters 25, 29, 30 Sept. 1924.

51. Royal Artillery, Central Committee Minutes, 12 Nov. 1924.

52. Sheffield Record Office, CA 653, especially (1)–(6) and (16).

53. Sheffield CA 653 (16), letter from E. V. Harris, 10 Mar. 1924.

54. Ibid., letter to E. V. Harris, 14 Mar. 1924.

55. Atkinson Brierley Papers, Box 108, War Memorial Enquiries, letter from H. M. Wellington, 30 Apr. 1918.

56. Atkinson Brierley Papers, Box 56, Pudsey War Memorial, letters from W. Shackleton, 21 June and 14 Oct. 1920. The question of naming the dead is discussed in Chapter 7.

57. Durham, D/Br/E 45 (8) and (9); Clwyd, P/45/1/379.

58. Powys, R/UD/LW/234, circular received 9 May 1921.
59. Clwyd, P/45/1/379, letter to Vicar of Northop, 21 June 1919.
60. Leeds University, Brotherton Library, Film 131, f.9, letters from Sadler to Gill, 14 and 31 Jan. 1920, and C. Cross to Sadler, 10 Sept. 1917. See also G. R. Kent, 'Sadler, Gill and the Money Changers', in University Gallery, Leeds, *Michael Sadler*, Leeds, 1989, pp. 34–8.
61. J. Glaves-Smith, 'Realism and Propaganda in the Work of Charles Sargeant Jagger and Their Relationship to Artistic Tradition', in A. Compton (ed.), *Charles Sargeant Jagger: War and Peace Sculpture*, London, 1985, p. 52.
62. See p. 107.

6

War Memorial Imagery

Memorial committees and members of the public looked mainly to precedent and tradition when choosing or judging designs for the memorials they erected,[1] but the meanings which they saw in them were often not those which would have sprung to viewers' minds in earlier times. The interpretation of even long-familiar objects was transformed in order to make them relevant to the unprecedented circumstances of the Great War. At the same time, a number of new forms of monument were developed which were intended to have special relevance to the war. The most widely used of these were the Cenotaph designed by Sir Edwin Lutyens, and the Cross of Sacrifice designed by Sir Reginald Blomfield for the Imperial War Graves Commission. Both these designs became part of the canon of monumental types.

This chapter considers the new interpretations which were given to traditional styles of memorial, and how innovations were absorbed into the repertoire of memorial forms. Although some interpretations took their cues closely from the actual appearance of a memorial, this was not necessarily the case. As we shall see, many derived from literary or other verbal, and even ceremonial, associations, which became strongly associated with particular symbols without any obvious reference to their formal details.

The process of interpretation was doubly important because it also served to involve members of the public actively in choices about designs, helping to make them popular and respected objects. We have already seen that the public contributed to the discussion of memorial projects in committees and in the press. Many interpretations were publicised by people with special authority in their fields, in order to suggest ways in which the public might find memorials relevant to the experience of war;

but non-specialists also had the opportunity to insist on their own standards of relevance.

Traditional Form and Contemporary Meaning

The process of transformation through which traditional forms acquired connotations relating them specifically to the recent war was most conspicuous in the case of the cross. In 1921, Charles Jagger declared that the cross 'has been, and probably always will be the symbol of the Great War'.[2] It acquired these connotations mainly as a consequence of the use of Christian ideas in wartime propaganda, and members of the public were likely to understand them immediately.

As a religious symbol, the popularity of the cross was relatively recent. It had been regarded with suspicion in England for much of the time since the Reformation; but nineteenth-century archaeologists and local historians had revived interest in it as a form of monument associated with historic rural communities.[3] The restoration of village crosses was a minor Victorian movement which accompanied the better-known vogue for church restoration,[4] and in the late nineteenth century the cross joined the traditional headstone as a common funerary monument. Crosses (frequently Celtic, to avoid any Catholic associations) had been used as memorials to the dead of the Boer War, and even, though rarely, as in the parish churchyard at Hawarden, Clwyd, a crucifix.

The cross came to be particularly associated with the idea that death in the war was a superlative example of self-sacrifice.[5] The Bishop of London described it as 'the emblem of sacrifice' in his speech dedicating the war memorial cross at Saint Mary's church, Stoke Newington.[6] The cross was already the symbol of sacrifice in the form of Christ's redemptive sacrifice for humanity. In a study of ancient Dartmoor crosses, published in 1892, William Crossing wrote, 'An object that could turn the thoughts to an event of such importance as the great sacrifice once offered for mankind, was peculiarly fitted for setting up in such places as the wayfarer should pass'.[7] During the war, however, the term 'great sacrifice' had changed its meaning. It came to refer in most people's minds to the supposedly willing and generous laying down of their lives by soldiers in defence of their country and their ideals.

The Great War was often justified, especially in its initial stages, as a purgative blood-sacrifice which would cleanse the world not only of political, but also of social and moral evil. This was not a particularly Christian idea, but it could be likened to the redemptive sacrifice of Christ by those who wished to give it a Christian inflection. In the war, said the Bishop of London in 1916, the blood of the dead, 'mingles with the Precious Blood which flowed in Calvary; again the world is being redeemed by precious blood'.[8] Or, in a more orthodox sense, the connection between Christ's sacrifice and that of soldiers was made by suggesting that the soldiers were imitating Christ in their devotion to duty and to the good of others.

The deaths of soldiers and the redemptive sacrifice of Christ were connected in a lithograph by James Clerk, published in the *Graphic*[9] at Christmas 1914, depicting a dead infantryman lying at the foot of a ghostly cross, with the crucified Christ looking down at him. It was entitled ambiguously 'The Great Sacrifice', leaving it uncertain whether the words refer to the dying Christ or the dead man. It became very popular.[10] Queen Mary bought the original, and distributed copies of it as gifts to a number of parishes during the war. Several still hang in churches today. One is on the wall of Saint Cross Hospital chapel at Winchester, over a wooden battlefield cross, in memory of a parishioner. Another was used as part of the war memorial at Marner Street school in east London.[11]

Street shrines also encouraged the association of military self-sacrifice with the cross. Amongst the patriotic symbols and lists of names, a cross could often be found, whether the shrine was home-made or bought from a professional manufacturer. In some cases a crucifix was used, although the *Evening News*, in its promotion of shrines, discouraged it, regarding it as a sectarian symbol exclusive to Catholicism.

The power of familiar wartime ideas to transform traditional symbols can also be seen in the image of the burning torch. An upturned torch - a light extinguished - was a classical funerary symbol. In connection with the war dead, at least so far as interpretations are available, torches were understood to connote the need to continue the struggle of those who had died. This meaning was taken from John McCrae's extremely popular poem 'In Flanders Fields', published in December 1915. One verse of the poem runs:

To you from failing hands we throw
The torch; be yours to hold it high.

To a member of Sheffield war memorial committee, this passage superseded the traditional classical meaning. He suggested a torch as the symbol to stand at the top of Sheffield war memorial, in place of the 'celestial crown' proposed by the designer, arguing that the torch 'has definite significance in these memorial matters'.[12] Lines from the poem were also used in the inscription on Chingford war memorial.

Obelisks and inscribed wall-tablets, both traditional forms of funerary monument, were frequently used as war memorials. As an urban monument, the obelisk fitted into the prevailing fashion for classicism in civic design. At Harrogate, the war memorial obelisk was incoporated into a new pattern of traffic circulation, cutting out a dangerous corner, and so formed part of a minor urban improvement scheme - a small step in the direction advocated by town planners like Stanley Adshead.[13] In the countryside, it was traditionally a form of monument used to commemorate great landlords or statesmen on their estates. Perhaps its aristocratic connotations influenced Lord Derwent, Walter Brierley's patron, in his choice of an obelisk as the village memorial at Hackness.[14] Brierley thought that an obelisk would be 'suitable to your surroundings', and that it ought to be 'prominent against the skyline',[15] as such aristocratic estate monuments had usually been. But obelisks had little association with the idea of a village community, and are not often found as rural war memorials.

Although long used by Christian society as a funerary marker, the oblelisk has no obviously Christian connotations; but as a war memorial it was frequently invested with a Christian meaning by adding a cross to it. R. Wynn Owen explained that he had placed crosses at the apex of the London and North Western Railway's war memorial at Euston Station (Figure 8), 'as the crowning feature of the design' to suggest the Christian principles for which the dead had fought and died. The *LNWR Gazette* stressed another Christian meaning: the inseparability of believers on earth from those now in heaven (the doctrine of the communion of saints). 'Marked by the cross on all sides, the memorial speaks to us of that sacred Christian unity, which is unbroken by death, untouched by the grave . . .'.[16] In a number of cases a cross was integrated more completely and subtly into the design of an obelisk. Lewisham memorial (Figure 9) has a cross on each face, but present only as a course of stone blocks, just proud enough of the rest of the structure to cast a suggestive shadow in direct sunlight.

In the case of the tablet, the form of the monument itself was not given any special connotation. It was the names inscribed on it which mattered. They carried the essential meaning of the memorial, and the treatment of them was the primary design consideration. Critics frequently recommended simplicity both in the wording and the cutting of inscriptions, although monumental masons and ecclesiastical architects like Walter Brierley offered designs in both gothic and classical styles as well.

Familiar forms of figurative sculpture, either realistic or allegorical, are a frequent feature of war memorials, although these too acquired new significance in some respects. As Nicholas Penny has written, the purpose of war memorial sculpture was 'to portray the typical, indeed the common, victim or participant'. They were, in this respect, distinct from the civic tradition of memorials to prominent citizens, whose qualities were represented as peculiar to them as individuals, not as the attributes of a group. Some memorials to individuals, Penny allows, may also stress the qualities of the typical victim, such as George Frampton's memorial to Edith Cavell in central London. The monument in Whtehall to Earl Haig is not in this category, as it celebrates the particular rather than the typical individual.[17]

This change of focus from the particular to the typical created a number of difficulties and ambiguities in designing and interpreting what were, after all, still civic memorials. In memorials which commemorate a group of people collectively, personal portraiture is not a practical proposition. Photographs of individuals might conveniently be incorporated into a memorial if the numbers involved were small, and institutions such as clubs sometimes did this. Where a community chose to have a fine piece of monumental sculpture as its memorial, in the tradition of monuments to its worthy citizens, some use of the figure other than an individual portrait was required.

Many figurative monuments do not include a figure to represent the dead at all. They are referred to, instead, in an inscription or a list of names, attended in some way by conventional allegorical figures which were conceived as statements about the

Figure 8.

Figure 9.

war or the dead (Figure 27), or by figures mourning. The place of allegorical figures could be taken by military figures, who thus acquired, at least in part, an allegorical role (Figures 6 and 29). Perhaps the most common of these was the soldier with rifle reversed (Figure 8); but others are common, often soldiers standing at ease, as if guarding the site sacred to the dead (Figure 25). In certain ambiguous respects these figures do also represent the dead. They illustrate their supposed qualities, not through classical allusions as allegorical figures do, but by illustrating their martial character and bearing. Often their physique and posture suggest determination and watchfulness, physical health and strength.

This kind of illustrative figure may also appear not as a supporter, but as the central figure of the monument, that is, in the position which should be occupied by the person to whom the memorial is dedicated. Here, its meaning becomes more ambiguous. The soldier with rifle reversed is again common in this position (Figure 10). The figure, however, is quite explicitly doing homage to the dead. In strict point of iconography, therefore, it depicts not the dead but those who mourned them, first and foremost their former comrades, showing respect for the dead through an appropriately military gesture. Other figures in the central position on a monument, such as John Tweed's for the King's Royal Rifle Corps memorial at Winchester (Figure 11), might more plausibly be seen as generalised representations of the dead themselves.[18] However, it is important to recognise that who or what is depicted by many of these figures is ambiguous. This absence of clear definition is characteristic of much memorial symbolism, and is the result of adapting existing artistic conventions - in this case the civic monument to an individual - to a novel situation.

There was considerable resistance in memorial committees to the idea of showing a dead body itself, even though recumbent figures as tomb sculptures or personal memorials had remained quite common in Britain into the early twentieth century. (They were also popular in Germany as war memorials.)[19] Depictions of bodies do occur, sometimes supported by angelic or allegorical figures, as at Stalybridge or in the Allerton memorial in Lady Hill Park, Bradford, where the supporting figure is Death; but they are not common. When Charles Jagger proposed to add a corpse to his design for the Royal Artillery memorial (Figure 12) at a

Figure 10.

Figure 11.

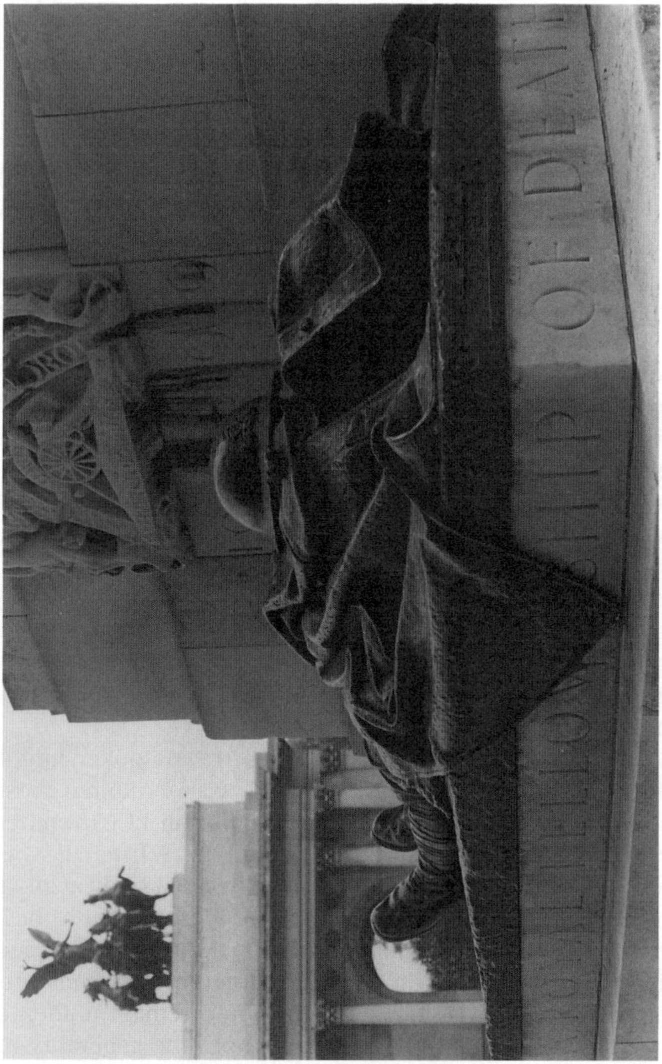

Figure 12.

late stage in its development, a number of committee members found fault with it. The figure is covered casually by a greatcoat, obscuring the face, and so left in a kind of limbo, as if awaiting disposal. One criticism was that a figure of this sort was inappropriate in a memorial which should, first and foremost, console the bereaved; another was simply that it was 'rather on the gruesome side'. A third, advanced by a number of members of the regiment, was that if there was to be 'a recumbent figure, it should be of a man just shot down', presumably because it would appear a more heroic and active image, in a manner derived from popular illustration.[20] The Cameronians' memorial in Glasgow includes a figure of this sort (Figure 13). On the other hand, two such figures which Gilbert Ledward had included in sketches for the relief panel of gunners in action on the Guard's Division memorial were removed before the design was executed.[21]

By covering the face, Jagger ensured that the body remained anonymous and its depiction of death was given the greatest possible generality. Edwin Lutyens achieved the same anonymity for a recumbent figure in a number of his memorial designs by lifting the body high above the viewer, on top of the memorial, so that no individual portraiture could be expected. The official description of Lutyens's design for Southampton memorial stressed the value to the bereaved of the anonymity of the figure at its top. All of them, it said, could imagine that the figure specifically depicted the individuals they personally mourned.[22]

This anonymity, as a means by which the onlooker might identify more closely with the memorial, was exploited most dramatically in the burial of Unknown Warrior on 11 November 1920,[23] the same day that the Cenotaph in Whitehall was unveiled. The warrior's tomb does not represent a body at all. It appears only as a marble slab in the floor of Westminster Abbey. The crucial image was not the tomb itself, but the story of the selection of the body from the cemeteries on the Western Front, in circumstances which guaranteed it would remain unidentifiable. Press accounts of the burial stress both the generality of the anonymous body, and the possibility of imagining that it was someone you yourself had known.[24] More local unknown warriors were wanted in some places. A Leeds alderman suggested that the city should have both its own cenotaph and

Figure 13.

unknown warrior, replicating the symbolic ensemble in central London.[25] Lutyens's first use of the anonymous recumbent figure, at Southampton, unveiled a few days before the burial of the Unknown Warrior, probably owes nothing to it; but Jagger specifically cited it as a precedent for his figure.[26]

The reception of Jagger's recumbent figure seems once again to point to the uncertainty created by the conjunction between old and new sources in the symbolism of remembrance. In this case, we see a clash between traditional civic allegory and the direct appeal to individual imagination associated with the Unknown Warrior. Jagger's figure had a special value in the eyes of several members of the Royal Artillery committee, because it seemed to connect the memorial more clearly with the dead. One remarked that, without it, the only approximate reference to death was the driver with outstretched arms, who appeared 'crucified'. Another thought it showed 'at once it was a memorial to the dead'.[27] The other figures on the memorial (Figure 6), although well calculated to express solemnity, were revealed, by contrast with the corpse, to make this essential connection only weakly. The frank statement it provided gave the memorial full value as a tribute to the dead.

In this case, the powerful but ethically inexpressive image of the unknown body turned the characterisations represented in the standing figures into marginal details. It is possible that the very absence of specific moral content in a recumbent figure made it an unsatisfactory choice for most people. Here, on the other hand, it highlights the lack of resolution in the meaning of the figurative sculpture of war memorials, which may have allowed room for viewers to form their own interpretations of these monuments in a way which earlier civic sculpture did not.

Inventing Conventions: The Cenotaph and the Cross of Sacrifice

One common type of war memorial was new, and seen to be new. It was derived from the Cenotaph erected in Whitehall for the Peace Day military parade held on 19 July 1919 to celebrate the signing of the Treaty of Versailles (Figure 14). The Whitehall Cenotaph had two incarnations. The first was a temporary structure of wood and plaster, marked to look as if it was made of stone blocks, carrying flags and wreaths, with the inscription

Figure 14.

'The Glorious Dead' and the dates of the war. It provided an object for the parading soldiers to salute in honour of their comrades who had been killed. Its site and position in the street were determined by its place in that day's ceremonies. It had to be on the route of the march, somewhere conspicuously visible to the crowds who attended, in reasonably impressive surroundings. It was informally unveiled the day before the parade, and people laid wreaths at it, most of which had to be removed again for the march past.[28] On Peace Day, the choir of Westminster

Abbey sang 'anthems and hymns' near it, striking 'the note of solemnity'.[29] It was saluted not only by the marching soldiers but by the Allied commanders, Foch, Haig and Pershing amongst them. On subsequent days people came to lay more flowers at the monument's base.

Press accounts of the Peace Day parade paid a great deal of attention to the Cenotaph. The *Manchester Guardian* gave a highly poetic account of it, saying that in its vicinity 'a light was shining in the daylight like a light on an altar'. It seemed at first 'a tiny object in the distance, but as the procession went on with all its separate associations of great deeds done and of those who had died in doing them, it loomed larger and larger in people's minds'.[30] The *Morning Post* was positively mystical. 'Near the memorial', it reported, 'there were moments of silence when the dead seemed very near, when one almost heard the passage of countless wings. Were not the fallen gathering in their hosts to receive their comrades' salute and take their share in the triumph they had died to win?'[31] In *The Times*'s judgement, 'no feature of the Victory March in London made a deeper or worthier impression than the cenotaph . . .'.[32]

Within days a movement was under way in Parliament and the press to have a permanent version of the Cenotaph produced. *The Times* of 21 July carried a letter from 'RIP', dated the day before the peace parade (the day the temporary monument was unveiled), arguing that it should be retained. Captain Ormsby-Gore asked a question in the House of Commons, proposing a permanent, exact replica.[33] Twenty-three MPs signed a memorandum to the First Commissioner of Works asking that it be re-erected on the same site.[34] The permanent stone version which now stands in Whitehall was unveiled by the King as part of the Armistice Day ceremonies in 1920.

When the temporary Cenotaph was commissioned, the Prime Minister was determined that it should be a work of high artistic quality, not merely part of the street decorations erected by the Office of Works for the parade. He insisted that it should be the work of 'some prominent artist'.[35] By implication, a brief was set for the design: Lord Curzon specified a simple pylon, which, at the same time, 'might be made sufficiently impressive', and Lloyd George wanted it 'sufficiently high to be impressive'.[36] Lutyens gave them what they asked for: an apparently simple object with a subtle composition intended to enhance its visual impact. To judge from Lutyens's sketches of the monument, which exaggerate the vertical perspective, he envisaged the slight stepping back of the upper part of the structure as a way of increasing the sense of recession, and so of height.[37] Slight curves in the horizontal and vertical surfaces were introduced in the stone replica, and were not in the original.[38]

The Cabinet was so specific about the form which the monument should take, not essentially for aesthetic reasons, but because it was keeping tight control of all the arrangements for the Peace Day parade. Arrangements for a salute to the dead were regarded as sensitive. Cabinet members were not prepared to leave such an important symbol entirely to the discretion of an artist, however eminent. Not all of the Cabinet had thought the project a good idea, and Curzon was afraid that the monument might be desecrated.[39]

Subsequently, the Cabinet was concerned to preserve the consensus which developed around the Cenotaph at its first appearance. It permitted hardly any noticeable changes to be made to the design when it was reproduced in stone, and would admit none of the additions which were proposed to express some sort of religious sentiment, either Christian or more universal.[40] Lutyens was not even allowed to replace the real silk flags with carved and painted stone ones, something he very much wanted to do.[41]

The Cenotaph was invested with its own particular meaning. It especially connoted death and mourning. Sir Alfred Mond understood the Cenotaph to be predominantly associated with bereavement when listing arguments for and against making it permanent. It might, he said, 'be of too mournful a character as a permanent expression of the triumphant victory of our arms'.[42] Benjamin Lloyd supported his proposal for a cenotaph as the Llandrindod Wells memorial by saying that it 'depicts the anguish of the nations engaged in the great war', and called it a 'more solemn form'.[43] Sir John Burnet, too, saw it as largely connoting mourning. He told Glasgow war memorial committee that, although they had asked for a cenotaph, he believed the monument should express 'not only grief . . . but the spirit of sacrifice and achievement', and so he proposed to include other elements in the design.[44]

Many people thought the Cenotaph was a good design and appropriately expressive. When J. W. Simpson, President of the

RIBA, presented Lutyens with the Institute's gold medal in 1921, he said,

> To me, as an architect, the Cenotaph is the most remarkable of his conceptions. Precisely suited to its site and its surroundings, austere yet gracious, technically perfect, it is the very expression of repressed emotion, of massive simplicity of purpose, of the qualities which mark those whom it commemorates and those who raised it.[45]

The Cenotaph's apparent simplicity was especially attractive. The *Morning Post* described it as 'of an austere simplicity that is profoundly impressive'.[46] Sir F. Hall of the Royal Artillery liked it because 'it is so simple'.[47] The *Staffordshire Advertiser* praised the reproduction cenotaph at Stoke as 'strikingly beautiful in its simplicity of design'.[48] The liking for simplicity accorded with an influential current of contemporary critical thinking, which valued directness of statement and clarity of form. A. C. Benson, poet and Master of Magdalene College, Cambridge, in his keynote address at the opening of the Civic Arts Association's exhibition of memorial designs in 1916, had recommended simplicity of statement 'so that the gazer can see at once that the matter recorded is great and significant and desires to know more'.[49] The Royal Academy of Art recommended that 'in all memorials simplicity, scale, and proportion should be aimed at, rather than profusion of detail or excessive costliness of material'.[50]

Simplicity also had a moral meaning. A Civic Arts Association pamphlet on war shrines published in 1918 recommended simplicity because it conveyed sincerity. 'Neither magnitude nor magnificence can adequately express a nation's gratitude to its sons for the vast sacrifices they have made on its behalf. Such simple records, as these proposed and now being used, . . . meet the case in a much better way. They are impressive because they are sincere.'[51] Simplicity was also understood to represent an important and admirable quality in the dead themselves, making simple monuments especially appropriate for them. Discussing the LNWR's memorial obelisk (Figure 8), the *LNWR Gazette* said, 'The simple grandeur of the structure corresponds with the simplicity and grandeur of those to whom it is raised . . .'.[52]

The liking for simplicity in commemorating the dead reached beyond the realm of specialist art criticism into newspapers and the opinions which private individuals expressed in war memorial committees. It was not applied only to permanent memorial structures, but to any acts and objects associated with the commemoration of the dead. The *Evening News* insisted that street shrines put up as a result of its fund-raising campaign 'are to be of the simplest character'.[53] Two years later, when it announced that the public was invited to lay flowers on the war shrine in Hyde Park, it added that 'the simpler the tribute the better'.[54] Mr Riddle, a Labour councillor in Carlisle, and secretary of the local Co-operative Society, told a public meeting called to discuss the city war memorial that, 'the finest feelings were expressed in the simplest terms',[55] while Mr C. C. Frank of Leeds, who claimed to speak 'with no authority, only as a man in the street', believed that 'the less fussy and the more plain and simple and unified the design the better'.[56]

The aesthetic qualities of the Cenotaph were only one reason for its popularity. Another powerful reason was that it marked a sacred site, the site of the salute to the dead by the soldiers amd Allied commanders in the Peace Day parade. The sanctity it acquired on that occasion remained an important part of many people's attitude to it, reflected in public support for the idea that it should remain in its original position, and not be removed to a quieter or safer site. As Alfred Mond said, 'no other site would have the same historical or sentimental association'.[57]

Moreover, in spite of its formal originality, it readily fitted the convention established by war shrines. It was seen from the very first as a shrine. Lord Curzon had referred to the Cenotaph in a Cabinet meeting as 'a temporary shrine',[58] and members of the public showed that they saw it in the same way by placing flowers at it both before and after the military parade on 19 July. Londoners in particular had been paying homage to war shrines for the previous three years, and they knew what to do with them. Thus there was no hesitation in the public response. It was immediately surrounded by floral tributes.[59]

Lutyens had himself been involved in the shrines movement at the end of the war. As we have seen, he was commissioned to design a replacement for the makeshift structure erected in Hyde Park in August 1918; but the scheme met with opposition. His first proposal envisaged construction methods like those used in the temporary Cenotaph; then, in November of that year, Sir Samuel Waring asked him to design a permanent shrine for the park, allegedly to the cost of £50,000.[60] Elsewhere, the idea of replacing temporary by permanent shrines had been put forward. The Vicar of Longton had proposed it in 1916,[61] and the shrine donated by Charles Higham to the Borough of Islington was in certain respects a permanent version of the original Hyde Park shrine.[62] To make the temporary Cenotaph permanent was not, therefore, a particularly original suggestion. What was unique in this case was the consensus which existed about the suitability of the design, and that it suited the authorities to accede to pressure for a permanent structure.[63]

It was subsequently taken by newspapers as a focus for their accounts of the first Armistice anniversary commemoration on 11 November 1919. The *Morning Post* wrote, 'as with a single impulse, all thoughts converged on the National Cenotaph in Whitehall'.[64] Other papers published highly coloured and emotional accounts of the behaviour of people around it on that occasion.

The combined influence of its form, original purpose and association with war-shrines, provided strong cues for understanding the Cenotaph, but did not fix its meaning absolutely. Other interpretations were quite possible, not all of them favourable. Some saw it as an imperial or national symbol. Douglas Haig described it as the 'symbol of an Empire's unity',[65] and *The Times* said of it, 'Simple, massive, unadorned, it speaks of the qualities of the race . . .'.[66] It was also seen, by a writer in the *Catholic Herald*, as a pagan monument, insulting to Christianity.[67] In 1930, a peace activist asserted that young men who refused to raise their hats to it 'say the Cenotaph celebrates victory and is an excuse for proud emotion, and is not a symbol of old, unhappy, far off things'. This remark was occasioned by a controversy over whether or not a military presence was proper at the Cenotaph on Armistice Day.[68] It saw the monument's significance as deriving from the routine official ceremonies. Perhaps it saw the flags at full-mast, not half-mast, and the word 'glorious' in the inscription. A younger viewer in 1930 might remember little about the wartime shrines or the Peace Day salute to the dead which had prompted the initial public response to the monument, and not be susceptible to the sacred and grief-laden associations it had originally had.

A cenotaph was one option frequently considered by local memorial committees. Some wanted cenotaphs which were direct imitations of the one in Whitehall. At Stoke-on-Trent an 'exact replica' was unveiled in November 1920. (Its inscription differed from the one on the original in referring to 'our', not 'the' glorious dead, if the press account is correct.) It was made of timber, expanded metal and a 2" coating of cement.[69] The Lord Provost of Glasgow suggested a reproduction of the Whitehall Cenotaph as the memorial for his city in 1921.[70] More often, while approving the general idea of a cenotaph, local committees wanted it adapted so as to be a recognisably individual monument. Sir John Stirling-Maxwell thought that merely to replicate the object in Whitehall was 'scarcely worthy of a great city like Glasgow'.[71] However a monument related to the cenotaph (and 'of artistic design', the committee said) had already received the support of the majority, including Stirling-Maxwell himself.[72]

Public enthusiasm required artists to incorporate the general form of the cenotaph into the repertoire of monumental types which they could offer to their clients. Artists who used it included practitioners of Lutyens's own standing in the architectural profession. Sir John Burnet provided the design for Glasgow cenotaph. Sir Robert Lorimer provided a version of it with an Egyptian character for the Cumberland and Westmorland joint counties' memorial at Carlisle. In normal circumstances, both men would probably have been reluctant to borrow from a design so closely associated with a professional rival. Even Reginald Blomfield, who had a number of professional conflicts with Lutyens, offered the city of Leeds a design whose classical detail, vertical emphasis, rectangular plan, and sarcophagus at the top suggest a large debt to Lutyens's idea. A Leeds alderman certainly saw this as 'like the Cenotaph in London'.[73] The willingness of such designers to exploit the Cenotaph for themselves is a measure of how far it had become common property. From being a characteristic and personal work by Lutyens (which he continued to develop for a number of clients), it had rapidly become a convention in its own right.

There were qualities in the original Cenotaph which made it an especially suitable model for other monuments. Although it was clearly different from the familiar types, its actual form was not easy to grasp or describe. It was very plain in its details. Apart from its verticality, and the presence of wreaths and flags, there was little about its shape or decoration which was likely to impress itself immediately and unmistakably on viewers, especially if they had to judge from the photographs of it published in newspapers.

People seem to have been prepared to see a wide range of not very similar objects as being like the Cenotaph. Initially, this may have been because press descriptions of the temporary version had led to confusion about its appearance. The day before the peace parade *The Times* carried a misleading account of it, describing it, correctly, as a pylon, and giving dimensions, but continuing, 'groups of flags will be arranged on each of the four sides . . . On the side fronting the pavement will be hung laurel wreaths . . . It is proposed to place at the top of the column' (the pylon was now a column) 'an altar containing a brazier from which will rise a tall flame'.[74] (Curzon had tentatively asked Lutyens for a flame, but they later abandoned the idea.)

The Times gave no source for its information, but it might have come from someone who had seen an earlier proposal from the Office of Works which the cabinet rejected. Alfred Mond had shown some unattributed drawings to the Cabinet at a meeting on 4 July, when Lloyd George in particular had expressed his keenness that a leading artist should be given the job.[75] The *Morning Post* interpreted the monument as a pedestal without its statue.[76] *The Times* continued to see its top as an altar.[77] It was, in fact, both a sarcophagus - a motif taken from classical architecture - and a coffin lying in state, draped in the Union Jack, according to the ceremonial practice for burying dead soldiers. It is also possible that people assumed the Cenotaph to be more like the war shrine erected in Hyde Park the previous year than it actually was.

Early attempts to reproduce the Cenotaph also suggest confusion about its appearance. At Stockport, a shrine to the dead of a local firm, S. R. Carrington and Sons, was erected for the Peace Day celebrations, consisting of a squat obelisk on a tall base, with flags on each side, a wreath on the face, and various pictures and inscriptions. Afterwards, the *Stockport Advertiser* called this a 'cenotaph', and described it as 'similar in nature to the one which was erected in London'.[78] In October 1919 a temporary structure was provided in Enfield market place to accompany a memorial service, and the public was invited to lay flowers at it. The *Enfield Gazette* had announced that this structure would be a replica of the Cenotaph, but it was, in fact, a squat obelisk with a flat top.[79]

A memorial committee's request for a cenotaph was usually no more than a request for something conforming to a vaguely defined type. Designers could treat the request with considerable flexibility. Some produced fairly close imitations, like that for Edmonton in north London (Figure 15), others produced assemblages of explicitly classical features, mimicking tombs, as at Enfield (Figure 16). Lutyens himself executed cenotaphs with a variety of sculptural additions, including recumbent figures on the top, and some designers followed his precedent in using the cenotaph as a basis for sculptural elaboration. There are a number of war memorials, like those at Barnsley and Pudsey (Figures 5 and 19), whose most eye-catching feature is a figurative sculpture, but where this is placed on a stone base so large as to be out of all proportion to it. Although the Cenotaph was not mentioned in the commissioning and design of either of these, it seems likely that they were conceived to some extent on the model of a cenotaph enhanced with sculpture, and should be understood as owing their overall form to that model.

Like the Cenotaph, the 'Cross of Sacrifice', designed by Sir Reginald Blomfield for the Imperial War Graves Commission,[80] is a symbol especially associated with the Great War. Blomfield took an existing conventional type of monument and gave it a new inflection to suit it more specifically to the commemoration of the war dead. It established a visibly new version of the traditional form - a new style - intended to match the novelty of its post-war connotations, and it was readily recognised as such by memorial committees and the general public.

Blomfield's cross has a severe, unornamented form, an octagonal section with capped ends to each limb, and a bronze sword pointing downwards on its face (Figure 17). He explained the meaning he intended for it in a speech at the opening of an exhibition of war memorial designs held by Leeds Civic Society in 1920. A memorial should 'speak of its own time', he said, for which 'an abstract statement of the purpose of the memorial' was necessary, in simple forms and without archaeological details. In his view 'runic monuments or gothic crosses had nothing to do with the grim terrors of the trenches'.[81] He was appealing to memories of the war as a time of grim austerity. Vera Brittain had evoked this experience in 1915 when she wrote in her diary, in words which foreshadow Blomfield's, of 'our present life - its agony and absence of ornamentation'.[82]

The Cross of Sacrifice embodies, in many respects, the ideals of simplicity and expressive functionalism we have already seen

Figure 15.

Figure 16.

Figure 17.

advocated by critics like Arthur Clutton-Brock,[83] and could be regarded as having a particularly modern character. Eckhard Gruber argues that the simplicity constantly recommended for memorials, in Germany as much as Britain, was a response to the confusing plethora of images which assault the eye in the modern urban environment.[84] It is, however, difficult to generalise about the modernity or otherwise of these aspects of style and taste, not only in war memorial design, but in the sculpture of the period more generally.[85] Simplicity and directness of statement had been touchstones of progress and renewal in design since the later nineteenth century. In literature, Josephine Guy points out, they could, on the contrary, epitomise the moralism of high Victorian writing as opposed to the revitalising commitment to originality, even wilfulness, in language which had been advocated by the Aesthetic Movement.[86] Given that literary sources were so influential in the interpretation of war memorials, simplicity and directness could have been appreciated in either of these contrary senses.

Blomfield's design is no less ambiguous. Even if it appears to stray from tradition, it is firmly rooted in classicism. In fact, it may well have been borrowed directly from an eighteenth-century source at Playden church, near Rye, which has a lead cross on its spire, remarkably like Blomfield's design. It is plain, with simple capped ends to the limbs, and, though cylindrical in section, looks, in strong light, as if the surface consists of flat facets. Blomfield must have known it well. He had a house in Rye from 1912, and a plaque in Playden church commemorates his association with the congregation there. It would have offered him an ideal precedent for a contemporary image, sanctioned by the historic architectural style which he admired most.

The Cross of Sacrifice, again like the Cenotaph, became common property. Memorial committees commissioned identical designs in a number of places. Blomfield maintained that he personally supervised the erection of about forty.[87] Its influence can be seen in the work of other artists. Walter Brierley offered the village of Bolton Percy a design which sounds very like it. 'The motif of the Cross', he wrote 'is a large base, on which the names will be legibly cut, and on which stands a bold and simple cross of sacrifice with a sword of defence on the face of it, with a shield on which the years of the war would be cut'.[88] Blomfield commented later that 'the design is, of course, my copyright, but I have come across horrible travesties of it in many local memorials apparently executed by the local mason from illustrations of the cross given in the papers'.[89] The sword, which he applied to the face of the cross, became a common feature of memorial crosses which in other respects bear no resemblance to his design.

However good the designs of the Cenotaph and Cross of Sacrifice may have been, in order to acquire the status of familiar monumental conventions, and to be accepted as appropriate and desirable forms of memorial, they had to be brought forcefully to the attention of the public. This occurred as a result of their connection with an organisation or a location which would ensure widespread public exposure. In the case of the Cenotaph, this exposure was assured by government's sponsorship of it, and the siting of it amongst the government buildings of Whitehall, by its place in the official Peace Day parade, and by the consequent interest of the press and members of Parliament.

The Cross of Sacrifice was distributed widely by the Imperial War Graves Commission in war cemeteries abroad, where it became the presiding symbol. The Commission also used it in a large number of civilian cemeteries in Britain where service personnel were buried. It would have been seen in the illustrations of designs for the war cemeteries issued while they were under discussion in Parliament in 1919 and 1920. It thus became a familiar object through the exposure given to it by the Commission, and its special association with the war dead was probably heightened by its physical proximity to their bodies in the war cemeteries.

Stylistic Nationalism

Most British memorials were executed in styles so familiar that they could be regarded as inherently part of a British national tradition, and as an affirmation of moral or political values characteristic of British culture. Heightened nationalism, stimulated by war, had created a prejudice against styles of work which did not belong to this tradition, and against foreign artists.[90] It was a prejudice which some British artists encouraged, for fear that foreigners might be given the best memorial commissions. In 1917, the council of the Royal Society of British Sculptors heard that Jacob Epstein, an American by birth, and well-known as a modernist, might be engaged to produce a memorial to the recently dead Lord Kitchener. The council proposed writing to the promoters of the memorial, arguing that 'in justice to British sculptors now serving at the front, no commission should be given for any national memorial till after peace is declared', and that any such memorial should be 'of the British school, and executed by a sculptor of purely British descent'.[91] Sir George Frampton, a past president of the society, wrote to *The Times* to warn that foreigners 'may be given preference and allowed to suck the juice from the grape (which should be the birthright of our own flesh and blood) leaving but the dry husk to the men of our race, whose development we have watched with such pride and pleasure'.[92]

In 1925 a rumour spread in Barnsley that John Tweed's bronze figure for the town's memorial had been cast in Germany, and protests were made to the committee. It had in fact been cast by the Compagnie des Bronzes of Brussels, one of Europe's leading foundries. The *Sheffield Mail* commented, 'It is not pleasant to realise that a figure in memory of Britishers was made by alien hands', although it added that 'it is infinitely preferable that it should have been made by our allies than by our erstwhile enemies'.[93] The mayor of Barnsley added that he could not understand why foreigners were employed; he thought British workmanship was best.

The effect of such views was that work in a style which did not look familiar might well be understood as un- or even anti-British. This was especially true if the work in question appeared to be in some way Teutonic. During the war, critics and artists publicly condemned recent German art as typifying a ruthless and dangerous national ethos. In 1916, Stanley Adshead had lectured on 'the significance of the war memorial in its relation to national and political outlook', and had concluded that the monuments of the Second Reich were 'strong, uncivilised interpretations of the power of the warlords'. He cited, in particular, the work of Bruno Schmitz[94] (Figure 18). A writer in *Architectural Review* also maintained that, 'in the memorials of war of modern Germany we see exemplified in the most appalling manner that creed of ruthless domination which has left such a tale of human misery in the stricken lands over which the German army has trampled'. Schmitz was again condemned.[95]

Figure 18.

By implication, anything which seemed to follow the example of art in the German Empire must be inappropriate for commemorating Britain's part in the war.[96] A particular object of criticism was the Siegesallée in Berlin (an avenue created to celebrate the Prussian defeat of France in 1870, containing monuments to the victors). In 1916, the *Church Times* insisted, 'We shall naturally avoid imitations of the Germania monuments and the atrocities of the Siegesallee, known among Germans themselves as the petrified slaughterhouse . . .'.[97] After Charles Pawley had exhibited his proposal to redevelop central Westminster as a national war memorial, the writer Lawrence Weaver criticised the scheme for showing a likeness to Prussian monumental planning. He said 'it would, if carried out, cover Westminster with a fine reminiscence of the "Siegesallee"'.[98] This dislike of commemorative art which appeared to be outside a British national tradition reinforced the existing tendency to aesthetic conservatism, and made it all the more likely that well-worn forms would be pressed into service in new causes.

Interpretation and Participation

The discussion of art was as necessary to the participatory character of war memorial projects as the more general discussion of the purposes of memorials which we examined in Chapter 3. Memorial committees had to discuss designs both with their artists and with members of the public who needed to be convinced of the propriety and quality of what the artists produced. In this, the aesthetic conservatism of so many memorial designs was positively useful, as recourse to well-established forms of art made it all the easier for people without artistic sophistication to interpret and judge the designs for themselves.

Sculpture representing the contemporary soldier, or some aspect of military life, was especially effective in engaging the interest of people who had become familiar with military life and its trappings, and who wanted a memorial which appealed to their experience. When the Royal Artillery's war memorial committee was discussing a design submitted to it by Lutyens, based on the Cenotaph, a demobilised gunner objected that the memorial should be something to represent 'the views of every gunner, not only the officers, but those who come to London with their families etc.' He wanted something which was recognisably connected with the Artillery, such as a team and gun, rather than something which seemed to him to appeal only to an upper-class taste.[99]

One reason for liking figure sculpture was that it offered an historical record of the contemporary soldier. Edward Warren had written in his pamphlet for the Civic Arts Association that figure sculpture was 'an endless opportunity for effective and historically valuable presentment'.[100] W. G. Storr-Barber recommended one of his figurative designs to Llandrindod Wells memorial committee on the grounds that it would show future generations 'the British soldier as he was in the Great War'.[101] Artillerymen seem to have appreciated Jagger's memorial for the regiment very much in this spirit, reminiscing about the details of their wartime work which the figures called to mind.[102] The requirement for historical accuracy in such a memorial allowed committee members to become closely involved in the development of a design through the opportunity this gave to discuss technical details of its appearance. Committees could generally find someone with sufficient military expertise to check the accuracy of figurative work for them. At Llandrindod Wells a general who lived locally supplied equipment for Benjamin Lloyd, the memorial's sculptor, to use as a model, and when the committee visited the studio, the general attended as well to give advice[103] (Figure 10).

Historical accuracy became a matter of contention between the sculptor Henry Poole and the memorial committee at Pudsey, where the question was not so much concerned with strict authenticity as with the recognisability of the image. Poole had originally proposed the figure of a soldier walking with his rifle slung over his shoulder and his bayonet fixed[104] (Figure 19). Some committee members took exception to this on the grounds that if he was 'marching easy', as he appeared to be, the bayonet would not have been fixed. Poole justified his design by referring to photographs, taken in battle, of men advancing against the enemy behind an artillery barrage in just this attitude, with their bayonets fixed.[105] They might even be smoking cigarettes, he said. He thought this 'very typical of the modern methods of warfare', and hence true to actual experience. But the committee would not accept Poole's use of 'a special and occasional attitude for perpetuation . . . instead of a more familiar one'. It would 'create a wrong impression and misconception' in future viewers. 'Not one person in a thousand today, will be aware of the *special* method adopted in the latter part of the war . . . and none of the future generations will be aware of it or appreciate its meaning'.[106] It was also argued that the bayonet would attract lightning. In the end it was omitted. It is possible that the bayonet was disliked simply for being a bayonet, with all its violent connotations. Bayonets proved to be a problem in nearby Bradford two months later, as we shall see.

Artists appreciated the need for an accessible public discussion of their proposals, and they presented them in a way which lent itself to verbalisation, creating programmes of meaning which could readily be explained to clients or described in the official programmes of unveiling ceremonies. This was as true of the purely formal elements of a design as of any images incorporated in it. R. Wynn Owen explained the formal qualities of his design for the LNWR memorial (Figure 8) thus: it dealt with matters which were sacred and which

> should . . . be approached in a spirit of humility, so the structure which is surmounted by the crosses and wreaths takes the form of a simple obelisk, entirely devoid of ornament, to the end that the eye is led up to the crowning element of the design [four crosses, one on each face of the obelisk] without distraction.[107]

In an equally literal manner, Charles Carus Wilson intended the flagstaff, which is the main feature of his design for Sheffield war memorial (Figure 7), to express aspiration,[108] presumably by reaching upward. The finial on the mast is a 'celestial crown' providing the culmination of the symbolism – presumably that to which the dead had aspired.[109] Memorial committee members followed the designers' lead and took a similarly literal view of the meaning of the formal elements of designs. Wakefield memorial committee claimed that in its selection of a design (Figure 20), 'An effort has been made to obtain a memorial which, whilst simple and dignified in outline, suggests that firmness and strength symbolical of the undoubted spirit of those who fought and fell in their country's cause.'[110] The memorial is a rectilinear stone pylon, slightly tapering upwards, suggesting the batter of a fortress wall, with carved wreaths in recesses in the upper stonework which could be read as a minimal castellation.[111]

The tendency to interpret form literally made it relatively easy to find quite full meaning in monuments which contained little

Figure 19.

Figure 20.

or no explicit allegory, and to convey a sense of their possible meanings to the public. By full, I mean that the meaning understood by a viewer should seem sufficient to account for the existence and form of the monument as a whole. Its form and imagery did not present obvious problems of interpretation by containing prominent inexplicable features. Such accessibility to a large public meant that arguments, especially concerning details of figure sculpture, were very likely to occur. In certain respects this made the business of choosing a design more difficult. At the same time, it was only through the work of resolving differences of perception and opinion that the production of a memorial could become a genuinely participatory act.

Although familiar styles of art were so useful to memorial committees in creating consensus, we should not take it for granted that public taste in war memorials was, of necessity, aesthetically conservative. We can find a number of memorials whose precedents lie outside the normal repertoire of civic monumental forms, and outside the western Christian tradition. Some are cairns of rough stone (Figure 21), some are roughly finished monoliths, both harking back to a remote pre-classical and pre-Christian past. Indeed, the monolith used for the village memorial at Westwell in Oxfordshire was thought actually to be a prehistoric monument[112] (Figure 22).

The memorial erected on the Green at Tynemouth in 1938 is hard to locate in any recognisable tradition (Figure 23), and has a distinctly modern look. Its form is partly utilitarian, the circular base of the pylon being intended as a seat; but this does not compromise the abstract quality of its design.[113] Eric Gill created a number of memorials incorporating simplified, archaising figure sculpture, carved directly in stone, rather than modelled and cast (Figure 24). These were characteristic of his sculptural technique, which constituted an important step in the development of modernist sculpture in Britain.[114] Gill had acquired some notoriety from his presence in pioneering exhibitions of modern art in the years immediately before the war, especially on account of his willingness to combine or juxtapose sexual and religious themes in what some critics saw as a scandalous manner.[115] His work was, nonetheless, well regarded as a vehicle for expressing the morality appropriate to war commemoration by a number of patrons. To Michael Sadler, at Leeds, this was because he admired Gill and liked his views.[116] To others it may have been

Figure 21.

Figure 22.

Figure 23.

Figure 24.

because his technique embodied the simplicity of design and direct, unsophisticated, supposedly honest, approach to the handling of materials advocated by Arthur Clutton-Brock and other influential critics.

The use of archaic or highly simplified forms of memorial was an enlargement of the vocabulary of civic monuments beyond classical and Christian models which, in some respects, ran parallel to modernist developments in art appreciation. Some modernists reinterpreted the idea of tradition itself to include ancient and non-European art, in order to justify departures from aesthetic convention by appealing to an extended sense of the continuity of human culture.[117] Similarly, innovations in commemorative art, towards greater abstraction and a more indefinite symbolism, could be placed in an accessible interpretative framework by invoking an enlarged sense of cultural tradition. However, it was probably the habit of making ethical, rather than merely aesthetic, judgements about memorials, often basing them on a very literal-minded formalist reading of the design, which encouraged memorial committees occasionally to accept decidedly unconventional proposals.

Notes to Chapter 6

1. For a detailed study of the forms of monumental art which have been applied to war see A. Borg, *War Memorials from Antiquity to the Present*, London, 1991.

2. Public Record Office, RAIL 258/447, Report by J. Burnet, T. Tait and C. Jagger, 21 Feb. 1921.

3. See, for example, W. Crossing, *Old Stone Crosses of the Dartmoor Borders*, London, 1892; A. Pope, *Old Stone Crosses of Dorset*, London, 1906.

4. A. Rimmer, *Ancient Stone Crosses of England*, London, 1875, p. 140; *Churchman's Family Magazine*, May 1863, p. 596.

5. See Chapter 7 for a further discussion of the importance of the idea of self-sacrifice.

6. *Hackney and Stoke Newington Recorder*, 15 Oct. 1920.

7. W. Crossing, *Old Stone Crosses*, p. xii.

8. Quoted in A. Wilkinson, *The Church of England and the First World War*, London, 1978, p. 190, where Wilkinson also discusses the analogy with Christ in depth.

9. *The Graphic*, 5 Dec. 1914.

10. See Wilkinson, *The Church of England*, p. 191.

11. *Hackney and Kingsland Gazette*, 30 Aug. 1916; *East London Advertiser*, 17 March 1917; London Borough of Tower Hamlets, Photos LH 85/16.

12. Sheffield, CA 653 (17), letter from W. Mackenzie-Smith, 19 Feb. 1925.

13. Harrogate Corporation Minutes, Aug. 1921, p. 4 and Sept. 1921, pp. 2 and 5.

14. Atkinson Brierley Papers, Box 105, Hackness War Memorial, letter from Derwent to Brierley, 20 Mar. 1919.

15. Ibid., letter 21 Mar. 1919.

16. *LNWR Gazette*, vol. 10, no. 111, Nov. 1921, p. 245.

17. N. Penny, 'English Sculpture and the First World War', *Oxford Art Journal*, vol. 4, no. 2, 1981, p. 37. One might add the memorial to Edward Horner, by Edwin Lutyens and Alfred Munnings, at Mells, to the category of monuments which represents individuals as typical figures.

18. Depiction of the dead in figurative sculpture is discussed from a different point of view, with particular reference to the technique of modelling as a way of reconstituting their bodies, in C. Moriarty, 'The Absent Dead and Figurative First World War Memorials', *Transactions of the Ancient Monuments Society*, vol. 39, (1995), pp. 8–40; and at greater length, also considering the question of portraiture, in C. Moriarty, 'Narrative and the Absent Body: The Mechanics of Meaning in First World War Memorials', unpublished D.Phil. thesis, University of Sussex, 1995.

19. The tombs of Lord and Lady Leverhulme at Port Sunlight, of Sir Redvers Buller in Winchester Cathedral, and Eric Kennington's monument to T. E. Lawrence at Wareham take this form. For Germany see U. Berger, '"Immer war die Plastik die Kunst nach dem Kriege": Zur Rolle der Bildhauerei bei der Kriegerdenkmalproduktion in der Zeit der Weimarer Republik', in R. Rother (ed.), *Die Letzten Tage der Menschheit: Bilder des Ersten Weltkrieges*, Berlin, 1994, p. 430.

20. Royal Artillery, Central Committee Minutes, 12 Nov. 1924, letter from Col. Lewin and comments by F. Mercer and General Newton.

21. Fine Art Society, *Gilbert Ledward, RA, PRBS: Drawings for Sculpture, a Centenary Tribute*, London, 1988 (pp. 3 and 7–8 of unpaginated catalogue). No discussion of this change appears to have survived.

22. Quoted in D. Boorman, *At the Going Down of the Sun: British First World War Memorials*, Dunnington Hall, 1988, p. 121.

23. Details of the arrangements for this ceremony are in A. M. Gregory, *The Silence of Memory: Armistice Day 1919–1946*, Oxford, 1994, pp. 24–6; see also K. S. Inglis, 'Entombing Unknown Soldiers: From London and Paris to Baghdad', *History and Memory*, no. 5, 1993, pp. 7–31.

24. *The Times*, 11 Nov. 1920; *Daily Mail*, 12 Nov. 1920.

25. *Yorkshire Evening News*, 19 Nov. 1920. Gloucester considered the possibility of burying an unknown warrior, see Moriarty, 'The Absent Dead', p. 17. Moriarty argues that the liking for memorials depicting soldiers was related to the popularity of the Unknown Warrior's tomb (ibid., p. 15).

26. Royal Artillery, Central Committee Minutes, 12 Nov. 1924.

27. Ibid.

28. *Manchester Guardian*, 21 July 1919.

29. *Morning Post*, 21 July 1919.

30. *Manchester Guardian*, 21 July 1919.
31. *Morning Post*, 21 July 1919.
32. *The Times*, 26 July 1919.
33. *Evening News*, 21 July 1919; *Parliamentary Debates*, fifth series, vol. 118, p. 1366, 23 July 1919.
34. Public Record Office, WORK 20/139, undated memorandum.
35. Public Record Office, CAB 23.11, Minutes, p. 2, 1 July 1919.
36. Ibid., Minutes, p. 7, 4 July 1919.
37. C. Hussey, *The Life of Sir Edwin Lutyens*, London, 1950, p. 384.
38. Allan Greenberg discusses the formal qualities of the Cenotaph at length in A. Greenberg, 'Lutyens' Cenotaph', *Journal of the Society of Architectural Historians*, vol. 48 (1989), pp. 5–23.
39. Public Record Office, CAB 23.11, Minutes, p. 7, 4 July 1919.
40. Public Record Office, CAB 23.12, p. 43, memorandum 23 Oct. 1919.
41. Public Record Office, CAB 24.109, memorandum 5 July 1920. In my view the Cabinet was entirely right in its judgement. The painted flags on Lutyens's Leicester city war memorial are reminiscent of the decorations on an ice-cream van.
42. Public Record Office, CAB 24.84, GT 7784, 23 July 1919.
43. Powys R/UD/LW/234, letter from B. Lloyd, 15 Sept. 1920.
44. Strathclyde, G4.1, Glasgow War Memorial, Minutes, 8 June 1921.
45. *Journal of the Royal Institute of British Architects*, series 3, vol. 28, 25 June 1921, p. 474.
46. *Morning Post*, 21 July 1919.
47. Royal Artillery, Minutes, 30 July 1920.
48. *Staffordshire Advertiser*, 19 Nov. 1920.
49. A. C. Benson, *Lest We Forget*, London, 1917, pp. 12 and 13.
50. 'Suggestions for the Treatment of War Memorials', Royal Academy, *Annual Report*, 1918, p. 67.
51. G. Jack, *War Shrines*, Burnley, 1918, p. 5.
52. *LNWR Gazette*, vol. 10, no. 111, Nov. 1921, p. 245.
53. *Evening News*, 9 Oct. 1916.
54. Ibid., 3 Aug. 1918.
55. *Carlisle Journal*, 28 Mar. 1919.
56. *Yorkshire Observer*, 2 July 1920.
57. Public Record Office, CAB 24.84, GT7784, 23 July 1919.
58. Public Record Office, CAB 23.11, Minutes, p. 7, 4 July 1919.
59. The great public reverence stimulated by the Cenotaph is described in D. W. Lloyd, *Battlefield Tourism: Pilgrimage and the Commemoration of the Great War in Britain, Australia and Canada, 1919–1939*, Oxford, 1998.
60. Public Record Office, WORK 16/26 (8), especially letter from Lutyens to Mond, 12 Nov. 1918, and press cutting with unidentified letter, 18 Nov. 1918.
61. *Challenge*, 28 July 1916.
62. See Chapter 2.
63. Alan Greenberg is wrong, I think, to say that the Cenotaph 'became the focus of four years of pent-up sorrow which had been waiting . . . to be released'. People had been expressing public sorrow, combined with other ideas and feelings, at war shrines for some time. Their response to the Cenotaph continued something which had become a common practice by the end of the war. What

might have been exceptional on this occasion was a sense that the killing had now – more or less – stopped. (A. Greenberg, 'Lutyens' Cenotaph', p. 11).

64. *Morning Post*, 12 Nov. 1919.

65. *The Times*, 10 Nov. 1920 (quoting Haig's message to schoolchildren published in *Teachers' World*).

66. *The Times*, 11 Nov. 1920.

67. Gregory, *The Silence of Memory*, p. 199.

68. Quoted in Gregory, *The Silence of Memory*, p. 125, where the associated controversy is also described fully.

69. *Staffordshire Sentinel*, 10 Nov. 1920. The original was replaced in 1938, but a contemporary photograph shows it to have been very close to its model, Hanley Library, S.I.850 A (6).

70. Strathclyde, G 1/3/1, letter from Sir John Stirling Maxwell, 4 Feb. 1921.

71. Ibid.

72. Strathclyde, G4.1, Glasgow War Memorial, Minutes, 13 Feb. 1920 and 18 Sept. 1919.

73. *Yorkshire Evening Post*, 19 June 1920; *Yorkshire Observer*, 2 July 1920.

74. *The Times*, 18 July 1919.

75. Public Record Office, CAB 23.11, Minutes, p.7, 4 July 1919.

76. *Morning Post*, 21 July 1919.

77. *The Times*, 19 July 1919.

78. *Stockport Advertiser*, 25 July 1919.

79. *Enfield Gazette*, 10 Oct. 1919 and 17 Oct. 1919.

80. P. Longworth, *The Unending Vigil: A History of the Commonwealth War Graves Commission 1917–1984*, London, 1985, p. 36.

81. *Yorkshire Post*, 17 Apr. 1920.

82. V. Brittain, *Chronicle of Youth, Vera Brittain's War Diary, 1913–1917*, ed. A. Bishop, London, 1981, p. 202, entry for 26 May 1915.

83. See Chapter 5.

84. E. Gruber, '". . . death is built into life." War Memorials and War Monuments in the Weimar Republic', *Daidalos*, no. 49, (1993), p. 77.

85. J. Glaves-Smith, 'The Primitive, Objectivity and Modernity: Some Issues in British Sculpture in the 1920s', in S. Nairne and N. Serota (eds), *British Sculpture in the Twentieth Century*, London, 1981, p. 81.

86. J. Guy, *The British Avant-Garde: The Theory and Politics of Tradition*, London, 1991, especially pp. 87–92 and 107–11.

87. R. Blomfield, *Memoirs of an Architect*, London, 1932, p. 180.

88. Atkinson Brierley Papers, Box 105, Bolton Percy War Memorial, letter to the Bishop of Beverley, 15 March 1919.

89. Blomfield, *Memoirs*, p. 180.

90. This outburst of cultural nationalism was not confined to Britain. The subject has been explored at length by Kenneth Silver; see K. Silver, *Esprit de Corps: The Art of the Parisian Avant-garde and the First World War*, Princeton, 1989.

91. Royal Society of British Sculptors, Minutes of Council, 28 June 1917.

92. *The Times*, 28 July 1917.

93. *Sheffield Mail*, 18 Aug. 1925.

94. *The Times*, 27 Jan. 1916.

95. 'Memorials of War VIII: German', *Architectural Review*, vol. 40, 1916, pp. 107 and 109.

96. The artists who designed a temporary monument to the dead to stand in the Champs Elysées in Paris for the French celebration of the signing of the Treaty of Versailles in 1919 suffered from this problem too. Silver, *Esprit de Corps*, pp. 222–3.

97. *Church Times*, 3 Mar. 1916.

98. *Builder*, vol. 116, 6 June 1919, p. 563.

99. Royal Artillery, Extraordinary General Meeting, Minutes, 30 July 1920. Lutyens's design, with sculpture by F. Derwent Wood, is illustrated on the cover of *Report of the RA War Commemoration Fund and the Royal Artillery Association,* 31 Dec. 1920. It has somewhat the character of a classical eighteenth-century tomb.

100. F. Warren, *War Memorials*, London, 1919, p. 2.

101. Powys, R/UD/LW/234, letter 14 Sept. 1920.

102. J. Glaves-Smith, 'Realism and Propaganda in the Work of Charles Sargeant Jagger and Their Relationship to Artistic Tradition, in A. Compton (ed.), *Charles Sargeant Jagger: War and Peace Sculpture*, London, 1985, p. 78.

103. Powys, R/UD/LW/234, letters from B. Lloyd, 7 March 1921 and to Lloyd, 30 April 1921.

104. Atkinson Brierley Papers, Box 56, Pudsey War Memorial, letter from H. Poole, 22 Dec. 1922, enclosing drawing.

105. Ibid., letter from Poole, 11 May 1922.

106. Ibid., letter from W. Shackleton, 13 May 1922.

107. Public Record Office, RAIL 1057/2868, LNWR, Papers relating to the unveiling of War Memorial, Euston, letter, 6 Nov. 1921.

108. Sheffield, CA 653 (16), untitled and undated press cutting. The newspaper report acknowledged that this was an 'unconventional design', but gave a precedent by describing it as a Venetian mast, on the model of those standing in front of the basilica in the Piazza San Marco.

109. Sheffield, CA 653 (17), letter from C. Carus-Wilson, 3 Mar. 1925.

110. Wakefield Library, untitled and undated press cutting.

111. This monument is also an obelisk with crosses attached.

112. B. R. Mitford, *Westwell (Nr. Burford), Oxfordshire. A Short History of the Prehistoric Henge, Church, Manor and Village, BC 1700?–AD 1951. Largely compiled from the researches made in 1928–9 by the late General Bertram Revely Mitford, CB, CMG, DSO*, no place, 1952.

113. Association of Northumberland Local History Societies, War Memorials Survey, Appendix I, 1996. The Association's extremely thorough survey of the county is available at the National Inventory of War Memorials, Imperial War Museum, London. I am most grateful to Nick Hewitt for these and other details.

114. See J. Collins, Barbican Art Gallery, *Eric Gill: Sculptures*, London, 1992.

115. Collins, *Eric Gill*, p.23.

116. See Chapter 5.

117. Glaves-Smith, 'The Primitive, Objectivity and Modernity', p. 77.

7

The Canonisation of Common People

Commemoration of the dead did not simply encourage people to remember who they had been and what had happened to them, but to remember them in a particular way. It made assertions, explicitly or by implication, about them. Through its memorial images and figures of speech, commemoration expressed the fundamental assumption that the dead should be respected and that what they had done in the war should be valued. It attributed a number of virtues to them in order to justify holding them in honour. This chapter will examine the broadly accepted depiction of the dead which was propagated in commemoration, explore reasons why various groups of people should have found it credible, and consider its sources.

Characterising the Dead

We saw in Chapter 3 the wide variety of purposes people believed their war memorials should serve; but whatever secondary purposes they might have been given, they were judged first of all by the contribution they made to prompting the right kind of memory, and the right kind of feelings and actions, in those who saw or used them. Memorials and ceremonial acts supplied focal points to conjure up the memory of the dead; but much more was said about them in the sermons, speeches and writings associated with memorial unveilings and other ceremonies. Thus memorials and ceremonies took on as much a didactic as a commemorative character.

Mourners were encouraged to moderate or escape from grief by cultivating positive emotions towards the deaths of their friends and relatives. Pride in their achievements and in their character was especially emphasised. Alderman Raley of Barnsley said, unveiling Cudworth war memorial, that the memories retained by the bereaved were 'poignant but proud'.[1] In 1920 the Wesleyan Conference issued a statement saying, 'There is a pride that is permissible, a pride whose constituents are love and honour and high thought and deep feeling; and we are proud of the sons who have fought our battles and given their lives. But we mourn for them . . .'.[2] Inscriptions and images on memorials often explicitly stated that the memory of those whom they commemorated was special - proud, honoured, glorious. Sedgfield war memorial, County Durham, reads: 'Pass not this stone in sorrow but in pride, . . .'. The design sub-committee for Barnsley war memorial extended the inscription suggested by both the sculptor and a committee member - 'to the memory'[3] of the town's dead - to read 'in honoured memory'. At Llanymynech on the Shropshire–Montgomeryshire border 'in proud and grateful memory' was substituted for plain 'in memory'.[4] The point was not simply to remember the dead, but to insist that they had been special, and that their memory was especially honourable.

Designs for memorials shared in the attempt to lift the thoughts of viewers above physical death. Heart, Son, Peart and Co. of London wrote to the vicar of Northop, Flintshire, that they were 'trying as far as possible to get away from the funereal appearance of tablets and especially in the case of War Memorials to make them somewhat varied in colour without being tawdry'.[5] The sculptor W. G. Storr-Barber proposed a design for Llandrindod Wells memorial in which he represented 'the British soldier as he was in the Great War', pointing out that the expression on the face of the figure would be one of 'hope and thoughtfulness rather than one of mournful sorrow or regret'.[6] The village war memorial at Stanway, Gloucestershire, carries an inscription that amounts to a table of appropriate transformations of feeling for those who contemplated the dead.[7] It reads:

For a tomb they have an altar
For lamentation memory
And for pity praise.

One justification for holding a great national ceremony in memory of the dead, and for the many more local commemorative events, was to give more than a purely personal significance to their memory. Even if only as a consolation to the bereaved, there was a desire to give the awareness of death a greater sense of importance than a purely personal loss. The simple fact that the community honoured the dead would help to console the bereaved, the *Enfield Gazette* said. 'Be it ours to pour in the balm of consolation to the stricken, and to convince them that, as a people, we hold in honour the gallant and unforgettable dead.'[8] Speeches at unveilings and on other ceremonial occasions frequently proposed characteristics which the public should attribute to the dead, principally: self-sacrifice, comradeship and the love of peace. At Saint Michael's church, Poplar, Major General Sir Nevill Smyth VC told the congregation for the unveiling of the war memorial that, 'We honour these men of Poplar today not so much for what they did as for what they were. Under their ever cheerful demeanour smouldered the fires of patriotism and self-sacrifice.' They were 'always honourable, merciful, gentle and chivalrous'.[9] (These remarks were greeted with cheers.) The audience at the unveiling of Stockport memorial was told that the dead had, 'without flinching, faced the horrors and deprivations of war, and willingly gave their lives for others and for the country they loved so well'.[10] Mr Alec Paterson, holder of the Military Cross, told the congregation in Saint Mary Magdalen, Bermondsey, when he unveiled the memorial there, that the dead 'were men of peace; they had no wish for war, but when danger threatened the homes of the people, they left behind all they counted most dear . . . Cheerfully they fought, cheerfully they endured, and uncomplainingly they fell.'[11]

The self-sacrifice of the dead was said to have made the most crucial contribution to victory. At the unveiling of the North Eastern Railway memorial in York, Lord Plumer, one of the British commanders in France, said, 'We all know that it was not we, no matter in what rank, who went out to the various theatres of operations and came back that won the war. It was those who went out and did not come back. It was their sacrifice which gained us victory.'[12] Their self-sacrifice had also been a great moral achievement. By becoming the victims of war they had triumphed over it, and by losing their lives they had acquired spiritual strength. In an article entitled 'The Meaning of the Silence', published in 1930, the *Daily Mail* explained that 'they faced Evil, and . . . though their bodies were destroyed by it, their souls overcame it' and achieved 'victory over violence and wrong'.[13] According to the programme for the opening of Birmingham's Hall of Memory, in 1925, the dead had 'been made mighty by sacrifice'.[14]

Self-sacrifice, an individual virtue, was accompanied by the collective virtue of comradeship. The inscription on Cheltenham war memorial says of those it commemorates: 'If they were strangers to one another here in their common home, they served and wrought and died in many lands near and far as a band of brothers.' The solidarity amongst fighting men was elevated, in the imagery of remembrance, into an ideal of brotherly love, modelled on the Christian ideal. Probably the most popular of moralising inscriptions applied to war memorials combines brotherly love and self-sacrifice as interdependent virtues. It is some words of Christ's to his disciples from Saint John's Gospel: 'Greater love hath no man than this, that a man lay down his life for his friends.'

In general, the achievement of the dead was represented as an ethical triumph over evil rather than a military triumph over other people. The soldierly nature of their triumph was only ambiguously acknowledged. Artists generally avoided images which might suggest violence. The military figures on Keighley war memorial, unveiled in 1924, were praised for being 'so balanced in poise as to give an impression of alertness and vigour, yet without any hint of aggressive force'[15] (Figure 25). The same effect may have been intended in John Tweed's figure for the memorial to the King's Royal Rifle Corps in Winchester, 1921 (Figure 11). The postures of William Goscombe John's figures for the Port Sunlight memorial, 1921, suggest waiting for an attack, rather than preparing to make one (Figure 26).[16] Figures on guard, like these, are far more common than scenes of action.

The dead were frequently honoured as victors, but the depiction of victory was a delicate matter. Artists sometimes disclaimed any wish to celebrate military triumph, even in memorials of strongly traditional design. R. Wynn Owen wanted onlookers at the LNWR memorial to notice that 'the monument is essentially a memorial to the fallen and is devoid of any element which might mark it as an emblem of victory'[17] (Figure 8). H. C. Fehr's design for Leeds war memorial, unveiled in 1922, originally included a figure of victory brandishing a sword above her head, but before it was complete he modified the figure so that she held the sword

Figure 25

NOT DEAD
NEVER DIE
PANELS ARE INSCRIBED
OF THOSE
AND WORKS OF
BROTHERS LIMITED
COMPANIES OVERSEAS
AND ALSO FROM PORT SUNLIGHT
LIVES IN THE GREAT WAR
1914 1919

Figure 26

before her, by the blade, with the handle uppermost, as if it were a cross. 'The explanation is that the sculptor proposed in the first place to show the sword held as if in token of triumph, but later modified his design.'[18] The inverted sword became a very common memorial symbol, present in allegorical figures, on obelisks, cenotaphs and crosses which took their cue from Reginald Blomfield's Cross of Sacrifice.

When victory was mentioned in imagery or inscriptions, it was frequently given an ethical rather than a military connotation by invoking the Christian, and distinctly ethical, idea of victory over death through self-sacrifice. One of the inscriptions on Leeds war memorial, 1922, is 'Invictis Pax' - peace to the undefeated. It could mean either undefeated in war or undefeated by death, or both. An equally ambiguous expression, substituting the moral attribute of manliness for the religious conception of resurrection, was used at Gateshead: 'Unconquerable manhood'.

The ethical dimension of victory was also emphasised by combining it with a reference to peace. Keighley memorial is surmounted by a female figure 'symbolising by the wreath in one hand and the palm branch in the other a "Peace Victory" won through service and sacrifice'.[19] A winged victory at Finsbury, carrying the same attributes, unveiled in 1921, was 'symbolical of Peace and Victory'.[20] These figures connoted either the victory of peace, or peace secured through victory. Thus, the purpose of the great struggle, and hence of those who had died in it, was represented as the achievement of peace, rather than victory for its own sake. Some memorials celebrate peace more explicitly. At Leeds, there is a figure of peace who was originally intended to hold a palm branch; but Fehr's revisions to the design included replacing this by a dove perched on one of her fingers, perhaps to make her identity unmistakable. The memorial at Eccleshill, a suburb of Bradford, by Harold Brownsword, unveiled in 1922, consists of a bronze figure of peace 'taking away the sword of strife and bestowing the laurel wreath of honour'[21] (Figure 27). There was, nonetheless, considerable ambiguity in these allusions to peace. They could be interpreted either to mean that the dead had served the achievement of peace, who now honoured them, or that, as a result of honourable deaths, the dead were now at peace, freed from the strife of the world.

Through these ambiguities, memorials could celebrate at once

Figure 27

a triumph of arms and a triumph of a higher order - moral, even religious - which could not be achieved through armed force, but only by its rejection, by a triumph over violence itself. It was a characterisation of the dead which ignored important aspects of the wartime experience of many, if not all, soldiers. It ignored the need to cultivate aggression, the weaknesses induced by fear and strain, the problems of discipline, the consolations of sex and drink, in order that the achievements of the dead could be presented as the outcome of moral and spiritual, rather than physical or political force. This purified memory of the dead did not, however, eradicate awareness other aspects of conduct in war, for it co-existed with alternative accounts of the war which deliberately stressed them. Such accounts, often in memoirs or novels, were frequently repudiated as dishonouring the dead, because they could be understood as a challenge to the elevated view which public remembrance propounded.

Controversy on the subject was most intense in the years around 1930,[22] but this was not the first time that anti-heroic accounts of the war had appeared. Philip Gibbs's *Realities of War*, first published in 1920, was probably very widely read. Soldiers had been trained, Gibbs wrote, 'until they became automata at the word of command, lost their souls, as it seemed, in that grinding machine of military training'. The men he had met at the front were disguising 'their fear of being afraid, their hatred of death'. They had been aware that much of what they did was morally indefensible. He quoted one as mocking the propagandist's analogy between soldiers and Christ, saying, 'I wonder if Christ would have stuck a bayonet into a German stomach - a German with his hands up? That's what we're asked to do.' He described in lurid detail the killing of 200 fleeing Germans, by British soldiers who 'were mad now, not humans in their senses . . . They were beasts of prey, these decent Yorkshire lads.' He also mentioned that they went to prostitutes.

Gibbs's account is equivocal about the moral qualities of soldiers, but he did not condemn them. He believed that training and propaganda induced a 'nervous stimulus', which could prompt them to do 'freakish and fantastic things of courage'. Yet he accepted that the men whose lives he described had indeed been courageous. He honoured them not as moral heroes, but as ordinary people caught in an extraordinary tragedy, and he wanted the true nature of the tragedy to be known to everyone. The book was intended, he said, 'as a memorial of men's courage in tragic years'.[23]

Gibbs acknowledged, at least tacitly, that the distinction between moral heroism and failure was unclear, though this need not cast doubt on the idea that suffering and death in war was a moral achievement. Apparent moral failure induced by combat might itself be seen as another of the sufferings inflicted on the hero-victim. A. P. Herbert's novel *The Secret Battle* was published in 1919, telling the fictional story (though compiled from actual experiences) of an honest and courageous volunteer officer whose nerve cracked and who was shot for cowardice. In 1928 Winston Churchill was invited to write an introduction to a new edition. Churchill discussed the book as if it were a memorial to the war dead, a common position for reviewers to take when writing about the literature, fictional or otherwise, of war experience.[24] The book was, Churchill said, 'a monument of the agony not of one but of millions, standing impassive in marble to give its message to all . . . who need a word of warning in their path. It speaks also with that strange note of consolation, often underlying tragedy, to those who . . . can never forget.' He suggested that the story would inspire rather than appal future generations, saying, 'ardent, virile youth . . . will not be deterred by its story from doing their duty by their native land, if ever the need should come. They will face terrors and tortures, if need be, with the simple faith that "What man has done, man can do."'[25] There was, however, a distinction between different kinds of anti-heroic war narrative. Some, like Gibbs's, were accounts which pointed up the human frailty of soldiers, many of whom had been killed. In others, most famously Eric Maria Remarque's *All Quiet on the Western Front*, which appeared in 1928, the principal protagonists were killed. The latter were explicitly portraits of the dead, appealing to the sense of tragedy and the sympathy generally attached to the war dead. They therefore posed a more direct challenge to the image of the dead as moral heroes than books which merely described the nastiness of war as a whole.

Two defences were possible against the threat posed to the moral stature of the dead by anti-heroic narratives. These seem broadly to match a political division between conservative, imperialist, and liberal, internationalist, views of the purpose of commemoration.[26] The first was to deny that this view of the war dead had any general validity. It might represent the experience and character of a few, but they were exceptional. In 1931, there was a correspondence in *Headway*, the League of Nations Union's journal, about the current spate of 'bad war books', *All Quiet on the Western Front* in particular. A correspondent signing himself 'Anzac' asked,

> What will be the effect on the rising generation after reading some of the war literature? The death of a parent or relative is a very precious and revered memory in many households throughout the Empire, but the sons and daughters of fathers who went through the war, and in many cases were killed, are being told that the men whom they loved and admired were practically all drunkards or beasts, and that anyone who laid down his life was a fool.[27]

The authors, he believed, were, 'hysterical neurotics who could not stand the strain of war, and who feel compelled now to unburden their minds regardless of the fact that they are sullying the imperishable memory of the fallen and putting into the minds of the rising generation a distorted conception of the lives of the British troops who took part in the late war'.[28] He argued that such books should be subject to the same kind of censorship as films. For him, remembrance of the dead provided the basis on which revelations about the corruption and unpleasantness of wartime behaviour could be set in the context of a deeper 'truth' which centred on moral achievement, suffering for others, the teaching of an essential lesson at the price of their own destruction.

A more liberal view, which accepted that the anti-heroic account of the war had much truth in it, was expressed by correspondents in *Headway* who replied to Anzac's criticism. One had read *All Quiet* and found it a revelation. 'I quite see the danger', she wrote, 'of coming generations generalising from these hysterical books, but everyone ought to know the unmentionable side which none of the decent men will speak about . . .'.[29] Another thought that the authors wanted to show the inevitably debasing results of war. He wrote, 'No one believes the fallen were "practically all drunkards and beasts", but every truthful man knows that war is capable of dragging men down to a depth of degradation which would be a disgrace if they sought it willingly.'[30] One could, indeed should, acknowledge the awful truth about people's behaviour in war, without thereby impugning their characters.[31]

Naming

An important part of the imagery of many memorials is a list of names of the people commemorated. In large urban communities the addition of names to a monument might be ruled out by the number required and the cost. Even then, the names of the dead would be recorded somewhere, probably in a roll of honour in book form especially commissioned by the municipality or the war memorial committee. The names of the dead were invested with a transcendental importance. Memorials frequently carried the assertion 'Their name liveth for evermore', or the commandment 'Let those who come after see to it that their names are not forgotten.' The sanctity of their names was enhanced, in many cases, by banishing from memorials the names of others who might traditionally have expected to be mentioned. Mayors, committee members, town clerks, architects, and building contractors, had, in the past, commonly been named on monuments for which they were responsible. This was not frequently done on memorials of the First World War. It was still acceptable for sculptors and architects to discreetly sign their work, but many deliberately did not. The names of donors and organisers of memorials rarely appeared.

While the sanctification of their names appeared to elevate the dead over the living, this way of commemorating them also celebrated their ordinariness. If we examine the growth in the practice of naming ordinary military personnel on public monuments, we can see that it occurred in recognition not of service beyond the call of duty, but rather of faithful performance of an allotted role. Ordinary soldiers were increasingly being honoured for just doing what they were supposed to do. This practice had the same meaning as the insistence in speeches like General Smyth's at Poplar[32] that the dead were honoured 'not so much for what they did as for what they were'. In Britain, this practice of honouring ordinary people for simply performing their allotted role to its uttermost conclusion, arose as an essentially military, not civilian, convention. Monuments which publicly displayed the names of the servicemen killed in the various wars of the nineteenth century had been largely the responsibility of the services themselves, not of civilian authorities or voluntary organisations. Nicholas Penny has pointed out that the idea of naming dead soldiers of all ranks was considered in France in the earliest revolutionary years, in order to identify the dead as full citizens of the revolutionary state. It was rapidly adopted by others for their own purposes, for example, by the Prussian monarchy, to whom the idea of the soldier as citizen in the revolutionary sense cannot have had a strong appeal.[33]

British political leaders, however, did not adopt the practice at that time. When such a general naming was mooted in Parliament to honour the dead of Waterloo it was turned down. Lord Castlereagh proposed to the House of Commons in 1815 that a monument to the Waterloo dead should be erected,[34] and, in response, Mr Wynn suggested naming all ranks who had died. He argued that the prospect of posthumous honours had played an important part in encouraging officers to exemplary acts of self-sacrifice, out of a desire to emulate heroes honoured in the past. He implied, though he did not say this directly, that the same consideration would be effective with other ranks.[35] Mr W. Smith agreed that 'recording the names of all who had fallen . . . would have the best possible effect'.[36] Castlereagh had himself suggested that if the dead officers could give their opinion 'nothing would be so gratifying to their feelings as to see some plan adopted which should include the commemoration of their brave soldiers, that they might also live in the gratitude of posterity, and of an admiring world'.[37] But whatever he meant by this, he was never persuaded that giving the names of all ranks killed was the right thing to do. Most of the people involved in commemorating the Napoleonic War seem to have felt the same way, and the publicly subscribed memorials which were erected celebrated military leaders such as Nelson and Wellington, not the ordinary soldier.[38]

There were some memorials of the 1850s, associated with the Sikh and Crimean Wars, which named all ranks of the dead. One is the Chilianwallah column standing in the grounds of Chelsea Hospital, erected in 1853, which names all the dead of a badly mismanaged battle in India. The memorial was subscribed for by the officers of the regiment involved, but there is no clue to their motive.[39] In the British military cemeteries in the Crimea, many unit memorials do name all ranks, although many also do not, giving only officers' names and perhaps simply the number of dead other rankers.[40] It thus appears that the practice of commemorating all dead ordinary soldiers by name was first adopted on memorials initiated and paid for by the military themselves. Only later did it become common practice in civic commemoration. In Britain, it was not initially a celebration of soldiers as citizens.

Even if commemoration of other ranks killed in battle was intended principally to improve military morale, as Wynn and Smith had argued, it had another significance as well. It served to confer an enhanced status on the ordinary men as members of the military community. The officers who erected the Chilianwallah memorial saw to it that the dead were commemorated all and sundry, not just their brother officers or those men who had achieved special distinction and so stood out from the mass. Within the regimental community, and without contradicting its hierarchy (officers and men are grouped on different faces of the monument) all the members who had lost their lives were acknowledged to be worthy of personal attention. All shared a common place of honour as individuals specified by name. What made them worthy of honour was not class, leading role or exceptional performance. It was simply that they had done the duty incumbent upon them as soldiers, as members of the military community which now commemorated them. Naming them was a recognition that the dead had all been equally valuable members of that community, because they had performed their allotted tasks to the extremity of death, even though they were not equal in any formal sense.[41] Honour did not depend on achieving special renown as an individual. Fidelity and reliability as a member of one's community became the essence of heroism, and these were virtues which were within the reach of all.

After the Boer War, local military memorials were widely subscribed to by the general public. By then it had also become normal to name all ranks of the dead, and women were included. Two nurses were named on the Yorkshire county memorial at York, unveiled in 1905.[42] The Boer War had required the raising of some 200,000 recruits, many of whom joined volunteer units especially formed for that war.[43] In this respect the army serving in South Africa had a certain amount in common with the volunteers who provided the idealised soldier of the Great War. A new development following the First World War was the frequent omission of the military ranks of the people commemorated, or at least the listing of all names in alphabetical rather than rank order, if ranks were given. This was taken to connote 'equality of sacrifice', the idea that all those who had sacrificed their lives possessed an equality of moral achievement which transcended any other distinctions, especially distinctions of class or rank. Walter Brierley advised Pudsey war memorial committee that 'we think it will be wise to adhere to the more usual custom of inscribing the name only, without either rank or regiment, and thus admitting equality of sacrifice'.[44]

Equality of sacrifice was an important point of commemorative etiquette. It emerged as an especially significant matter in 1919 and 1920, when the House of Commons held debates on the plans of the Imperial War Graves Commission not to allow repatriation of the bodies of the dead, but to bury them in specially constructed military cemeteries abroad. There was opposition, both to the general policy, and to the actual proposals for the design of cemeteries, led by Robert and Hugh Cecil in the House of Commons, and by Lord Balfour of Burleigh in the Lords. A public campaign against the Commission was conducted by the British War Graves Association, for whom Lady Maud Cecil became a spokeswoman. The Cecils' chief objection was that the state had no right to make rules about the disposal of the dead, and that the bereaved should have liberty of choice in the memorial to be placed over each grave, while Balfour of Burleigh wanted there to be a standard alternative, in the form of a cross, to the headstone which the Commission intended to provide for everyone.

Both points were debated at length, and supporters of the Commission's policy won the argument largely by maintaining the importance of equality of sacrifice. W. Burdett Coutts, MP for Westminster, who was their most effective spokesman, argued that the Commission's proposal gave a moral meaning to the commemoration of the dead which would be absent from an unorganised cemetery in which monuments of different sorts and sizes distinguished the dead according to the ability of their nearest and dearest to pay for a tomb. A unified design for the cemeteries, using standard components, would assert that all were equally worthy of honour, 'great and lowly, peer and peasant, rich and poor, learned and ignorant, raised to one supreme level in death by common sacrifice for a common cause'.[45]

Pious Fictions and Experience

The main ethical ideas applied to the memory of the dead in commemoration had been put to work extensively in wartime propaganda, and so their association with war service was already familiar. The most important of these for the post-war remembrance of the dead was a tendency to use the idea of self-sacrifice to represent the war as a purgative moral struggle, and participation in it as a personal moral triumph for the individuals involved. The idea that war was a force which could purge and renew society, and that self-sacrifice was a supreme contribution to this, appeared in the patriotic rhetoric of the war effort. Lloyd George invoked them in a speech in September 1914, saying,

> the stern hand of Fate has scourged us to an elevation where we can see the everlasting things that matter for a nation – the high peaks we had forgotten, of Honour, Duty, Patriotism, and clad in glittering white, the great pinnacle of Sacrifice, pointing like a rugged finger to Heaven. We shall descend into the valleys again; but as long as the men and women of this generation last, they will carry in their hearts the image of those great mountain peaks whose foundations are not shaken, though Europe rock and sway in the convulsions of a great war.[46]

It became a commonplace that the war was having a positive moral impact through the opportunity it provided to rise above the mundane concerns of peacetime life, and through the suffering which it inflicted (though by no means everyone agreed).[47] Proponents of this view believed that there was a spiritually constructive side to the war which would restore the nation or the world to a state of moral health. A writer in the London County Council Staff Gazette expressed the opinion that as a result of the war, 'crude materialism' and 'uninspired spiritualism' had 'given place to larger thoughts', and that 'class distinctions and old political boundaries have been removed'.[48] The Bishop of Carlisle, more dramatically, regarded the war as 'the agony in the womb of the morning; of a new birth of mankind to a life of higher truth and nobler liberty'.[49] This view was not confined to the home front. Some of those, like the poet Rupert Brooke, who joined the armed forces also saw the war as a cleansing and renewing experience. Gilbert Talbot, son of the Bishop of Winchester, who was killed in action in 1915, wrote to his parents, 'It's all magnificent really – it's purging us all.'[50] It was through self-sacrifice, through willingly accepting the need to suffer, that these desirable transformations could be brought about.

The ideals of self-sacrifice and purgation were intended to add to the moral acceptability of the war, and also give meaning to its unexpected destructiveness and the suffering it caused. Although certain branches of the newspaper press were complacent and unrealistically optimistic in their accounts of the war on many occasions, the public became aware that the war was enormously destructive and that soldiers' experiences were often profoundly dreadful. There was a widespread sense of the war's horror even amongst those who were not, or not yet, the victims of it, either personally or through the loss of loved ones.[51] The idea that war was a form of moral service and entailed martyrdom for a great ideal provided a way of making sense of suffering and actual or threatened loss in such a context. It was taken up by sensitive and anxious private individuals as well as by recruiters and propagandists. In her diary for 1915 Vera Brittain invoked 'the few great things which are all we have to cling to now – honour & love and heroism & sacrifice' to console herself in the grim circumstances of the time.[52]

The other key quality attributed to the dead – comradeship – derived partly from official military emphasis on *esprit de corps*, and appeared in recruiting propaganda from an early stage in the war. In a pamphlet first published in 1914, Kipling described the war service of volunteers as an 'all-embracing brotherhood' and asked what would become of 'the young man who has deliberately elected to outcast himself' from it.[53] The comradeship which was being cultivated through the war effort, like self-sacrifice, was seen as a redeeming virtue achieved through suffering. In a letter to *The Times* early in 1917, a retired bishop wrote: 'The trenches have made fellowship and brotherhood a reality in danger and hardship and sacrifice.' It was 'a principle which, like all things worth getting, has been begotten in travail'.[54]

War-time usage also provided a precedent for exhortations to moderate the feeling of grief or to transform it into something else. Bishop Cecil of Exeter, in 1915, tried to represent the loss of a loved one as a moral achievement in itself. He said 'let us doff our hats to the parents of the brave dead, and offer them our congratulations'.[55] Some soldiers, too, adopted this outlook.

A letter from one to his parents before the opening of the Battle of the Somme asked them, if he was killed, to 'look upon it as an honour that you have given your son for King and Country'.[56]

However, the values attributed to the dead were not founded only on propagandist rhetoric. The idea that the dead were special has, to some extent, a sociological source. Those who enlisted earliest in the war appeared to be the most willing to serve the country. They had shown the readiest appreciation of their duty, and the greatest generosity. The standards of physical fitness required for enlistment were higher at the beginning of the war, and were progressively reduced as the war continued. Those who enlisted early were the most likely to be killed, and as casualties mounted, so did anxiety that the human stock of the nation was being eroded, the morally and physically healthy part of the nation drained away. Thus an assumption could grow that the best were those who had been killed. The idea of comradeship, too derived as much from the personal experiences of soldiers as from recruitment campaigns. Tony Ashworth has described the importance to soldiers of 'small, informal friendship cliques which provided for their members emotional and material welfare not forthcoming from the military organisation'.[57] Denis Winter notes that a circle of 'mates' provided 'the chief prop' against cracking under the strain of combat.[58] This system of support encouraged a sense of mutual appreciation and esteem which in itself could be seen as valuable. 'Comradeship redeemed war from absolute condemnation even where combatants were extremely critical' of it.[59]

The rhetoric and experience of war offered organisers, artists and other participants in the commemoration of the dead a number of key moral ideas which directed their activity. They were used first to approach the problems of suffering and death in connection with street shrines and remembrance ceremonies during the war, and subsequently provided the basic common assumptions on which the co-operation necessary in war memorial projects depended. They also provided a common understanding and sense of shared purpose between war memorial committees and the artists they employed. Artists were trusted to give expression to by now familiar values without having to be told what to express. They were experts who could be relied on to say the things everyone knew must be said. They could satisfy their clients in this role because they already shared their expectations and sense of propriety. Everyone involved had been subjected to four years of intense effort to represent death in the war as a moral achievement, and many of them had assisted actively in the effort. But the common assumptions thus provided were not closely defined, and allowed considerable room for interpretation. Conflicts between rival interpretations frequently became visible, and these will be examined in the next chapter.

Notes to Chapter 7

1. *Barnsley Chronicle*, 31 July 1920.
2. Hackney, SN/W/1/25, untitled press cutting, 16 July 1920.
3. Barnsley, Town Clerk's In Letters, File 35, letters from Tweed, 1 Jan. 1925, and from Ald. Raley, 12 Aug. 1925.
4. Shropshire, 1919/1, Minutes, 6 June and 15 June 1921.
5. Clwyd, P/45/1/379, letter, 5 June 1919.
6. Powys, R/UD/LW/234, letter, 14 Sept. 1920.
7. The words are taken from an epitaph by Simonides on the dead of the battle of Thermopylae. I am grateful to David Phelps for this information, and to Dr Tom Gretton for drawing my attention to the memorial.
8. *Enfield Gazette*, 18 July 1919.
9. *East End News*, 10 Dec. 1920.
10. Stockport, B/AA/4, Opening and Unveiling Ceremony, 15 Oct. 1925.
11. Southwark, YX 14, untitled press cutting, 1923.
12. *Yorkshire Herald*, 16 June 1924.
13. *Daily Mail*, 10 Nov. 1930.
14. *Birmingham Post*, 4 July 1925.
15. *Keighley News*, 6 Dec. 1924.
16. Note, in the Rifle Corps figure, the clenched fist, and the weight on the back foot, connoting determination to resist an opposing force, but not aggression. The principal figure at Port Sunlight also has his weight on the back foot.
17. Public Record Office, RAIL 1057/2868, copy of description of design by R. Wynn Owen.
18. *Yorkshire Evening Post*, 16 Oct. 1922.
19. *Keighley News*, 6 Dec. 1924.
20. *Finsbury Weekly News*, 16 Sept. 1921.
21. *Yorkshire Observer*, 12 June 1922.
22. See R. M. Bracco, *Merchants of Hope: British Middlebrow Writers and the First World War*, Oxford, 1993, pp. 3 and 32.
23. P. Gibbs, *Realities of War*, London, 1920, pp. 59, 61, 82, 89, 129, 133, v.
24. R. H. Mottram and Richard Aldington also wrote books conceived as

memorials: see G. Dyer, *The Missing of the Somme*, Harmondsworth, 1995, p. 33. Bracco's account of the critical reception of R. C. Sherriff's play *Journey's End* illustrates how far war literature was judged by standards derived from commemoration of the dead (although this is not an argument she actually puts forward): see Bracco, *Merchants of Hope*, p. 153.

25. A. P. Herbert, *The Secret Battle*, London, 1928, pp. 6–7.

26. The division may appear obvious at first sight, but given the degree of flexibility which existed in the political interpretation of commemoration (see Chapter 8), it should not be taken for granted. It would have been possible for political Conservatives to subscribe to the liberal view here, even if the reverse were unlikely.

27. *Headway*, vol. 13, no. 7, July 1931, p. 128.

28. Ibid.

29. *Headway*, vol. 13, no. 8, Aug. 1931, p. 159.

30. Ibid.

31. A writer in the *Manchester Guardian* (11 Nov. 1930) believed, with some justification, that the anti-heroic books of the late twenties and early thirties were not as severe a condemnation of military service as they seemed: the recent 'remarkable output' of war literature did not 'romanticise war in the old sense' and did record its horror, but 'there is a curious kind of admiration for war in them as well', as if it were 'an experience not to be missed'.

32. See p. 175.

33. N. Penny, '"Amor Publicus Posuit": Monuments for the People and of the People', *Burlington Magazine*, vol. 109, no. 1017, Dec. 1987, p. 794.

34. *Parliamentary Debates*, first series, vol. xxi, p. 1049, 29 June 1815.

35. Ibid., p. 1052.

36. Ibid., p. 1054.

37. Ibid., p. 1051.

38. A. Yarrington, *The Commemoration of the Hero, 1800–1864: Monuments to the British Victors of the Napoleonic Wars*, London, 1988, *passim*.

39. Public Record Office, WORK 20.30.

40. A large number of the inscriptions in these cemeteries are given in J. Colborne and F. Brine, *Graves and Epitaphs of our Fallen Heroes in the Crimea and Scutari*, London, 1857.

41. Olive Anderson has noted a new concern for the individual souls of the soldiery in the religious evangelisation of the army which followed the Crimean War. During that war the British army was first hailed as a people's army. From the 1850s the army was represented increasingly as a respectable career, and in the 1860s, in pursuit of a better quality of recruit, there was an effort to make army life comparable to that of the 'respectable' working classes, especially in its spiritual aspect. A heightened respect for the individuality of soldiers who died in the performance of the duties which devolved on them as ordinary members of their community – their regiment – would have been consistent with this trend. See O. Anderson, 'The Growth of Christian Militarism in mid-Victorian Britain', *English Historical Review*, vol. 86, (1971), pp. 46–72.

42. *Yorkshire Herald*, 3 Aug. 1905.

43. See Chapter 2.

44. Atkinson Brierley Papers, Box 56, Pudsey War Memorial, letter to A. E. Evans, 29 June 1920.

45. The controversy is described at length in P. Longworth, *The Unending Vigil: A History of the Commonwealth War Graves Commission 1917–1984*, London, 1985, pp. 29–55, but he has confused Lord Balfour of Burleigh with Arthur Balfour, who was not involved. Hugh Cecil, in spite of his libertarian argument in the Commons in favour of freedom of choice for the bereaved, was far from liberal-minded in such matters. He wanted memorials to the dead to be explicit assertions of Christian belief, and he condemned the memorials to Muslim and Hindu soldiers, which the Commission was to build in France, for following the funerary traditions of those two faiths. He thought that, 'Christians cannot be asked to further the actual practice of the worship of such religions.' He was clearly out of sympathy with the religious pluralism which was characteristic of the commemoration of the war dead (Lambeth Palace Library, Davidson Papers, vol. 377, ff.267 and 268, 12 Feb. 1920). There is a letter from E. R. Lindsay expressing similar sentiments: 'Christians ought not to be deprived of their rights either through concession to heathen sentiment or through fear of democratic tyranny' (ibid., f.263, 18 Feb. 1919).

46. Quoted in A. Wilkinson, *The Church of England and the First World War*, London, 1978, p. 29.

47. Hugh Cecil expressed his scepticism in a sermon at Saint Martin-in-the-Fields, London, in November 1916 (*Church Family Newspaper*, 24 Nov. 1916), and the writer Caroline Playne thought the war debased the sensibilities of the public (Wilkinson, *The Church of England*, pp. 170 and 190).

48. J. G. Arrow in *LCC Staff Gazette*, vol. 17, Feb. 1916, p. 22.

49. Quoted in A. Marrin, *The Last Crusade: The Church of England in the First World War*, Durham, North Carolina, 1974, p. 212.

50. Quoted in Wilkinson, *The Church of England*, p. 186.

51. See, for example, the personal correspondence of the Essex schoolmaster, Robert Saunders, quoted in T. Wilson, *The Myriad Faces of War: Britain and the Great War 1914–1918*, Cambridge, 1986 pp. 166–7; Vera Brittain's diary frequently gives the same impression.

52. V. Brittain, *Chronicle of Youth: Vera Brittain's War Diary 1913–1917*, ed. A. Bishop, London, 1981, p. 202, entry for 26 May 1915. The idea that propagandist rhetoric was an important means of individual reassurance is discussed at length by Stuart Sillars: see S. Sillars, *Art and Survival in First World War Britain*, London, 1982, pp. 154–63.

53. Quoted in P. Buitenhuis, *The Great War of Words: Literature as Propaganda 1914–1918 and After*, London, 1989, p. 26.

54. *The Times*, 12 Jan. 1917.

55. Marrin, *The Last Crusade*, p. 213.

56. J. Laffin (ed.), *Letters from the Front: 1914–1918*, London, 1973, p. 6, quoted in Wilkinson, *The Church of England*, p. 189.

57. T. Ashworth, *Trench Warfare 1914–1918: The Live and Let Live System*, London, 1980, p. 155.

58. D. Winter, *Death's Men: Soldiers of the Great War*, London, 1978, p. 137.

59. Ashworth, *Trench Warfare*, p. 156.

8

Moral Obligation and Politics in the Commemoration of the Dead

Many people expected the commemoration of the dead to have a beneficial effect on the behaviour of the living. To do adequate honour to the dead, it was thought necessary to understand what they had died for and to follow the example they had set. The dead had died for others, and by emulating them the living could show that they were, indeed, worthy of the sacrifices the dead had made on their behalf. The vicar of Enfield told the audience at a remembrance ceremony in October 1919 that they could only 'do worthy homage' to the qualities shown by the dead if they applied the same 'vision and hope and faith' to opposing 'all manner of evil in all places in the world'.[1] The inscription on Cheltenham war memorial concludes, 'Learn from them so to live and die that, when you have followed them and are no more seen, you may like them be remembered and regretted.'

The requirement to emulate the dead was given added force by fear that their sacrifices might otherwise prove to have been in vain. If the dead were remembered, and their example of virtuous conduct was followed, then it would be possible to ensure that they had died to some purpose. Some people did express the fear that all the suffering had been in vain, because the world was not a whit improved after the war. The Bishop of London referred to this fear when unveiling a parish church war memorial in October 1920. He quoted a letter from an officer's widow who had written, 'I would not mind if I saw a better world, but I feel that my husband died in vain. That is the cause of my bitterness.'[2] The bishop's answer was that only the future could show whether or not it had all been a waste of life. He added significantly that whether or not the future finally did give retrospective meaning to the war deaths 'would . . . largely depend upon what the people in that church did to make the sacrifice worth while'. The living thus had an obligation to emulate the dead, in order to give continuing meaning to their deaths. Effective emulation required the living to understand and interpret the wishes and ideals of the dead, and to act accordingly. Consequently, a large part of the speech and writing which accompanied the ceremonial acts and symbolic objects of commemoration consisted of attempts to interpret those wishes and ideals and apply them to the post-war world. Interpretations took the form of political homilies reflecting on the state of the nation, and on how the work of the dead could be furthered by those who survived them. This chapter will examine the various inflections which were given to the idea of an obligation to the dead, and the political uses to which they were put.[3]

War and Citizenship

Because commemoration emphasised the moral rather than the military aspects of war death, the example of the dead was seen as a universal moral one, not specifically related to military issues. At the same time, the emphasis placed on their comradeship directed attention towards the moral aspect of collective relationships, in the form of loyalty and service to one's community. As a result, the obligation to emulate the dead was frequently discussed in terms of the individual's responsibility to the community.

The example of comradeship set by the dead was seen as essential to solving whatever problems the future might hold for the nation. The Duke of York, unveiling Saint Michael's war memorial, Poplar, in 1920, said, 'If we can do our duty with the same unselfish comradeship with which these splendid dead did their task, there can be nothing dark in the difficulties which the future may hold for our country.'[4] At the unveiling of the London and North Western Railway memorial at Euston station in October 1921, Charles Lawrence, the company chairman, made a more specific application of this idea. He said,

> we, the survivors, should dedicate ourselves anew to the service of our country, and that, especially in our characters of employers and employed, we should strive to act in a spirit of mutual sympathy, of mutual forbearance, of absolute rectitude of purpose, and even of

> magnanimity if we wish to assist in binding up the wounds of our common country, and so prove ourselves worthy of the sacrifice these men have made for us.[5]

Speakers and writers laid emphasis on the individual's place in the community or nation, in other words on his or her 'citizenship'. The memory of the dead would be treasured as that of ideal citizens, the *Enfield Gazette* maintained in 1919: 'Being dead, they will speak for all time to future generations, a perpetual reminder of, and incentive to, that Duty to the State which is the reasonable service to be rendered by each and every citizen.'[6] It was by being a good citizen that one could best emulate the dead. The Archbishop of York told railwaymen at a commemorative service in Stockport, in 1919, that they should repay their debt to the dead 'by filling their citizenship with a new spirit worthy of that with which these men met their death'.[7]

Education in citizenship, known as 'civics', was a subject of considerable concern in the inter-war years. E. M. White, a lecturer in Civics, reviewing the available textbooks on the subject in 1923, gave a comprehensive definition which stressed continuity between generations through the emulation of past examples. 'The citizen . . . can utilize all the achievements of his ancestors for a foundation on which to build his own contribution to the advancement of civilisation.' Civics should be 'an inspiration to service'. 'Modern Civics', he concluded, 'may be said to date from the war, when a quickening – not an initiation – of social questionings, suggestions, determinations and experiments took place.'[8]

This educational programme was aimed at a nation in which political rights had recently been very considerably extended. The 1918 Representation of the People Act increased the electorate from some seven million to twenty million. With the extension of rights, new voters had acquired influence in the exercise of political power. At the same time, there was considerable anxiety about social disorder in the aftermath of war, and the economic power of employers was challenged by major strikes in the mining industry and on the railways. On the left as well as the right, there was a fear that disgruntled ex-servicemen might resort to political violence.[9] Many ex-servicemen showed an aggressive unwillingness to put up with unsatisfactory living and working conditions, and decisions by the authorities which they thought unreasonable. At Luton, it was alleged, a refusal by the town council to allow ex-servicemen to use a park for a drumhead memorial service had led to the burning down of the town hall.[10]

Political participation was now available to people who had not previously been entitled to it, and local élites met this apparent challenge to their predominance with appeals to the idea of responsible citizenship, and to the memory of the war effort. In 1919, the *Enfield Gazette* challenged the new Labour-controlled district council to show its fitness to hold office by demonstrating 'their conception of Civics in practical administration'.[11] Commenting on the crisis in the mining industry, the *Barnsley Chronicle*, from the heart of the south Yorkshire coalfield, hoped that 'patriotism and love of country will even now prevail over the fatuous folly of heading this country - for which so many have valiantly fought and died - straight for irretrievable national disaster'.[12] At many a memorial's unveiling, political, military and industrial leaders juxtaposed these two ideas to form a civic creed of remembrance. With a conscious eye on the state of the nation, they put forward an ideal of citizenship which had little to do with the desires, complaints and sectional loyalties which go to make up normal domestic politics. The model citizen represented by the dead was a person who gave everything for the common good, above all for the good of a local community or an institution of which he or she was a recognised member. The commemorative ideal offered a citizenship consisting of service and sacrifice, as distinct from the struggle for one's own rights and power, or for the interests of the particular section of the community to which one belonged.

Although the idea of citizenship implied in commemoration was frequently invoked in defence of the social and political status quo, it was not confined to that use. The duty required of a citizen-soldier, and hence of his commemorators, was the performance of one's allotted role to its uttermost, regardless of the consequences to oneself. This appears, initially, to have distinctly conservative overtones. What was celebrated was deferential citizenship. However, the doctrine of equality of sacrifice could be turned against deference. As commemoration amounted to a public demand that the service and sacrifice of those commemorated be recognised and valued, it became a medium through which social groups whose rights had previously been relatively limited could claim equality with those who were more privileged.

They made this claim on the strength of their sacrifices in the war effort, represented by 'their' dead – people from their own social groups who had made the supreme sacrifice. A letter to the *Daily Herald* in November 1924 from a hiking enthusiast directed just such a claim against the rights of landowners to exclude the public from their properties. He wrote: 'throughout the kingdom memorials of stone have been erected' to the war dead. But why, he asked, were 'Trespassers will be prosecuted' signs 'multiplying throughout the land' and barbed wire stretching 'for miles of the woodside? Is it to resist the encroachments of the kith and kin of those to whom the memorials of stone have been erected?'[13] The reference to barbed wire, in connection with the war dead, was particularly poignant, as it suggested that the war being waged by landlords against the unpropertied was as monstrous as the world war had been.

Moreover, men in the armed forces were not the only ones who had made sacrifices and done their duty. Various groups of non-combatants could be set alongside those had died in the services as having also made great sacrifices in their own way, especially the families of the dead. Opening the East Vale Wesleyan memorial hall at Longton, the Revd A. Woodward said that, while remembering 'the courage of those who had gone out to fight at duty's call', they also remembered 'the patient heroism of those who sent them with a sob in their hearts, but a "God bless you" on their lips'.[14] The *Birmingham Post* maintained that the city's Hall of Memory was also a memorial to 'parents and wives and children who acquiesced, unmurmuring in risks and in sacrifice'.[15]

Women, whether in the forces or not, were the most significant group of non-combatant adults to whom the virtue of self-sacrifice was thus extended. Women were commemorated both on memorials with servicemen, and on their own memorials.[16] Nurses were recognised as a service in their own right. At Menston, Yorkshire, the war memorial was a cottage for a district nurse, and at its unveiling the local MP said, 'In the lives of nurses there was heroism that was never told.'[17] All women throughout the Empire who had been killed in the war were commemorated by the restoration of the Five Sisters Window at York Minster, a project which began as a county memorial to women. The *British Legion Journal* called it 'a women's cenotaph'.[18]

There was no individual figure used to symbolise a general conception of active female service which might compare with the frequent sculptures of infantrymen. This absence was, to some extent, compensated for in other ways – ways which implied a claim by women to recognition of their own idealism, service and sacrifice. Many women's organisations took an active part in commemoration, and thereby enacted a living image of female service through their organised, often uniformed, presence at ceremonies, and through their work for war memorial committees. Female medical and military services, and the women's sections of the British Legion, took formal part in ceremonies, and sometimes women's civic organisations initiated memorial projects.[19] By taking a prominent part, they affirmed their awareness of an obligation to take an active part in creating a world worthy of the sacrifices of the dead as their comrades and successors.

Even children were recruited into the ranks of the honoured dead. At Poplar, where 18 school pupils had been killed by German bombs in 1917, the victims were commemorated as the equals of dead service personnel and represented to other children as suffering comrades from whom they should learn lessons. A memorial appeal was launched the same year, in which the mayor asserted that 'These dear little ones died as truly for their country as any of our gallant men.'[20] When their memorial was unveiled, General Ashmore told those present, 'They died for their country and had set an example which should never be forgotten.'[21] Servicemen had borne the brunt of the suffering, but their achievements were shared by others to some degree. The bereaved, and non-combatants who were killed by enemy action, especially women and children, were closest to, perhaps matched, the moral achievement of the dead soldiers.

Entire communities were also expected, through commemoration, to show their worth, to celebrate their service, and to claim the honour and virtue due to their wartime sufferings and losses. When making appeals for memorial funds, civic leaders expressed concern that local memorials should be worthy not only of the dead, but also of those who commemorated them. Lord Leverhulme told a general meeting of his employees at Port Sunlight that, 'A memorial was desired that would be for all time a pride and stimulus . . . Any other type of memorial should be brushed aside as scarcely worthy of our fallen heroes or ourselves.'[22] The worthiness and idealism of the living was to be expressed through their connection with the dead, as comrades, friends and mourners. If the war had been a purging and morally elevating experience, it had been so for all, not only for the dead, and commemoration acknowledged this. J. M. Barrie implied something of the sort when he wrote to Lutyens about the Cenotaph, 'I stand cogitating why and how it is so noble a thing. It is how the war has moved you and lifted you above yourself.'[23] The monument, in other words, owed its quality to the impact of the war on its designer's work. He had shared some, at least, of the spiritual elevation of the war experience epitomised by the dead, and had expressed its impact on himself in honouring them.

Those who participated in commemoration were not merely tutees and beneficiaries of the dead, but also guardians of their achievements and comrades in their struggle, sharing, to some extent, their spiritual achievement, and taking responsibility for its preservation. They had an obligation to be active citizens, builders of a new world in honour of the dead, charged with creating a community imbued with their values, in which the work the dead had begun would be continued. All who participated in commemoration could claim the right to be heard, and to have their views and actions respected, in the process of remaking the post-war world, by virtue of their comradeship with and loyalty to the dead.

The End of War

It was widely held that the best the living could do to prevent the deaths of those they remembered from being squandered was to prevent war occurring again. General Sir Charles Harington told his audience at the unveiling of Keighley war memorial in 1924, 'Those whom we are honouring today trusted us, and we are in honour bound to carry on their great work . . . the preservation of peace.'[24] One of the inscriptions on Barnsley war memorial reads: 'and we in faith keep that peace for which they paid'. The chief lesson taught by the suffering of war was now taken to be the necessity for peace.[25]

The Great War appeared to many people, combatants and non-combatants alike, to have been an unprecedented horror. Whether or not veterans had been prepared to discuss their experiences with others, enough had become known, both during the war and after, for the idea to pervade almost all discussion of the war. The position was clearly put by a reviewer of the first published collection of Wilfred Owen's poems. The poems showed, he said, 'a great range of realities . . . which, because of the horror and anguish associated with them, men do conspire to glose over and hush up. War . . . involves savagery; it demands of men such cruel outrage against their human instincts that as a moral experience it is essentially unbearable.'[26] Awareness of the horror gave dramatic substance to the idea that military service had been a moral triumph for those who had undertaken it. In facing it, the soldier-martyrs had endured hell for their faith and friends, and were heroic at least as much for their capacity to face the horror as for their courage or skill in combat. What distinguished post-war from pre-war attempts to give moral significance to the experience of war was the post-war recognition that war was horrible.[27]

While the horror of war contributed to the image of the war dead as martyrs, it also posed the urgent political question of how to avoid such a catastrophe in future. There was great anxiety in the inter-war period about the destructive effect of a future world conflict. Concern focused especially on the aerial bombing of civilian populations and the use of poison gas. Neither of these had been developed into strategically effective weapons during the First World War, and experience of bombing was extremely limited; but the mere knowledge of their possibility caused a great deal of alarm. Imaginary accounts of their effects were published either in explicit disarmament propaganda or in fiction.[28] In his expectations for any future war, published in 1924, Philip Gibbs even imagined a new horror, which he presumably regarded as a credible technical possibility in the near future. He feared that 'some "death ray" projecting wireless force may sweep a countryside with heat that would turn everything to flame and then to dust and ashes'.[29] This image probably owed more to memories of H. G. Wells's *War of the Worlds* than to the recent war in Europe. Much of the fear of future weapons was derived, not from anything actually experienced in the war, but rather from the enormous technical potential for destruction which the war had revealed. What was derived from the war experience was the general idea that combat and enemy occupation were horrible, and that the application of modern technology to warfare could produce the ultimate catastrophe. The possibility of air attack meant that in a future war such horrors would be extended even to Britain.

Many shared Gibbs's thought that a public reminder of how terrible war was should be central to the commemoration of those who had suffered most in it,[30] and memorials were widely regarded as standing in some way for the horrors of war, even though they rarely contained any images which remotely suggest horror. The clergyman who officiated at the unveiling of Brancepeth war memorial, an entirely conventional gothic cross devoid of any reference to violence (Figure 28),[31] told his audience that 'a cross reminded them of the horrors and the wickedness of war', and consequently 'helped them to the declaration "never again will the earth be blasted by this terrible curse"'. It was a sign 'that they should each do their part to produce a peaceful atmosphere'.[32] The Dean of Leeds Roman Catholic cathedral made the same point, at the unveiling of the city's war memorial in 1922, when he prayed that the monument 'may serve to fill us with a horror of war'.[33]

The attention thus drawn to the devastating danger of war made commemoration of the dead into an occasion for discussing armaments policy, international relations, and how peace might be preserved. Its focus on these issues was orchestrated and exploited by activist organisations. In 1922 the League of Nations Union (LNU), a voluntary organisation led by Lord Robert Cecil and dedicated to encouraging popular support for the League,[34] began to focus on the period around 11 November as a time for putting itself before the public. The move was led by the Welsh National Council of the Union, under the chairmanship of the coal millionaire David Davies, Lord Davies of Llandinam, who believed strongly in the virtue of properly organised campaigning. At its first annual meeting in 1922 the Welsh National Council suggested a year-long timetable for branches, stressing the use of the period around Armistice Day. It recommended a recruiting effort in October to culminate in Armistice Week, and asked 'can the branch make Armistice week, the Enrolment week, the renewal week, *the week of its year*?'.[35] In 1925 LNU headquarters in London asked branches to do a house-to-house canvass in Armistice Week. There were big rallies organised in Manchester,

Figure 28

Hull and Grimsby, and in Derby the union branch organised a civic demonstration which was said to include 'representatives of practically every interest in the town'.[36] In the thirties, recruiting campaigns continued to be mounted in early November. In 1936 Peace Weeks were held in several places, and the one in Bolton, in late September, included illumination of the town war memorial.[37] British Legion branches frequently co-operated with branches of the LNU in their campaigns.

In the 1930s, pacifist organisations such as the Peace Pledge Union and Quakers held meetings and distributed literature on Armistice Day to the large crowds who assembled for the two minutes' silence. In 1933, against resistance from the British Legion, the Co-operative Women's Guild began to sell white poppies as emblems of peace in an attempt to introduce a new and specifically pacifist symbol into the rituals of remembrance. On the other hand, many of those who commemorated the dead, and accepted that modern war was evil and should be avoided, were not prepared to draw the conclusion that a vigorous defence policy, a military career or the values of military life were themselves questionable. The Conservative MP, Robert Boothby, issued an Armistice Day address to his constituents in 1934 in which he argued that air rearmament was now necessary, and that by combining it with 'a wise and constructive foreign policy we can still save the world from war'. If Britain failed to take a lead, and opened itself to attack, he said, 'everything which makes life worth living will be swept away'.[38]

To some veterans, in particular professional soldiers, willingness to come to the armed defence of the nation, as the dead had done, remained important, although they accepted that a crucial element in the nation's defence was preventing conflict. They had in certain respects enjoyed their time in the armed forces, and regarded the experience as positive. In an article entitled 'Let's Be Frank About the War',[39] published in 1933, Oliver Locker-Lampson, an MP and former naval officer, confessed that, though he hated war, 'I am afraid I occasionally like fighting.' War, he believed, also had the 'virtue' of producing a sense of national purpose and co-operation. Nonetheless, such people could see a side to war, represented by the suffering inflicted on women and children, rather than on the men involved in the fighting, which made it imperative to avoid future wars. Locker-Lampson continued, 'If only for "the mother and kids" there should be no more war. The woe of women would exceed as never before the agony of men.' In 1932, Sir Ian Hamilton wrote in the *British Legion Journal* that he had enjoyed his career as a soldier, and his attitude to warfare changed only after the Great War, when he discovered the extent of the bereavement it had inflicted on women and children. 'The widows and orphans are the people who have overcome my admiration for feats of arms', he said.[40] In any future war all sides would, in effect, be losers because of the domestic destruction which would occur, and the suffering of non-combatants which that would entail. By adopting this conception of the horrors of war, career service personnel, veterans who continued to value their war experiences, and politicians who wanted to maintain strong national defences could agree that war was terrible and should be avoided, without abandoning their approval of the military life. They could thus join wholeheartedly in a form of commemoration which represented war as one of the greatest evils facing civilisation.

The idea that war was horrible was shared by a wide range of people, but when reflection on it prompted discussion of the means by which it might be prevented in future, consensus gave way to the divisions of practical politics. As Stanley Baldwin was reported to have said in 1933, 'It is not difficult to choose peace . . . But to make your choice effective – that is not so easy.'[41] The question of how to achieve an effective peace was rehearsed in the press and in political speeches year after year in the period around Armistice Day.

Whose Side Were They On?

If the legacy of the dead was to be preserved, the issues of post-war politics had to be approached in an appropriate spirit. However, those who wished to commemorate the dead, and recognised an obligation to preserve their supposed achievements, were far from agreed on what the appropriate spirit actually was. They tended to interpret the moral obligation imposed on the living by the memory of the dead in a way which accorded with their particular political commitments. Newspaper articles and letters, sermons and memorial unveiling speeches all provided opportunities to give interpretations of the basic postulates of remembrance, specifying its relevance to contemporary problems. In them, writers and speakers supported whatever political outlook they wished to promote by suggesting that the dead would have thought the same way about contemporary questions, and by appealing to the obligation to remain loyal to their ideals.

Activists from across the political spectrum used commemoration to enlist the dead in their political battles. The *Daily Mail*, in 1920 - on an Armistice Day which included the burial of the Unknown Warrior - saw the elevated values of the war dead as the source of British national greatness. It asked, 'What makes a nation great? . . . the example of lives such as these [the dead's, that is] and the tradition of heroic deeds and faith even unto death to noble ideals . . . the comradeship and unselfish devotion which marked them'.[42] The *Daily Herald* agreed that the dead must be honoured, and adhered to the high moral evaluation of them which was central to commemoration; but it expressed quite different ideas about the war and Britain's greatness. In 1919 it saw no tradition of heroic deeds, but only 'the crime which called these men to battle' and 'the fond, glorious and tragic delusion under which they went'. Nonetheless, it referred to the memory of the dead as if it were a sacred and empowering talisman. It said: 'by the sacred memory of those lost to you, swear to yourself this day . . . that never again, God helping you, shall the peace and happiness of the world fall into the murderous hands of a few cynical old men; that never again shall you, or your children after you, be sent in arms against a brother man'.[43]

When political questions could intrude so conspicuously into people's understandings of the public desire to honour the dead, it is not surprising that interpretations of commemorative symbols differed widely. There were differing interpretations of the meaning of the military symbolism of ceremonies. The *Manchester Guardian* commented in 1930 on what it saw as muddled meanings in Armistice Day: 'presenting arms and intoning prayers, reverently laying down wreaths of flowers and stiffly lifting naked bayonets . . . expresses an incoherent sentiment'.[44] The *Daily Mirror*, however, saw nothing wrong in the military ceremonial. It noted 'the glitter of raised swords and fixed bayonets, the blaze of uniforms, the nodding bearskins - and yet no suggestion of militaristic display was conveyed'.[45] At Birmingham, there was controversy in 1925 over whether or not the unveiling ceremony for the Hall of Memory should include a specifically military element. A brigadier wrote to the press that, as there were no official plans to sound the Last Post and Reveille, the surviving comrades of the dead were being 'denied the usual beautiful and touching ceremonial which is the most sacred part of our Naval and Military life'.[46] In reply, a wartime army captain wrote from the University to argue that they should honour the dead, in 'these days of peace . . . without pomp and ceremony, quietly and dispassionately (just as they died), with all signs of militarism and strife removed'.[47]

The imagery of monuments was equally open to conflicts of interpretation. Bradford war memorial (Figure 29), unveiled in July 1922, included two bronze figures representing a soldier and sailor advancing with fixed bayonets. The posture of these figures caused a controversy because they appeared to some observers to celebrate aggression. After the unveiling a Baptist minister commented that 'the idea of the fixed bayonet was not

Figure 29

the motive which led some of our best to lay down their lives', and he wished Bradford 'had handed down to posterity not an affirmation of might but of ideals, not of physical but spiritual power'.[48] The Lord Mayor thought the figures were 'apparently too ready for restarting business immediately', and that they contradicted the motives of 'so many Bradford men [who] . . . laid down their lives – that the late conflict should be a war to end war'.[49]

On the other side of the question, the alderman who unveiled the memorial, already knowing that there was some criticism of its design, explained that it was 'not a glorifying image of militarism, but a monument to the self-sacrifice of Bradford men'.[50] An ex-serviceman wrote to the local press arguing that the figure of the soldier 'is in the position of short point: he is therefore ready for peace or war', meaning, presumably, that he is simply advancing at the ready, not attacking anyone. He went on to say that everyone would 'like to see war finished for ever', but the country must not 'be caught napping again . . . So I hope the bayonet will remind the young men of Bradford to be ready not to make war but to help to stop it if it should ever start again.' (His point, clearly, was that they should do this through military preparedness, not through a refusal to fight.) He ended by describing his sense of the motives of those who had volunteered to serve in the war. He and his comrades, he said, had joined up as a result of 'the fighting spirit of the British race and love of the old country and of adventure. I don't remember ever hearing of stopping war for ever in 1914.'[51]

Commemoration as Political Expression

Why did the commemoration of the dead have to bear such a burden of political issues? Why did it not become a politically neutral, essentially religious observance, in which people who wished to could simply mourn those they had lost and seek consolation? The civic tradition of commemoration was long-established as a vehicle for the propagation of political attitudes; but this is only part of the answer. A wide range of participants, not only civic leaders and opinion-formers in the press and pulpit, were concerned about the impact of the war on post-war social and political life. Many were moved either to speak or to act in public to express their concern. The kind and strength of the feelings engaged was unlike earlier commemorative practices. We need to explain not just the presence of a political element in commemoration, but why it was so important to so many people.

There were two reasons. First, the political platform which commemorations had always offered now became available to mass organisations especially concerned with the war and its aftermath, principally the British Legion and the League of Nations Union. These organisations had many local branches which took advantage of the regular opportunities for public display which Armistice Day offered. The Union's activities in this field have already been mentioned. The Legion, one of the mainstays of war commemoration, shared the widespread concern with current political issues. According to its first chairman, T. F. Lister, it

> is a Legion of Service, which men who have fulfilled one of the responsibilities of citizenship are asked to join, so that they may serve their country in another and not always an easier sphere. The Legion comes into being because of the problems associated with War. I believe it will flourish because it will tackle the problems of Peace.[52]

It set out to be an organ of citizen activism as much as a veterans' association. In 1925, an editorial in its journal expressed a commitment to propagating political values of a non-partisan, civic kind. The Legion, it said,

> exists to perpetuate in the Civil life of the Empire and of the world the principles for which the nation stood in the Great War: one of its chief objects is to inculcate a sense of loyalty to the Crown, Community, State and Nation: it sets out to promote unity amongst all classes and to make right the master of might.[53]

The Legion devoted much of its effort to the promotion of peace through the League of Nations. At the Legion's first delegate meeting in 1921 a resolution in support of the League of Nations was carried unanimously, which, according to its journal, 'did most emphatically denote that the men had retained a belief in the noble purpose for which the great war was fought'. In 1925 an editorial claimed that the Legion's special virtue of comradeship promoted peace: 'In many ways does the Legion manifest its allegiance to the cause of Peace: it stands for comradeship: that in itself is a seeking after Peace.'[54] The 1925 Annual

Conference passed a strong motion in favour of criminalising the manufacture and use of poison gas. Between 1931 and 1933 they supported international demonstrations in favour of maximum arms reductions through the Geneva disarmament conference.

The second reason why commemoration was so concerned with political questions lay in the emotional intensity of the experience of war, and of thought about it afterwards. Remembrance of the dead articulated for many a feeling that death in the war needed to be given a sense of purpose through the subsequent actions of those who mourned them. As much as anyone else, people who held strong views on the issues raised by reflection on the war and death wanted to remember, mourn and honour dead friends and relatives. They felt that making sense of death in the war entailed some form of political action, and insisted on saying clearly what they thought it should be. They also, perhaps, did not wish to see those friends and relatives incorporated into a national cult of whose aims they disapproved, and believed their dead would also have disapproved. Many joined the organisations which used commemoration as a platform for making their views heard, and did their best to dispute appropriations of the dead which they considered wrong.

If remembrance was to give retrospective meaning to death, it was bound to mean different things to different people. In the confusion of competing attitudes, they struggled to make the memory of the dead a right memory as they saw it. This entailed interpreting the symbols of remembrance in what seemed to each to be the correct manner, and arguing with others about their meaning. In a society deeply divided on fundamental issues, the opportunity to propose meanings for commemorative symbols was, inevitably, the opportunity for an argument.

One might ask how far the political dimension of remembrance shaped the conduct of contemporary politics. Evidence of the impact which it had on social discipline in general, and on the character of political belief and action, is elusive. It is hard to disentangle effects specific to it from the influence of other forms of thought about the war, or from the pressure of the economic and political circumstances of the post-war world. Writers who have addressed this question have tended to see the way in which war was represented generally, in everyday communication amongst individuals as much as in art, memoirs, fiction and journalism, as a means by which people internalised conservative or conformist attitudes. Bob Bushaway has seen the idealisation of the dead as inhibiting serious criticism of the social and political structure which took Britain into and through the war. The editors of the collection of essays on gender and war, *Behind the Lines*, argue that public reflections on the war, including commemoration of the dead, played an important part in the process of restoring conventional gender relationships after the disruptions of war.[55]

On the contrary, the general variety of interpretations given of commemorative symbols does not suggest that radical criticism was ruled out, nor does it suggest that commemoration conveyed a particular view of society or of the individual's position within it. We have seen that meanings were attributed to visual symbols, and to the verbal formulae which accompanied them, according to the circumstances of the people interpreting them. We have also seen how the interpretations which people expressed were frequently calculated to influence the actions of institutions or social groups in which they were participating, either to pursue particular interests within them, or to sustain their general coherence and effectiveness. As a result, the significance of their words was contingent on immediate and changing requirements. It cannot, therefore, be correct to see the ways in which the dead were represented as having a univocal determining effect on people's understanding or behaviour, nor as imposing a single subjective position upon them. This is a principle which, I think, applies to representation in general, and I share Timothy Clark's dissatisfaction with the idea that texts or images 'construct' the subjectivity of their audiences,[56] which is frequently implied in current discussions of the subject.

Idealistic rhetoric did not constrain people closely to any concrete social goals; but the way in which acts of remembrance were organised may have had a more distinct impact on political action, serving to sustain the moderate conservatism and deference which Bushaway attributes to remembrance. Commemoration encouraged active and organised discharge of the citizen's political responsibilities; but it did so within a civic framework which promoted co-operation, negotiation and inclusiveness. Those who had a case to make in connection with the remembrance of the dead had to make it within this framework to get the hearing they desired. On Armistice Day 1919 the organiser of the Manchester Branch of the National Association of Employed and Unemployed Ex-Service Men and Women asked the Lord Mayor if he might 'state the case for the living, in honour of the dead' to the crowd assembled for the Silence. The Lord Mayor thought this inappropriate, but he invited the ex-service representatives to a private discussion about unemployment with him after the ceremony.[57]

To benefit from their association with the dead, and the obligation owed to them, the ex-servicemen, like any other activists, had to accept the decorum of these occasions and tailor the protest they wished to make accordingly. More assertive action was likely only to brand protestors as extremists, unable to understand or appreciate the obligation to which they laid claim. It would rule them out of the community of mutual respect and co-operation which remembrance of the dead was supposed to constitute, at least in the early post-war years. By the 1930s, with the growth of organised pacifism and its connection with the political left, there seems to have been a greater tendency to arrange specifically political, yet decorous, demonstrations in connection with remembrance of the dead. Its symbols were no less respected than in official ceremonies; but those taking part made a far less ambiguous commitment to socially radical and anti-militarist ideas, and the controversial white poppy played an important part.[58]

While differing opinions were expressed through commemorative acts about the ideal society and citizen, the ideal of international peace was not contested. Differences of opinion about how to achieve the ideal did not impede consensus about the ultimate goal of policy. In this unanimity we may see a more decisive impact on contemporary affairs, for the emphasis placed on avoiding war was undoubtedly fertile ground for those who wished to maintain good relations with Mussolini's Italy and Hitler's Germany. Martin Gilbert has written, in his study of British policy towards Germany in the inter-war years, that 'a resolve never again to drift or fall unwittingly into war'[59] played a large part in appeasement of the Nazis. The pervasive representation of the war dead as martyrs for peace, who would be betrayed if another war occurred, was a powerful resource in rallying support for that resolve.

Notes to Chapter 8

1. *Enfield Gazette*, 11 Oct. 1919.

2. Hackney, SN/W/1/25, untitled press cutting, 15 Oct. 1920.

3. The appeal to give retrospective meaning to death in war by following some course of political or moral action was not new, although the scale of the world war, and the impact of its losses on a large proportion of the population, increased the number of people who might have been susceptible to it. Similar appeals had accompanied commemoration of the Boer War dead. Speaking at the unveiling of the Yorkshire Boer War memorial in 1905, Lord Wenlock had said that, though many people wanted to forget the war in South Africa, it was important to remember it as 'an incentive and a stimulus to determine that never again would they be compelled to undergo such a trial'. He meant that the difficulties and unpreparedness of the army in that war ought not to be repeated. 'If that were the outcome,' he went on, 'those men whose memory they were there to commemorate would not have died in vain' (*Yorkshire Herald*, 3 Aug. 1905).

4. *East End News*, 10 Dec. 1920.

5. Public Record Office, RAIL 236/418/1, draft of speech.

6. *Enfield Gazette*, 18 July 1919.

7. *Stockport Advertiser*, 1 Aug. 1919.

8. E. M. White, 'The Purpose of Civics, and How it is Served in Recent English Text-Books', *Sociological Review*, vol. 15, (1923), pp. 206–7.

9. S. R. Ward, 'Intelligence Surveillance of British Ex-Servicemen', *Historical Journal*, vol. 16, no. 1, (1973), pp. 178–88; D. Englander, 'The National Union of Ex-Servicemen and the Labour Movement, 1918–1920', *History*, vol. 76, no. 246 (1991), p. 41.

10. *Evening News*, 21 July 1919.

11. *Enfield Gazette*, 11 Apr. 1919.

12. *Barnsley Chronicle*, 22 Feb. 1919.

13. *Daily Herald*, 12 Nov. 1924, letter from A. Bond Saunders.

14. *Staffordshire Sentinel*, 19 July 1920.

15. *Birmingham Post*, 6 July 1925.

16. According to Colin McIntyre, women are more often listed separately on First World War memorials than integrated into the main sequence of men's names; see C. McIntyre, *Monuments of War: How to Read a War Memorial*, London, 1990, p. 154. I am grateful to Dr Catherine Moriarty for information on the subject derived from the National Inventory of War Memorials.

17. *Yorkshire Observer*, 29 May 1922.

18. *British Legion Journal*, vol. 11, no. 1, July 1931, p. 36.

19. Women's organisations in Tadcaster commissioned a memorial from Walter Brierley: Atkinson Brierley Papers, Box 108, letter, 13 Dec. 1919.

20. Tower Hamlets, 082.2, leaflet, Nov. 1917.

21. *East London Advertiser*, 23 June 1919.

22. *Progress*, July 1918, p. 79.

23. Letter 6 Aug. 1919, quoted in C. Hussey, *The Life of Sir Edwin Lutyens*, London, 1950, p. 393.

24. *Keighley News*, 13 Dec. 1924.

25. An idea that the justification for fighting the First World War was to end

war for ever was current from its earliest days. It had been advanced by J. L. Garvin, editor of *The Observer*, and H. G. Wells as an argument in favour of participation in the war. It continued to be used after the war to advocate support for the League of Nations as a way of honouring the moral obligation to the dead.

26. *Times Literary Supplement*, 6 Jan. 1921, p. 6.

27. Compare the pre-war publicity material of the National Service League quoted by Anne Summers in A. Summers, 'Militarism in Britain before the Great War', *History Workshop*, no. 2, (1976), p. 120.

28. See I. F. Clarke, *Voices Prophesying War*, London, 1970.

29. P. Gibbs, *Ten Years After: A Reminder*, London, 1924, p. 178.

30. See Chapter 3.

31. This memorial was designed by W. H. Wood, an architect with a largely ecclesiastical practice, and a considerable reputation, in Newcastle-upon-Tyne.

32. *Durham County Advertiser*, 10 June 1921.

33. *Yorkshire Weekly Post*, 21 Oct. 1922. The assumption that a memorial should be a warning about the nature of war was not approved by everyone. Col. Lewin, of the Royal Artillery, thought that, while determination to warn was entirely creditable, it was not appropriate to do this in a memorial, which should be a consolation to the bereaved and a reminder of the outstanding qualities of the dead (Royal Artillery, Minutes, 12 Nov. 1924).

34. The LNU was a large, cross-party organisation with many political and civic leaders and clergy of all denominations amongst its members. In social terms it was more than a pressure group, having many characteristics of a nationwide civic institution. See D. S. Birn, *The League of Nations Union*, Oxford, 1981.

35. *Headway*, vol. 4, no. 6, Jan. 1922, p. 119 (emphasis in original).

36. *Headway*, vol. 8, no. 12, Dec. 1925, p. 239.

37. *Headway*, vol. 18, no. 11, Nov. 1936, p. 218.

38. Quoted in P. Kyba, *Covenants without the Sword: Public Opinion and British Defence Policy 1931–1935*, Waterloo, Ontario, 1983, p. 123.

39. *British Legion Journal*, vol. 13, no. 3, Sept. 1933, p. 81.

40. Ibid., vol. 12, no. 5, Nov. 1932, p. 152.

41. *Morning Post*, 9 Nov. 1933.

42. *Daily Mail*, 11 Nov. 1920.

43. *Daily Herald*, 11 Nov. 1919.

44. *Manchester Guardian*, 11 Nov. 1930.

45. *Daily Mirror*, 12 Nov. 1930.

46. *Birmingham Post*, 3 July 1925.

47. Ibid., 4 July 1925.

48. *Bradford Daily Telegraph*, 3 July 1922.

49. Ibid.

50. Ibid.

51. *Yorkshire Observer*, 6 July 1922.

52. T. F. Lister, 'Our First Duty', *British Legion Journal*, vol. 1, no. 1, July 1921, p. 4.

53. Ibid.

54. Ibid., vol. 5, no. 2, Aug. 1925, p. 37.

55. B. Bushaway, 'Name Upon Name: The Great War and Remembrance', in R. Porter (ed.), *Myths of the English*, London, 1992, pp. 159–61; M. Higgonet, J. Jensen, S. Michel and C. Weitz (eds), *Behind the Lines: Gender and the Two*

World Wars, New Haven, 1987, pp. 4-8.

56. T. J. Clark 'Preliminaries to a Possible Treatment of "Olympia" in 1865', *Screen*, vol.21, no. 1 (1980), p. 23. In this instance, Clark appeals for support to a theoretical article by Paul Willemen. This reference is presumably intended specifically for readers of *Screen*, as it is untypical of Clark's generally far more empirical approach. Willemen relies on Lacanian assumptions about the constitution of subjectivity through representation, stressing its purely conjunctural, temporary and discontinuous nature, which also underlie the views he is criticising, but which I do not share. However, he insists on the importance of institutions in giving coherence to the relationship between individuals and images or texts, which is, I think, quite right. See P. Willemen, 'Notes on Subjectivity: On Reading Edward Branigan's "Subjectivity Under Siege"', *Screen*, vol. 19, no. 1, (1978), pp. 41-69.

57. *Manchester Guardian*, 12 Nov. 1919.

58. J. Gaffin and D. Thomas, *Caring and Sharing: The Centenary History of the Co-operative Women's Guild*, Manchester, 1983, p. 111; A. M. Gregory, *The Silence of Memory: Armistice Day 1919–1946*, Oxford, 1994, pp. 152-9.

59. M. Gilbert, *The Roots of Appeasement*, London, 1966, p. 9.

9

Sacred Union

Although participants expressed different senses of the meaning of commemorative symbols, reflecting their differences of purpose, they retained sufficient sense of unity amongst themselves for remembrance of the dead to remain an almost universal public observance. Their disagreements were secondary to the need to ensure that the dead were properly honoured. They all agreed to respect the sacred time - the Great Silence - set aside for honouring the dead, and the memorials dedicated to them. They shared the common acts of homage, such as laying wreaths and flowers before the names of the dead wherever they were recorded, and they joined publicly with others to show their reverence. This chapter considers how and why, in spite of all the differences, such unanimity was achieved.

Feeling and Commemoration

Originally, there was no reason to expect that the events and memorials which constituted public reflection on the Great War would be so overwhelmingly concerned with death. The royal proclamation which instituted the two minutes' silence specified that it was to 'afford an opportunity' to 'perpetuate the memory of the Great Deliverance' as well as 'of those who laid down their lives to achieve it'.[1] The committee which made the arrangements for the Armistice Day ceremony at the Whitehall Cenotaph in 1921 intended to set a tone to be copied throughout the country, and insisted in its recommendations that 'Armistice Day is not a day of National grief'. The committee's chairman, Lord Curzon, was convinced that 'in this and subsequent years the 11th November would not be a day of mourning but would be the commemoration of a great day in the country's history'.[2] The matter was extensively discussed in October 1925 in connection with a campaign led by the Revd Dick Sheppard to make Armistice Day a more solemn occasion.[3] A number of letters to the press deplored the tendency to make 11 November exclusively a day of mourning. It is clear from these letters that many people had not been treating it as such and resented pressure to do so. They were as much concerned to celebrate victory and their own wartime service as to remember the dead.[4]

In many people's minds, however, the outcome of the war could not be separated from the deaths which had occurred. The official Peace Day celebrations in 1919 combined celebration of victory with mourning in the salute to the dead made by the parading troops at the temporary Cenotaph. In planning the event, the Prime Minister had 'deprecated the idea of a national rejoicing which did not include some tribute to the dead'.[5] He did not feel that pleasure in the coming of peace could be separated from the cost of war. Not all the Cabinet agreed, but his view prevailed, and the salute to the Cenotaph became the most memorable aspect of the celebration.

For many, any pleasure there might be in recollections of the war or its ending was smothered by a sense of loss. As early as 1915, Vera Brittain recorded her awareness that this would be the case:

> I thought with what mockery and irony the jubilant celebrations which will hail the coming of peace will fall upon the ears of those to whom their best will never return, upon whose sorrow victory is built . . . I wonder if I shall be one of those who will take a happy part in the triumph – or if I shall listen to the merriment with a heart that breaks and ears that try to keep out of the mirthful sounds.

She believed that 'even if I do not lose directly, my heart will be too full of what others have lost to rejoice unrestrictedly'.[6] The eventual cessation of hostilities brought mixed feelings. Sir Arthur Conan Doyle, whose son died of wounds shortly before the end of the war, was deeply upset by the spontaneous celebrations at the declaration of the Armistice. It should be, he felt, 'a moment for prayer' not revelry.[7]

The fact of bereavement, and consideration shown for the feelings of the bereaved, profoundly affected the way most people reflected on the war; but the part bereavement played in shaping the commemoration of the dead was not straightforward. Some contemporaries noticed a decline in the emotionality of crowds on Armistice Day ceremonies in the later 1920s.[8] On the other hand, deep feeling did persist in many individuals. A significant number continued to express grief publicly for what must be reckoned an unusually long time, at least by comparison with research from the later twentieth century.[9] A resident of Liverpool who regularly passed the city cenotaph noticed in 1933 that 'Round about Armistice Day one will often observe . . . women in mourning quietly sobbing over the wreaths they have deposited.'[10]

The circumstances of death in war may have made the feelings associated with it harder than usual to resolve. The dead were largely young, and such promise as their lives might have held had not been fulfilled. Most were buried in distant places, if they had a known grave at all, and no final leave-taking had been possible. Writers who have discussed these matters have tended to see commemoration of the dead as an attempt to restore the regular pattern of mourning in difficult circumstances, and have understood it by reference to what is generally regarded as the normal form of grief-work. Jay Winter has suggested that ritual acts directed at memorials offered an escape from the melancholia which might otherwise overwhelm a bereaved person.[11] Adrian Gregory has seen the naming of the dead as part of the process by which the bereaved came to accept the absence of those who had borne the names.[12] Catherine Moriarty has discussed the production of memorials as a substitute adopted by the bereaved for actually burying their own dead.[13] All these suggestions are credible up to a point, and could have been important to at least some people; but there are also a number of characteristics of war commemoration which point in different directions, and suggest that normalisation of the grief process might neither have been sought nor achieved by the means which were actually used.

The forms and locations of memorials were rarely chosen to reproduce the symbolic sites of mourning characteristic of ordinary peacetime life. They are usually in public places: town or village centres, municipal parks, the entrances to commercial or institutional premises. By contrast, the nineteenth century had seen a migration of the places where individuals and families related to their dead away from the hubbub of everyday community life. The names of the war dead may be repeated on memorials in a variety of locations, represented in one place as a citizen of a town, in another as a member of a church, club, or military unit, or as an employee of a firm. Thus dead individuals might be fragmented into the variety of roles in which they had led their public lives. These sites seem poorly calculated to act as substitutes for the regular processes of grief. They seem, rather, to have a principally institutional significance. They were projections, into the space of everyday business, of a claim that the institutions responsible for them maintained a connection with the dead who were formerly their members.

One can imagine an alternative to this institutional and fragmentary form of remembrance, which might have followed the pattern of the wartime street shrines; remaining collective, yet coming nearer to the communities in which the dead were probably best known and most missed. It does, in fact, exist in the Abbey parish in Saint Albans, where memorials to people of the neighbourhood stand in several streets; but public memorials with such a local, even familial, character are very hard to find. As we have seen,[14] permanent replacements for street shrines were suggested during the war; but, apart perhaps from the established church, no institution had, any longer, a great interest in acting at such a local level to create them. Significantly, it appears that the Saint Albans street memorials may owe their existence, at least in part, to local clergy.[15] A permanent street memorial in Cyprus Street, Bethnal Green, was erected by an ex-servicemen's benevolent club. It is an indication of how far the erection of memorials was determined by institutional rather than personal imperatives that permanent memorials on this neighbourly scale are so rare.

Commemoration of the dead was also drawn out in time. To judge from announcements in *The Times*, memorial services for the dead, individually or collectively, were quite common from 1916 onwards. A high proportion of these would presumably have been for members of high-status social groups, but we may also presume that the memorial element reported in a regular Easter service at Stoke Newington in 1916[16] was not merely an isolated example. After the war, further memorial services, and the unveiling of memorials in the variety of institutions I have already described, continued this diffusion of mourning. It is hard to see how any one out of this number of ceremonies could form a definitive taking leave of the distant dead.

Perhaps disturbances to the normal patterns of mourning,

dispersing it in space and drawing it out in time, presented no special problems to the bereaved in negotiating their period of grief. Geoffrey Gorer's influential study of modern bereavement is often taken to imply that a formalised and public mourning process is by far the most effective for the bereaved, and is in some way a natural necessity. In fact, he observes a range of successful mourning practices, some of which do not require a formally structured period of mourning.[17] The matter is an individual one. For some, as David Cannadine has argued in the case of Victorian mourning, a heavy emphasis on ritualisation may be oppressive.[18] Adrian Gregory cites a couple, an ex-soldier and his current wife whose first husband had been killed in the war, who found the regular observation of Armistice Day deeply painful.[19] According to the psychological literature on the subject, events or objects that appear to perpetuate the existence of the dead can be both helpful and unhelpful to the bereaved.[20] It seems that there could be just as much variety in emotional responses to formal occasions for remembering the dead as in intellectual responses to them.

Repeated remembrance ceremonies, inescapably included in the national calendar, may themselves have generated much of the emotion recorded by contemporaries. According to Richard Lamerton, 'for several years occasional brief periods of yearning and depression may be precipitated by reminders of the loss', and illusions of the presence of the mourned person may continue 'at intervals for a decade or so'.[21] Up to a point, therefore, the expression of grief in public could be self-perpetuating. In this context, there are good reasons for regarding the expression of grief as the satisfaction of a political as much as of a psychological need. Much of the moral meaning of remembrance of the dead was predicated on its capacity to renew appropriate emotions. It was on people's feelings towards the dead that the sense of moral obligation to them was based. The expression of grief acted as a sign of the sincerity of commemoration by showing that these feelings were genuine. To wear mourning or hold ceremonies are conventional acts. By contrast, an outburst of grief appears natural and from the heart. It was, therefore, important that at least some people should continue to express it. Its expression was valued and, in effect, welcomed by many of the newspaper writers who presented the public with a moralising commentary on remembrance ceremonies every year. Breaking through the otherwise reticent act of commemoration, grief was an important part of commemorative symbolism. Commemoration thus played on the pathological aspects of grief, and set out deliberately to prolong them, in order to improve, morally and politically, post-war society.

Emotional states other than grief were also of enormous importance in the remembrance of the dead. Some veterans appear to have felt a guilt like that now known as 'survivor syndrome', closely related to grief but also to anxiety for one's own safety. Harold Macmillan wrote many years later, 'We almost began to feel a sense of guilt for not having shared the fate of our friends and comrades.' To alleviate this he resorted to the familiar idea of an obligation to the dead. He continued, 'We certainly felt some obligation to make some decent use of the life that had been spared to us.'[22] Eric Leed has argued that mourning rituals were a medium through which ex-combatants could express the loss of the idealised visions of war service and of the home they were supposed to be defending; losses which they incurred both through the actual experience of fighting and through a sense of estrangement from non-combatants. 'This organised mourning, . . . was the most acceptable way in which the war continued to define the identities of combatants' he writes. 'The mourning of soldiers for the dead, . . . was reinforced in pageants, memorials, rituals, and songs of veterans groups.'[23]

However, the observable behaviour of their organisations is not necessarily evidence of a general feeling amongst veterans. Only a minority of ex-service personnel joined British veterans' organisations. Not all of those had experienced the front-line fighting which is central to Leed's argument, and many of those who had experienced it cannot have joined. The British Legion managed to recruit only about one-tenth of those who had served in the armed forces during the war, and its membership included a large number of women who had not shared the experience of front-line fighting. Female membership rose from 6,560 in 1922 to 107,580 (slightly over a quarter of the total) in 1930.[24]

The particular feelings of ex-combatants should, therefore, not be overstressed in the formation and sustenance of a public cult of the dead. The need to mourn the dead and to honour a moral obligation to them may well have articulated the feelings of some ex-combatants, but the source of this feeling cannot simply be attributed to their fighting experience. The existence of a moral obligation to the dead was an idea shared with, and recognised and propagated by recruiters, politicians and clergy well before the troops returned from the war, and even before many of them had gone to it. Annual reiteration may also have stimulated the sense of guilt Macmillan mentions, in the same way that grief was revived. It is, therefore, not easy to know how far veterans' sense of guilt and obligation was the source and how far the product of the concentration on death, and on the moral superiority of the dead, which was enshrined in the official remembrance of the war.

A more general form of anxiety was involved in commemoration of the dead, on account of the political issues it raised. Winston Churchill expressed a sense of impending apocalypse, probably shared by many people, politically engaged or not, which had some similarities with the anxiety about nuclear weapons which has existed since 1945. 'Mankind', he wrote in 1929, 'has got into its hands for the first time the tools by which it can unfailingly accomplish its own extermination.'[25] The *Daily Mirror* imagined on Armistice Day 1935, amidst German rearmament and a mounting crisis in Abyssinia, that 'There must have been hundreds of thousands who prayed more fervently and more urgently for peace than at any time since the peace began.'[26] In her novel *South Riding*, set (and written) in the mid-1930s, Winifred Holtby depicts the spasm of anxiety which a sudden reminder of the war might arouse. The schoolteacher Sarah Burton is listening to children sing wartime songs in a theatrical show:

> Like many women of her generation, she could not listen unmoved to the familiar tunes which circumstances had associated with intolerable memory . . . With increasing awareness every year she realised what it had meant of horror, desperation, anxiety, and loss to her generation. She knew that the dead are most needed, not when they are mourned, but in a world robbed of their stabilising presence . . . and the world did ill without them.
>
> She was haunted by the menace of another war. Constantly, when she least expected it, that spectre threatened her, undermining her confidence in her work, her faith, her future. A joke, a picture, a tune, could trap her into a blinding waste of misery and helplessness.[27]

Holtby's description here probably combines feelings of her own with the experiences of friends like Vera Brittain, who lost her brother and many close male friends in the war. Sarah's feeling is not focused so much on her own loss, as on a sense of the enormity of the losses as a whole, and on anxiety that they might recur. The anxiety does not diminish but increases with the passage of time, through increasing realisation of the total cost of the war and the danger of another. It is exacerbated by the idea that those who had been killed would have contributed greatly to the stability of the world if they had survived.

There was anxiety of another kind, especially amongst people with a conservative social outlook, about the loss of a renewed sense of purpose which many had felt during the war. They were afraid that something which had been gained through the war effort was being thrown away. The vicar of Alsager, Cheshire, was expressing this anxiety when he wrote the following in his parish magazine in August 1919: 'The spirit of patriotism and comradeship which was so manifest during the dark days of the war seems to have given place to a spirit of reckless selfishness and disinclination for work . . . It will be deplorable if we lose by our folly and selfishness what our sailors and soldiers and airmen have fought and died to save.'[28]

We have seen these anxieties appear as themes in the speech-making and editorial-writing associated with the remembrance of the dead, expressed as exhortations to disarmament, rearmament, national unity, a sense of duty, a sense of international justice, and so on. They were, like grief, responses to death, though focused less on personal loss than on the sense of catastrophe which the war and the subsequent state of the world had impressed on the minds of many. Continued anxieties about the conditions and dangers of the post-war world found a ready form of expression through remembrance, loaded as it was with an emotionality which was revived with each passing year, and strengthened by continued revelations of and reflection on the costs of war.

The emotional power of remembrance was founded on personal griefs and anxieties; but these feelings need not have been acted out in ceremonies which repeatedly engaged the whole community, and which carried such an enormous burden of idealisation. In modern British culture the expression of grief and fear are generally consigned to the sphere of private life and personal relationships. The Victorian funeral had been a public event amongst all classes; but it was a one-off affair. The formal period of mourning had a definite limit, and was not sustained by repetitions of the ceremony. Besides, the conspicuous formality of nineteenth-century mourning had been declining before the First World War, and for many would have been neither expected nor desired.[29] Why then did remembrance of the dead become such an intrusively public and moralistic occasion?

Part of the explanation lies in the existence of the tradition of civic commemoration. Commemoration had become a feature of civic life in which civic pride was expressed and municipal rivalries were conducted. It offered a field in which civic leaders could perform to good effect in public, showing their sense of propriety and of occasion, and it was felt to encourage social cohesion. Any event of national importance could offer an opportunity to serve these purposes, and thus the development of a form of civic commemoration for such a major event as a great war could easily be predicted. In this instance, the matter may have had greater importance than usual for civic leaders. In the period before the introduction of conscription in 1916, they had taken a large part in the voluntary recruitment of troops, a system which depended on exerting moral, and sometimes economic, pressure on reluctant individuals through newspapers, the Church, employers and other organisations. Some employees had been offered financial inducements to enlist, others dismissed from their jobs to force them into the services.[30] When compulsion was eventually applied, the same social leaders devoted themselves to supporting the government's administration of it, and provided members for the local boards which adjudicated exemption cases. Their reputations as faithful stewards of the communal interest could be at stake if their part in the organisation of the war had been widely seen as unjust afterwards. To displace responsibility for deaths in the war from the state and its agents to the individual, by seeing it as a personal moral achievement, might reduce the possibility of blame.

There is some indirect evidence that their contributions to recruitment came back to haunt those who had conducted it. Success in recruiting and in the administration of conscription had been matters of considerable pride to them during the war;[31] but they did not claim conspicuous credit for it afterwards. Francis Dod, the Stoke Newington alderman, was a man who did not always choose his words very carefully, and he might be expected occasionally to say what others in his position would not. In a speech to a public dinner in 1920, he expressed a fear that his role as a recruiter could have been resented. Some months before, he said, he had addressed a meeting of ex-servicemen, many of whom 'had been sent into the army by me, and when that vast body stood up and sang "For he's a jolly good fellow" - meaning me - I thought they did not misunderstand me'.[32] It would clearly suit civic leaders like Dod that the citizen-soldier should see himself as willing and cheerful in his self-sacrifice.

The didactic purpose of commemoration also moved its organisers to make it a large-scale event. The more who came the better, and if people whose views were questionable could be made to join in, that was all to the good. There was a feeling that merely being present on these occasions would impress a right understanding of the war, and of one's duty as a citizen, on those who participated. A writer in the *British Legion Journal* in November 1929 thought that it was a pity to reduce the number of serving soldiers in the guard of honour at the Cenotaph. Most ordinary soldiers of the time would not have served in the war, so as many as possible should be given the opportunity of parading at the Cenotaph 'to be imbued with the spirit of sacrifice, devotion and comradeship which is of these observances'.[33] In 1930, the right-wing journalist Douglas Jerrold praised the ceremonial of Armistice Day as a 'wholesome and disciplinary experience'.[34]

But to concentrate on the motives of those who led public commemoration does not get us very far. Members of the public had to be willing to participate in the events which civic leaders organised if they were to be successful. They had, therefore, to find the view of the dead which they presented - as special people, whose deaths had involved a moral achievement - credible. For the bereaved, idealisation of the dead might help to make sense of deaths which could not be absorbed into the normal cycle of life and its satisfactions. The war dead had not lived out their allotted span. They had not been allowed to make of their lives whatever they could, and the bereaved could not console themselves that those they had lost had either led worthy and enjoyable lives, or were well out of bad ones. An alternative was to insist that they had died in a worthy cause, had contributed significantly to it in the process, and had even been given an opportunity for achievement which a life of peace might never have offered. For most of them, no record of any significant military act survived apart from their joining up and their dying; hence the moral strength willingly to serve and courageously to face death were the only constructive achievements that could be attributed to them.

The appeal of public commemoration was, therefore, not simply the opportunity to mourn, but the recognition which it conferred on the dead. The presence of a casualty's name on a local memorial satisfied the desire to mark the death as special, different from the normal run of mortality through the moral achievement it had entailed, whether or not the normal rites of mourning had been performed. This is the feeling expressed by Mrs Amy Merrick, whose husband died in the spring of 1922 of disease contracted on army service, and who wrote to Stoke Newington memorial committee to claim his equality with those killed in combat. 'I feel quite sure', she said, 'that I am not asking too much to have his name honoured among the fallen heroes, that met their death on the Field violently, after all, his fate was equally as bad to have fought and suffered and know and realise, that his end was near.'[35] Exclusion from the list of the honoured dead often occurred, usually because a death consequent on war service was regarded as too late. This caused resentment, because it denied an ex-combatant the recognition others had been granted.

There was also little choice but to make any ritualised mourning for the dead into some kind of communal occasion, not the conventional family affair. Church authorities tried to discourage the erection of private memorials to the war dead in their buildings, which were the most obvious sites for memorials to individuals. This was, to a considerable extent, a conservation measure,[36] but it also complied with a desire, encapsulated in the idea of 'equality of sacrifice', that memorials to the dead should show no social distinction and should recognise the comradeship of military service. Thus whatever emotional investment most people might have made in a personal memorial in a public place had to be transferred to an officially sponsored collective memorial, erected, as we have seen, to serve a local administrative entity such as the parish, municipality, or some kind of voluntary community. The memorial might be in a church, but it was, nonetheless, a public and shared product.

A moralised characterisation of the dead might have had the

same appeal to veterans of the war as it had to bereaved relatives. They may have had even more need to find some ethical or religious meaning in the suffering of comrades whom they had lost. The sense of guilt which some felt at having survived when others had perished may also have prompted them to see those who had died as morally superior. Veterans were presented with a number of challenges to their self-esteem after the war. Philip Gibbs recounted the brutalising effect which he thought hand-to-hand combat had on those who participated in it.[37] Official enquiries suggested that trench warfare could have an injurious psychological impact even on those who did not develop symptoms needing treatment. The psychological health of all who had fought was thus publicly questioned.[38] Against this, the moral example of the dead provided an elevated public image of the virtues of military service and of those who performed it. Fidelity to the dead as moral exemplars could help ex-service personnel reaffirm a sense of their own moral worth, and give them a reason for looking back on their service with pride and a sense of achievement which was not dulled by the widespread sense of horror at the destruction and destabilisation the war had caused. It might even help them to come to terms with things they themselves had done in the war by laying a moral cloak over them.

Some, however, like the writer Charles Carrington, wished neither to mourn nor to moralise. Carrington would not go to the Cenotaph ceremonies because he disliked what he saw as their pacifist message, and complained that 'the British Legion seemed to make its principal outing a day of mourning'. It became 'too much like attending one's own funeral'.[39] He confined himself to celebrating 11 November with like-minded friends. Carrington seems to have enjoyed the war. His outlook at its end may be inferred from the fact that he considered volunteering for the Auxiliary forces fighting against Irish independence, and for the British counter-revolutionary intervention force in Russia.[40]

It may be questionable, therefore, whether a general desire to mourn the dead in public existed amongst ex-combatants; but there is no doubt about its importance to ex-service organisations, who took a special interest in ensuring that the dead were properly honoured. They contributed to the erection of local war memorials, and conducted their own remembrance ceremonies. Here, once more, we need to avoid conflating the personal and institutional motives which lie behind public symbolic acts. A large-scale communal event offered activists of many sorts who were concerned with the war an opportunity, not only to pursue their campaigns, but to cultivate their own solidarity. We have already noticed the use made of Armistice Day by the League of Nations Union and other politically motivated bodies. Ex-service organisations found the same uses in it.

The British Legion was especially active in sustaining public commemorative ceremonial throughout the inter-war period. Its branches frequently paraded in public at memorials, not only in the annual Remembrance events, but on other military anniversaries (often the dates of battles in which local units had participated), or on Empire Day. A national ceremony was held at the Cenotaph each Whitsun to coincide with the Legion's annual conference. Armistice Day was also the occasion for a charity drive, selling poppies in aid of disabled ex-servicemen. In 1923 the *Journal* noted that the Legion's own Whitsun ceremony at the Cenotaph 'offered fresh opportunity to reconsecrate our lives to a noble cause'.[41] In 1932 a writer said that 'the service at the Cenotaph means . . . a spiritual revival, and a brotherly reunion'.[42] As well as providing a platform for putting forward their views, public displays gave such organisations a chance simply to show their size and degree of support, and to instil a sense of excitement and endeavour in their membership.

Common Ground

Although we can identify a variety of motives and political outlooks amongst those who participated in commemoration of the dead, all were united in their respect for the sanctity of the symbolic acts and objects on which it was centred. In general, this respect was made all the easier by the openness of their symbolism. Reticence, silence or simplicity, were regarded as appropriately expressive qualities. Collective reticence embodied the unity of all who honoured the moral power displayed through suffering and death, and avoided the controversial issues which commemoration raised.

The most universally performed expression of common purpose was the Great Silence. It was appropriate to all places, all activities and all attitudes. *The Times*, in its report of the crowds at the unveiling of the Whitehall Cenotaph, said that British silence had superseded the Periclean tradition of panegyric on the dead.[43] The dead were now recognised as heroic principally through the wordless memory of them, rather than by rhetorically enumerating their qualities. What they had actually been like, as soldiers or as ordinary people, was left, in this sacred moment, to individual memory or imagination. Silence was also regarded as an expressive element in other events or objects connected with the remembrance of the dead. At the unveiling of Enfield cenotaph, a reporter maintained that the 'voiceless stone spoke audibly to thousands of silent watchers'.[44] In contrast to the profane world of everyday noise, the presence of the dead was wrapped in sacred silence. 'Here in the heart of one of the greatest cities of the Empire, where the noise of everyday business life is continually heard, you have raised a monument – a silent sentinel – to the memory of those who were once of you', said Lord Derby at the unveiling of Manchester cenotaph.[45]

It was often suggested that the sites chosen for monuments should facilitate quiet reminiscence, in order to establish a special relationship between a memorial and the public, and to encourage a sense of its sanctity. Carlisle Citizens' League, which was responsible for organising the Cumberland and Westmorland memorial at Carlisle, thought that their cenotaph should stand in beautiful surroundings and away from the 'turmoil of the streets'.[46] In the House of Commons, a member expressed the opinion that the Cenotaph should be moved from Whitehall to a site which offered 'a quiet opportunity for contemplation' beside it.[47] In 1923 an experimental rubber road surface was laid round the Cenotaph in order to reduce traffic noise and provide an auditory image of its sanctity for visitors. The grouting failed, however, and it was removed the next year.[48]

The silence was more symbolic than real. Many an account of Armistice Day gives a prominent place to the sounds which occur in the silence, often the poorly co-ordinated signals for its beginning provided by neighbouring local authorities. *The Times*, in 1920, reported the arrival of the remains of the Unknown Warrior at Victoria station in an hallucination of silence. 'There was great silence – The silence deepened, for no one seemed to move. One heard a smothered sound of weeping. The smoke in the roof bellied and eddied round the arc lamps. The funeral carriage stopped at last . . .. Still it was so silent.'[49] In spite of these words, the scene was, in fact, accompanied by the noise of a steam engine and carriage coming into a large railway station. Rather than a physical condition, silence was the appropriate state of mind for those honouring the dead, a state in which differences were suppressed, and all concentrated on the transcendent fact of death.

Common purpose amongst all who commemorated the dead was also expressed in their recognition of the sanctity of memorials. The disagreement over Bradford war memorial, described in the last chapter, provides an excellent instance of how the sense of sanctity could transcend differences of motive and interpretation. Despite disagreement over the meaning of its imagery, supporters and critics of the memorial were alike concerned that its sanctity should not be compromised. Nor did critics wish to see it rejected by the public. One hesitated to criticise the 'crude and mistaken' figures because the memorial 'is and must remain a shrine of reverent remembrance . . . No man or woman among us should pass lightly or think without reverence of the dead.'[50] The clergyman who had first raised the issue of the figures nonetheless expressed his gratitude to all who had worked to get the memorial made.[51] Later, the alderman who had defended the memorial at its unveiling also appealed to the argument that the sanctity of the memorial ought to take precedence in people's minds over its other visible meanings. He said at the unveiling of another memorial (although it was obvious that he was referring to the previous controversy),

> what mattered in a memorial was not so much its form as the sacredness of the thing it stood for . . . Even though a memorial called attention to certain things that happened in the war – and the war was no kid-glove affair – we forgot that in a moment, and remembered that whatever the lads passed through, they did so to crush a tremendous evil.[52]

Participants could disagree profoundly about the moral meaning they believed a memorial to communicate, but still agree on the need to regard it as sacred. They appear to have believed that its sanctity depended on the respect the community showed it for the sake of the dead it commemorated, rather than on the ideas it was seen to express. All interested parties felt it necessary to encourage the public to see the memorial as sacred. This was all the more necessary if it had something in its form which could give offence to some people. They were willing to overlook opinions or images which they rejected so that they could continue to share in the commemorative act.

Time-honoured artistic conventions were used to mark out memorials as sacred objects. The most straightforward was the use of the cross, recognisable both as the sacred symbol of Christianity and as, by the early twentieth century, a common form of grave marker, more especially the typical marker used during the war to identify the graves of soldiers. Architecture could serve the same purpose. The mayor of Stockport, discussing the design of the town's memorial, explained that 'immediately on entering the porch they looked right along a distance of about sixty feet to the place where the sculpture group would be standing against the background of a stained glass window with the light from the main hall shining down upon it . . .. that alone would be something that would make people feel they were in a holy place'.[53] The window was not executed, but the effect is powerful nonetheless (Figure 4).

Through equally well-established conventions of reverence, individuals could assist in affirming the sanctity of a memorial. A report in the *Yorkshire Evening Post* saw the openly expressive actions of the public as essential in establishing the proper meaning of a memorial and making it something more than mere public art. The presence of the bereaved at the unveiling of the city war memorial, it said,

> gave to the memorial and to the simple little ceremony their deepest sanctity . . . each group of them carrying a wreath or bunch of flowers to lay at the foot of the shrine, showed that the beautiful work of bronze and stone is more than a work of art – that it is and will be the collective expression of the homage of the citizens . . .[54]

A resident agreed, writing to the paper a week later to complain of people's behaviour towards the memorial: 'You could see them reading the inscription "Honour the Fallen" and yet not one man of all the hundreds who passed did I see with sufficient respect to raise his hat for one moment.'[55] Men had regularly raised their hats to wartime street shrines[56] and subsequently to the Cenotaph. The writer clearly regarded such gestures as crucial to establishing the memorial's value, for he concluded: 'I would appeal to the citizens of Leeds to save this magnificent piece of work from degenerating into a mere adornment to the city, and to make it a memorial.'

Sir John Burnet, too, believed that appropriate gestures were important in establishing the sanctity of a war memorial, and in distinguishing it from other monuments. He hoped to encourage viewers to make a gesture of homage to the memorial he designed for Glasgow through the way it was laid out. One of the main features of his initial design was a horizontal stone slab, with a large palm branch and wreath carved on it, standing in a pit several feet below ground level. This arrangement was intended to prompt visitors to look downwards, as if bowing their heads before the memory of the dead. He explained that it 'seems not unfitting that such a monument should distinctly differ from other public monuments in so far that an attitude of reverence is secured by the eye being drawn down before the whole monument is seen'.[57] The city corporation refused to allow a pit, but some of his idea survives in the executed design. The stone slab was placed slightly above ground level, enclosed on three sides by a low wall which also serves as seats, looking down on it (Figure 30).

At best, observing conventions of reverence was a simple matter of right feeling, neither deliberate nor reasoned, with the least possible intellectual content. For some people, it was a powerful compulsion, making the sanctity of a war memorial seem a more or less physical experience. Charles Ffoulkes, first curator of the Imperial War Museum collection, described his response to the soldier's corpse on the Royal Artillery memorial at Hyde Park thus: 'The figure . . . has no trace of sentiment, it is just a poignant and tremendous statement of fact which makes the onlooker unconsciously raise his hat.'[58] A Liverpool resident described his response to the city's cenotaph as a mixture of aesthetic and religious feelings prompting an act of reverence. 'I have occasion to pass the Cenotaph every day', he wrote, 'and always it seemed to me so admirably suited to its position that I must take my hat off in passing because it is sacred ground.'[59]

Men, of course, were expected to doff their hats on entering a church, and some seem to have found the compulsion to observe this convention so strong that they claimed it was quite automatic. The travel writer H. V. Morton, recounting a visit to the supposedly haunted ruins of Beaulieu Abbey, where the old plan of the nave could still be made out in a field, wrote: 'In this

Figure 30

green meadow you instinctively raise your hat, for it still seems holy ground.'[60] A remembrance ceremony could prompt this kind of automatic acknowledgement of sanctity as well as a physical memorial. A *Times* writer, who claimed to have been cynical about the idea of a two minutes' silence before the first one had actually occurred, described his response to it, and that of his companions, like this: 'we, too, were on our feet and our heads were uncovered. None of us could say by what process of thought he came to that position . . . we did it half-consciously, as though moved by an uncontrollable impulse.'[61] In such an automatic recognition there was no place for interpretation, and understanding of it was postponed until after the sacred moment of homage. Like the public expression of grief, or the ritual silence, it helped to identify the moment of inarticulate sanctity as one in which all were united in a common feeling. In spite of their differences, all entered, in that instant, into a common relationship with the symbol.

Public Discipline

The conventions of behaviour expressing reverence for the dead, through which unity of action was made possible, were not sustained simply by public respect for them. They could be, and often were, physically enforced. Official and unofficial steps were taken to control the character of acts of remembrance, and to see that they were honoured by all, and their unity extended to all, including those who might otherwise have shown no interest in them or have been actively hostile. Restrictions placed on what participants could do to express feelings or opinions at the public events organised around the Great Silence assisted in giving it the character of a thoroughly consensual act. People who did not wish to participate might be disciplined by other members of the public if they made their refusal to join in perceptible.

It was difficult not to join in the Great Silence on Armistice Day if one was in a public place. Police stopped the traffic. Managers of business premises organised staff and customers to ensure they behaved appropriately. Outdoor and indoor space was temporarily subjected to the discipline of a remembrance ceremony. Officiants at ceremonies could suppress expressions of opinion which they deemed inappropriate. In 1936, the Proctors of Oxford University banned the University Peace Council from taking part in the ceremony at the war memorial in Saint Giles, and made restrictive stipulations about the wording of inscriptions on wreaths and the times at which they might be laid if that was to be done privately. In response both the University Conservative Association and the Labour Club protested at 'a very vigorous campaign . . . waged against the most elementary rights of self-expression'.[62] Where an oppressive discipline was imposed, it could, as at Oxford, be contested; but simply to defy it was liable to set one outside the commemorative consensus. This would be self-defeating for people who wished to take a place in the ceremonial of remembrance and claim that their interpretation of its meaning was sincere. To appear sincere, people had to show that they either shared for themselves, or respected in others, the feelings on which commemoration was founded. An element of compromise was thus necessary. To join in the ceremonies required at least outward respect for the feelings of the other people involved. To stand out against or disrupt the communal ceremony suggested that one neither shared nor appreciated those feelings.

Control of commemorative ceremonies was not left to official bodies alone. Ex-service organisations also concerned themselves with the propriety of commemorative symbols. Before the Women's Co-operative Guild started selling white poppies on Armistice Day 1933, as symbols of personal commitment to peace through non-violence, they asked the British Legion if they could sell alongside its red poppy sellers, thereby acknowledging a joint commitment to peace. The request was refused, however, and a Legion branch officer in Wellingborough explained 'that there was no need of a peace emblem in addition to the Flanders poppy, which brought memories which were in themselves the finest possible peace propaganda'.[63] Other participants also defended the sanctity of commemorative rituals, apparently on their own initiative. In 1920 the *Daily Mail* claimed that two clerks in the office of the socialist *Workers' Dreadnought* had disrupted the two minutes' silence by singing, dancing and banging tin cans. Their office was 'raided by angry people . . . and the women gave the offenders a good trouncing.'[64] The *Daily Herald* recorded a number of 'ugly incidents' in London on Armistice Day 1924.[65] In Moorgate a man was mobbed by some two hundred people and beaten for ignoring the signal at the beginning of the silence. 'Bleeding and dishevelled', he took refuge in a shop. A sailor who was mobbed by a crowd in Bow Street for ignoring the silence 'took off his hat and coat and offered to fight'. He was arrested, supposedly for his own protection, and brought before a magistrate, who told him he had behaved foolishly. His response was to ask, 'Why? Why all these demands? It is not in order. People can please themselves.' But in that belief he was mistaken. Pressure to conform made participation in the two minutes' silence more or less obligatory for all, whether or not they approved of or were interested in the ceremony.

Desire and discipline were both essential in producing a united public form of commemoration. The unity they created affirmed a community of feeling and a common purpose amongst all who were, whether willingly or not, subjected to it. Conventions of visual art and of personal or collective conduct provided a basis for distinguishing the sacred essentials of the commemoration of the dead from the partisan expressions of opinion which so closely accompanied it. They provided a repertoire of symbolic acts and objects which all could share, because they required no more explicit commitment than an act of reverence. Respect for the sacred acts and objects was demanded from everyone, and the power to police public spaces and places of work, exercised by local administrations, employers or crowd violence, enforced it.

Communities of Commemoration

We have seen that several types of community were alluded to in the rhetoric of commemoration: the community of the dead with the living; of the dead amongst themselves (expressed in their comradeship); of all mourners, or of those who now had the obligation to ensure the sacrifices of war were not in vain; of the nation (as the community which had mobilised the war effort), and most especially of the localities from which the dead had come – their homes. The idea of community was the basis on which a sense of validity, of meaning, for death in the war was constructed. Death could be made meaningful if it was seen as service to the community, as protection of it, purification of it, a warning to it, or restoration of it to an older and better identity. Loyalty to one's community provided an explanation of death in the war, a reason for seeing death as having intrinsic value, and a proposal for action on the part of the living which would keep that value alive. But, in commemoration, the idea of community, which provided a ground for the meaning of death, was far more than an abstraction or a general moral principle. The communities whom the dead had served, and the living should serve in their turn, were described as specific people in specific places, actual communities which could be recognised - town, parish, school, club, and so on.

Whoever the suffering was undertaken *for* and who, therefore, should acknowledge an obligation to the dead, was announced by naming them, just as the dead were named. War memorial committees normally organised the honouring of specifically local people by local people. Inscriptions dedicated memorials to, for example, 'the men and women of Barnsley who laid down their lives in the Great War', 'to the glory of God and in memory of Hampsthwaite men' or, 'to the men of Charfield who fought in the Great War'. Where the community was not mentioned by name, those commemorated were frequently claimed for 'this borough' or 'this parish'. Their service to the national community might be mentioned, but their connection with a locality was not submerged in it. Yarmouth war memorial was 'to perpetuate the memory of the men of this borough who died for king and country', and Clapham Old Church memorial commemorated 'the men of Clapham who died for England'. Commemorating the dead was thought of as a matter of specifically local importance, not merely the local performance of a national celebration. The Archbishop of Canterbury saw the erection of memorials as 'vital to the best local life'.[66]

This attention to actual and identifiable communities allowed the moral value of commemoration to be conceived in very concrete terms. It was not seen merely as a matter of propagating ideas and principles of action, but of creating relationships amongst the people who came together to commemorate the dead. The act of homage - erecting a memorial or conducting a ceremony - provided an occasion for overcoming divisions within the community created by the conflicting interests of everyday life. The anniversary of the unveiling of Llandrindod Wells war memorial, which was celebrated annually, on 1 July, from 1923 onwards, was hoped to provide 'one occasion of the year when all creeds and classes of the district can come together on common ground to do honour to those lads who have fallen for our common country, and this bringing together of those otherwise holding divergent views will be a noble result'.[67]

The idea of community can been used in different ways. It may be a sentimental or politically motivated fiction, or it may refer to groups with a substantial functional coherence.[68] Although sentiment and idealism were present in commemorative references to 'community', there was nothing fictional about the communities who created war memorials. They were founded not on common feeling or personal relationships, but on the possession of administrative power. They could confer honour on the dead because they had the power to create and maintain the symbols which expressed it. The possession of some form of executive power was essential if a communal statement was to be made, as it was the means by which the diversity of groups within its jurisdiction could be organised into a single act. Thus, 'The bringing together of those holding divergent views' was not merely a pious hope. With respect to its dead, each local or institutional community did draw together and form a united movement transcending its characteristic internal differences, and enacted the ideal civic vision of itself. At the same time, each community was drawn into a larger whole. The symbols, ceremonies, speeches and writing of commemoration proposed the existence of a greater community amongst all who commemorated the dead. Its fundamental principles of agreement were rehearsed in newspapers, speeches and sermons throughout the year, but on Armistice Day it took power over public spaces throughout the country and beyond, and obtained what appeared to be almost universal assent to its ideals.

From the local to the international levels, community of action was made possible by the symbolic element in commemoration: holding ceremonies and erecting memorials. The performance of these actions provided a goal around which an inclusive organisation could be formed, precisely because it transcended sectional differences. Many, who did not agree on their specific goals, could come together in agreement on the symbolic part of their activity, giving reality to the unity which they believed commemoration should establish.

Through commemoration, a movement was assembled which insisted on remembering the war and the dead, and assigning value to them. It also insisted that everyone else should do the same. It defined itself, if only vaguely, against all those who had forgotten or wished to forget. The movement could exert power over others (whether its members actually wished to or not), to protect the symbols around which it cohered, and to draw attention to those things which concerned it. It drew attention, especially, to the arguments amongst its members about the meaning of what they were doing, and hence provided a public platform for the different views held by participants. People joined together not because they shared a single attitude to the war, but in the belief that it was necessary to make something valid out of it, whether seeking consolation for personal loss, or out of a sense of political commitment, or often from both. Something of value must be saved from the wreck of so many lives, if only a lesson that the disaster of war must not occur again.

The commemorative movement was an activist one, not merely an expression of feeling, no matter how important feelings might have been in its conduct. It was concerned with either creating or preserving change. Participants might hold that the world had been changed by war and its suffering, and that the changes must subsequently be preserved, or that the war had shown how radically the world needed changing, and that change must now be brought to fruition. Even those who believed that the war had, or should have, restored an older Britain and revived lost values saw this as a change in social and moral life, the reversal of a process of decline. Many who commemorated the dead may not have had activist intentions; but the movement itself acquired an activist character through its public commitment to the pursuit of moral and political issues, and to the reformation of values.

The community of the nation was often alluded to in war commemoration; but was commemoration therefore a specifically nationalist activity? Writers on nationalism have given what might be called broad and narrow definitions of it. The broad view, taken by Elie Kedourie, is that the conception of nations as natural divisions of humanity, and the consequent belief that national groups should be self-governing, have become the basic assumptions of most Western political attitudes.[69] Hence, modern political activity tends to pursue implicitly nationalist goals, even when it does not advertise its nationalist credentials. However, Kenneth Minogue adopts a narrower definition, distinguishing strongly between patriotism and nationalism as between attachment to an actual and a fantasy community.[70] Anthony Smith also takes the narrow view, reserving the term nationalism for the programme of a political movement, and contrasting it with national sentiment, which he describes as a set of feelings including 'devotion to one's nation and advocacy of its interests'.[71] Valuing the nation as a unit of social solidarity does not, as Minogue and Smith see it, constitute nationalism. Furthermore, patriotism or national sentiment may amount only to awareness that one is a member of a national community, and that this community has benefits to offer. It need not automatically take precedence over other solidarities.

Eric Hobsbawm offers a useful way of judging the nationalist content of commemoration when he says that, for a nationalist, duty to one's nation 'overrides all other public obligations, and in extreme cases (such as war) all other obligations of whatever kind'.[72] British war commemoration did not, in general, assert any such thing. It insisted that the nation as a whole should recognise an obligation to the dead and emulate their moral achievements. It thus represented the nation as subject to certain moral values and imperatives; but the representation did not elevate the nation, its culture, or the particular qualities of its people, as themselves the source of value, and the ultimate object of loyalty.

Elsewhere, however, the case may have been different. George Mosse has concluded that 'the civic religion of nationalism'[73] was the pervasive theme of remembrance of the war dead, generalising to a large extent from the German experience. National commemorative practices were, in fact, less homogeneous than he suggests, but it seems true that the plurality of voices characteristic of British war commemoration only rarely appeared in Germany. Two studies of local memorials in Germany give some insight into this national difference. Martin Bach has noticed that large towns often had difficulty erecting a memorial to the war dead, a fact which he traces to political discontinuity and confusion in the urban politics of the Weimar republic. It was hard either to raise money or to obtain the necessary unanimity about what should be done. Significantly, he suggests that the success-rate in erecting memorials increased after the Nazis took power, a development which did a great deal to discourage disagreement.[74]

Gerhard Armanski, in a similar study, describes two localities in which memorial projects were dominated by civic leaders and ex-service organisations, without general participation from other sections of society. At Marbach, the Gemeinderat resolved in 1920 to erect a monument, and it set up a committee dominated by one veterans' association. In 1925, a local newspaper maintained that 80 per cent of front-fighters and bereaved in the town were against a monumental memorial, and a public meeting in support of one attracted only nine people. The project was abandoned until 1934, when the Nazi local authority took it in hand. At Windsbach, too, civic leaders and functionaries ran the memorial project without the participation even of representatives of the bereaved.[75] It appears that many German memorials of this period were erected by local movements which did not cater for the wide range of social groups typically involved in a British project, and hence did not need to allow for a plurality of attitudes to the war. If this was true, then they could be less equivocal in their commitment to a particular political doctrine, and might frequently have been dominated by nationalists.

It is true, as Mosse says, that 'the cult of the dead was linked to the self-representation of the nation';[76] but the link might be programmatically nationalist or it might not. It was hardly nationalist to say, as many did in Britain, that the nation should emulate its dead by defending freedom and justice; although the defence of freedom and justice might, in some circumstances, be used as the excuse for a nationalist crusade. Nationalism was no more than one possible form of national self-representation. The differences amongst them depended on the institutions and political practices of the societies in which commemoration took place. Thus, in a political culture which promoted the ideal of national distinctiveness and rivalry with other nations more aggressively, the case might very well be different from what we have observed in Britain, especially if the organisation of commemorative acts was less inclusive. In Britain, too, commemoration of the war dead was an opportunity for nationalists to rally, and the rhetoric of obligation was available for them to use; but the same was true for those without nationalist aspirations, and for those who consciously rejected nationalism.

In the wider sense of valuing cultural distinctiveness, attachment to one's community and place of origin, we might see commemoration as having a more direct and unambiguous connection with patriotism or consciousness of national identity. British commemorative practices were, and were seen to be, distinctively British; not surprisingly, as they were founded on a well-defined tradition, not only of imagery, but also of organisation. *The Times* saw the Great Silence as a particularly British commemorative idiom.[77] The Duke of Atholl intended the Scottish National War Memorial to be a source of pride in Scottish national distinctiveness, and hoped it would prevent Scotland's historic part in the war from being swallowed up in that of Britain as a whole.[78] Moreover, the idea of national distinctiveness was quite compatible with the ideals of international reconciliation and peace which many participants in commemoration regarded as its most important political purpose.

The extent to which commemoration developed from existing traditions, and then became embedded in British culture, may have helped to reinforce some people's attachment to national institutions, language, landscape, and other aspects of that culture by finding in some or all of them sources of meaning for loss; though that need not have promoted a sense of national rather than any other form of belonging. Commemoration derived the value it attributed to death at least as much from a local sense of place and community as from the nation, and much of the activism associated with it appealed to the wider international community represented by the League of Nations. The most that can be said is that it promoted a sense of belonging to a collectivity of some kind, and that this belonging entailed obligations to the others who also belonged; but people gave content to these broad propositions in various ways.

Notes to Chapter 9

1. Quoted in R. Coppin, 'Remembrance Sunday', *Theology*, vol. 68, no. 545 (1965), p. 525.

2. Public Record Office, HO45/11557/20, Observation of Armistice Day (Nov. 11th) Committee, Report of meeting, 12 Oct. 1921, pp. 1–2, and Recommendations of Committee, 13 Oct. 1921, p. 2.

3. A. M. Gregory, *Silence of Memory: Armistice Day 1919–1946*, Oxford, 1994, pp. 65–80.

4. *The Times*, 21, 22, 25 and 26 Oct. 1925.
5. Public Record Office, CAB 23/11, Minutes, p. 7, 4 July 1919.
6. V. Brittain, *Chronicle of Youth: Vera Brittain's War Diary, 1913–1917*, ed. A. Bishop, London, 1981, p. 198, entry for 16 May 1915.
7. Quoted in S. Weintraub, *A Stillness Heard Round the World, The End of the Great War: November 1918*, Oxford, 1985, p. 262.
8. See Chapter 1.
9. A. Wiener, I. Gerber, D. Battin and A. M. Arkin, 'The Process and Phenomenology of Bereavement', in B. Schoenberg, I. Gerber, A. Wiener, A. H. Kutscher, D. Peretz and A. C. Carr, *Bereavement: Its Psychosocial Aspects*, New York, 1975, pp. 53–65; R. Lamerton, *Care of the Dying*, Harmondsworth, 1980.
10. *Liverpool Post and Mercury*, 10 Jan. 1933.
11. J. M. Winter, *Sites of Memory, Sites of Mourning: The Great War in European Cultural History*, Cambridge, 1995, p. 115.
12. Gregory, *The Silence of Memory*, p. 23.
13. C. Moriarty, 'The Absent Dead and Figurative First World War Memorials', *Transactions of the Ancient Monuments Society*, vol. 39 (1995), p. 12.
14. See Chapter 6.
15. See A. Goodman, *The Street Memorials of Saint Albans Abbey Parish*, St Albans, 1987, especially p. 22.
16. See chapter 2.
17. G. Gorer, *Death, Grief and Mourning in Contemporary Britain*, London, 1965, p. 72 and 77–8.
18. D. Cannadine, 'War, Death, Grief and Mourning in Modern Britain', in J. Whaley (ed.), *Mirrors of Mortality: Studies in the Social History of Death*, London, 1981, pp. 190–3.
19. Gregory, *The Silence of Memory*, p. 165.
20. A. C. Carr, 'Bereavement as a Relative Experience', in Schoenberg *et al.*, *Bereavement*, 1975, p. 7; Lamerton, *Care of the Dying*, p. 189.
21. Lamerton, *Care of the Dying*, p. 183.
22. H. Macmillan, *Winds of Change 1914–1939*, London, 1968, p. 98, quoted in Cannadine, 'War, Death, Grief and Mourning', p. 212.
23. E. Leed, *No Man's Land: Combat and Identity in World War I*, Cambridge, 1979, p. 212.
24. G. Wootton, *The Official History of the British Legion*, London, 1956, p. 305.
25. W. S. Churchill, *The World Crisis: The Aftermath*, London, 1929, pp. 454–5, quoted in Cannadine, 'War, Death, Grief and Mourning', p. 202.
26. *Daily Mirror*, 12 Nov. 1935.
27. W. Holtby, *South Riding: An English Landscape*, London 1988, pp. 70–1.
28. Quoted in A. Wilkinson, *The Church of England and the First World War*, London, 1978, p. 62.
29. Cannadine, 'War, Death, Grief and Mourning', pp. 191–3.
30. Accounts of these methods can be found in C. Hughes, 'The New Armies', in I. Beckett and K. Simpson, *A Nation in Arms: A Social History of the British Army in the First World War*, Manchester, 1985, p. 102, and in J. M. Osborne, *The Voluntary Recruiting Movement in Britain, 1914–1916*, New York, 1982, pp. 24–8.
31. Osborne, *The Voluntary Recruiting Movement*, pp. 59 and 64–72.

32. *Hackney and Stoke Newington Recorder*, 12 Nov. 1920.
33. *British Legion Journal*, vol. 9, no. 5, Nov. 1929, p. 115.
34. *Daily Mail*, 11 Nov. 1930.
35. Hackney, SN/W/1/6, letter 15 July 1923. There is a similar letter from Mrs Trewinnard in the minute book SN/W/1/1, dated 19 Nov. 1924. She suggested a special tablet for the names of those who died after 1918.
36. See Chapter 3.
37. See Chapter 7.
38. Leed, *No Man's Land*, p. 181. See also T. Bogacz, 'War Neurosis and Cultural Change in England, 1914–1922: The Work of the War Office Committee of Enquiry into "Shell Shock"', *Journal of Contemporary History*, vol. 24, no. 2 (1989), pp. 227–56.
39. C. Carrington, *Soldier from the Wars Returning*, London 1964, p. 258.
40. Ibid., p. 252.
41. *British Legion Journal*, vol. 2, no. 12, June 1923, p. 298.
42. Ibid., vol. 12, no. 6, Dec. 1932, pp. 196–7.
43. *The Times*, 16 Nov. 1920.
44. *Enfield Gazette*, 4 Nov. 1921.
45. *Manchester Evening News*, 12 July 1924.
46. Carlisle, Ca/C10/12/1, circular dated Oct. 1919.
47. *Parliamentary Debates*, fifth series, vol. 122, p. 1201, 9 Dec. 1919.
48. Westminster City Council, Minutes, 26 Apr. 1923, 17 May 1923, 11 Oct 1923, 26 June 1924.
49. *The Times*, 11 Nov. 1920.
50. *Yorkshire Observer*, 3 July 1922.
51. Ibid.
52. *Bradford Daily Telegraph*, 31 July 1922.
53. *Stockport Advertiser*, 10 Dec. 1920.
54. *Yorkshire Evening Post*, 16 Oct. 1922.
55. Ibid., 23 Oct. 1922.
56. See Chapter 2.
57. Strathclyde, G4.1, Glasgow War Memorial, Minutes, 20 Apr. 1922. It is a great pity the design was not executed as intended, as the result would have been very striking. A number of German memorials, built and unbuilt, also exploited the idea of projection into rather than above the ground. They are discussed in J. Tietz, 'Monumente des Gedenkens', and W. Herzogenrath, 'Denkmäler wider das Vergessen', in R. Rother (ed.), *Die letzten Tage der Menschheit: Bilder des Ersten Weltkrieges*, Berlin, 1994, pp. 397–408, and 445–50.
58. C. ffoulkes, *Arms and the Tower*, London, 1939, pp. 143–4.
59. *Liverpool Post and Mercury*, 30 Jan. 1933.
60. H. V. Morton, *In Search of England*, London, 1929, p. 36.
61. *The Times*, 12 Nov. 1919.
62. *Daily Herald*, 12 Nov. 1936.
63. *The Times*, 30 Oct. 1933.
64. *Daily Mail*, 12 Nov. 1920.
65. *Daily Herald*, 12 Nov. 1924.
66. *The Times*, 12 Nov. 1920, supplement p. 3.
67. Powys, R/UD/LW/234, letter from A. G. Camp, 13 July 1922.

68. S. Hall, 'Variants of Liberalism', in J. Donald and S. Hall (eds), *Politics and Ideology*, Milton Keynes, 1985, p. 66.

69. E. Kedourie, *Nationalism*, London, 1966, p. 9.

70. K. R. Minogue, *Nationalism*, London, 1967, p. 23.

71. A. D. Smith, *Theories of Nationalism*, London, 1983, p. 168.

72. E. J. Hobsbawm, *Nations and Nationalism since 1780: Programme, Myth and Reality*, Cambridge, 1990, p. 9.

73. G. L. Mosse, *Fallen Soldiers: Reshaping the Memory of the First World War*, Oxford, 1990, p. 101.

74. M. Bach, *Studien zur Geschichte des deutschen Kriegerdenkmals in Westfalen und Lippe*, Frankfurt-am-Main, 1985, pp. 246 and 247.

75. G. Armanski, *"und wenn wir sterben müssen": Die politische Ästhetik von Kriegerdenkmälern*, Hamburg, 1989, 100–7, and 81–2.

76. Mosse, *Fallen Soldiers*, p. 105.

77. *The Times*, 16 Nov. 1920.

78. Scottish National War Memorial, Bundle 19, G. Swinton, 'Memorandum on a Scottish National War Museum, Home of Record and Monument', p. 2 (Atholl wrote to the *Scotsman* to this effect on 28 June 1917). To some extent, the expression of Celtic national aspirations in war commemoration was itself of more local than national significance. This is a complex issue, more to do with the uses of nationalist symbolism than with war commemoration, and cannot be explored here. For a study of Wales which is suggestive in this respect see A. Gaffney, '"Poppies on the Up Platform": Commemoration of the Great War in Wales', unpublished Ph.D. thesis, University College of Cardiff, 1996.

Conclusion

This book has presented the remembrance of the dead as a collective creative activity. It has considered the public not simply as consumers, but as the creators of culture, and culture not as something given, but something constantly produced by all who participated in it. The fundamental importance of war commemoration in the inter-war period lay precisely in its being such a socially comprehensive creative activity. The professional creative work of specialists was an essential part of it, but of greater significance was the effort put by all concerned into finding ways to understand the objects created. Although most memorials followed aesthetic and iconographical precedents, they were not left to speak for themselves in an established symbolic language. They were constantly given voices which spoke of their own time through the interpretations which were applied to them. As they were interpreted in a variety of different senses, no definitive meaning was established, and often clashing voices co-existed.

The symbolism of remembrance was, therefore, a very uncertain medium for conveying ethical and political ideas, and it was felt to be so by contemporaries. It was no longer possible to regard monuments as authoritative, because broadly agreed, bearers of particular meaning. One might connect this characteristic with the argument of Modris Eksteins that, in this period, the arts retreated from the role of public communication to become vehicles of private vision and individual assertion. Eksteins's idea is echoed by Tom Laqueur in his contention that memorials of the Great War evaded the task of giving moral or political meaning to death, which the memorials of former times had borne.[1] However, this view discounts the wealth of interpretation and critical exegesis which always surrounded such public symbols, and which remained deeply concerned with the rational communication of meaning. It would be truer to say that communication did not take place through the symbol itself, but through the confrontation between people and symbols, in which authoritative utterance gave way to debate. This did not necessarily reflect doubt or incomprehension amongst the public. Some individuals may have had doubts, but many held strong convictions which they expressed clearly in public, and it was on these expressions of conviction that the attribution of meaning to symbols was based.

Yet here also lay the strength of commemoration as a collective symbolic act. It was essentially inclusive, and it was recourse to the past which made it so. The form of organisation offered by the civic commemorative tradition made a virtue of the existence of differences amongst participants. Its organisation was founded on a forum in which differences were aired and a project negotiated, without participants' having to abandon strongly held views. All that was necessary was that they should share the overall aim of creating a public symbolic object of some sort. British civic commemoration valued the act of communal creation above the specific ideas to be expressed. It offered a basis for common action, not in a shared sense of the meaning of what was created, but in a shared desire to give meaning, via their interpretations of symbols, to the experiences which lay behind them. Continuity with past practices thus made collective expression possible; but continuity depended only in part on conformity to precedent. It also required re-interpretation of precedents – by revising standards of judgement, and talking about these revisions in order to make them familiar. There was nothing especially new about this, except, perhaps, its scale. The symbolic representation of the state and its relation to its subjects has probably never been free from arguments about the values it was supposed to embody. The history of artistic taste also shows continual re-definition of what was considered properly classical or properly Christian.

It is now widely accepted that commemorative symbols are subject to a variety of interpretations; but this has frequently been seen as a contest amongst different groups within a community to get their own preferred meaning accepted by the community at large, ultimately leading to the establishment of a single dominant form of understanding.[2] In the cases we have been studying, there clearly was active rivalry between opposed interpretations of commemorative symbols, but the final effect was not to enforce a dominant understanding. On the contrary, conflict between advocates of different interpretations served to highlight the characteristic and persistent differences between the groups who participated in commemorative acts. As a result of this variety of views, participants were offered many points of interest on which they might focus their attention, and this had the effect of emphasising the social and political inclusiveness of the communal celebration. It was by accepting the co-existence of a plurality of views that the community could be drawn into common action and share in the expressive and practical opportunities which commemoration offered. Thus the latitude which is apparent in the attribution of meaning to symbols played a key part in forming a commemorative movement which was diffuse in its aims and views, but shared a common sense of purpose and discipline.

The symbolism of remembrance was not so much a cognitive resource for a community, promoting common ways of seeing the world, as an instrument for creating desired forms of co-operative social relationship, in the absence of common values. While expressions of value were actively deployed to contradict each other, a fundamental unity of purpose was provided by the presence of controlling institutions. It was they who co-ordinated the constructive resources of participants, enforced rules which set the fundamental terms of participation, and defended the boundary between the sacred - embodied in rituals and memorial sites - and the secular business of interpretation.

Institutional control was of crucial importance to all who participated, and the rules which institutions set were, for the most part, accepted. Even for those with no ulterior motive beyond remembering and honouring the dead, the possibility of commemoration depended on the effective action of the organisations which promoted it. It was their power to create a special time or a special object for remembering the dead which sustained the assertion that they were special, and rallied public assent to it. Other participants acquiesced because they themselves had an interest in maintaining the commemorative consensus. The value of participation to them would be reduced if its value to others was reduced - either by excessive conflict, or by a reduction in its inclusiveness. The continuation of consensus required both tolerance of other people's positions and self-restraint in the expression of one's own. Where necessary, the rules could be imposed by force, although such cases were exceptional.

We can see, therefore, that the expressive possibilities of war commemoration were not shaped by a system of values encoded in commemorative symbolism, but by the nature of the institutions through which commemoration took place, and by the interests of participant groups, pursuing goals determined by their own sectional values. We cannot, therefore, regard representation as a system of power in its own right, with forms of social action as its consequences, as is sometimes argued.[3] The symbols through which war, and matters related to it, were represented relied for their own existence on the presence of power-bearing institutions through which they were created and manipulated. They did not so much prescribe a form of social discipline as provide an occasion on which certain forms of co-operation were put into practice.

I have not been able to treat any cases other than Britain in depth here. A systematic international comparison would throw a great deal more light on the way in which social institutions generate symbolic meanings, and on the practical effects of symbolic action. The issues raised in war commemoration might bear on many fields of civic and national life, and their focus varied according to differences of institutional context and political circumstances. In France, war commemoration may have played a novel part at the local level in the constitutional relations between Republic and Church, which have been such an important characteristic of French politics. Frequently, local secular authorities and clergy both participated in the organisations which erected French memorials. Disputes between the two sides could disrupt their work;[4] but the existence of joint organisations is itself suggestive.

In Britain and France, both popular and official thought stressed the ideal of averting future wars. Amongst the victors, this was something all could broadly accept. Even those with a nationalist or militarist outlook could agree that another war was more likely to disturb than to advance the causes they stood for. In Germany, it seems, in spite of widespread revulsion amongst veterans against belligerence, such agreement was not achieved. Richard Bessell[5] has discussed a range of ideological and psychological reasons for this. However, a detailed study of the forms of organisation behind public symbolic acts in Germany would be useful in explaining why a widespread feeling against war should have proved so ineffective politically. There may be a deeper cultural point at issue here. If Eksteins is right to see

Germany in the pre-war period as searching for new forms of culture and ethics, 'conceived not in terms of laws and finiteness but in terms of symbol, metaphor and myth',[6] it is worth asking whether symbolic action was not already rather different from its British counterpart. What forms of interpretation accompanied this increased recourse to symbolic expression? Did people readily commit themselves to explicit interpretations, or were symbols commonly used as rallying points for politically assertive public acts without articulate attachment to coherently conceived interests? Answers to these questions could suggest how far institutions of civil society possessed or lacked the capacity to produce a coherent sense of their own goals and values.

Commemoration of the dead was only one form of reflection on the war, and our sense of its meaning and function would be enhanced by a comparison with other forms of expression which I have only occasionally touched on. Political rhetoric is one obvious example; literature is another. The work of Paul Fussell and Samuel Hynes has tended to suggest that reflections on the war were polarised between a backward-looking view, unable to reach beyond the horizons of pre-war thought, and determined to idealise the aberrant experience, and a critical view which faced the awful facts, finally breaking with old attitudes. To take the latter view would have set the speaker or writer outside the framework of commemorative thought, with its tendency to sanctify and moralise, and would entail scepticism about the applicability of conventional expressions of value, no matter how they were interpreted. However, we ought not to be misled into thinking that there were necessarily two opposed mind-sets in reflection on the war: the critical, often ironic, and the pious.[7]

It may well be, as Fussell says, that soldiers cultivated an ironic view of their wartime situation in order to make it adequately expressible; but most of the literature which articulated this view was written several years later, with a well-established commemorative rhetoric and way of thinking as its background. Irony may have been a way of disengaging the self from what was unacceptable or unmanageable in experience; but it also disengaged one from what was being done in the social acts and relationships constituted through sacred, conventional and consensual symbolic acts. Were the two forms of expression in competition? How and when might speakers shift from one mode to the other, and what purposes might be served by doing so? Symbolic expression of the sort we have been considering here exists in symbiosis with other forms of thought and action, while retaining the distinct identity which gives it its particular use. It needs to be seen as one amongst a variety of possibilities in the repertoire of human communication, and also as one possible move, amongst others, in the conduct of social relationships and in the management of the institutions which constitute society.

Notes to Conclusion

1. M. Eksteins, *Rites of Spring: The Great War and the Modern Age*, London, 1989, especially pp. 43 and 219; T. W. Laqueur, 'Memory and Naming in the Great War', in J. R. Gillis (ed.), *Commemorations: The Politics of National Identity*, Princeton, 1994, p. 160.
2. See Introduction.
3. M. Poster, *Foucault, Marxism and History: Mode of Production versus Mode of Information*, Cambridge, 1984, p. 87.
4. J. Giroud and R. Michel, *Les Monuments aux Morts de la Vaucluse*, L'Isle sur Sorgue, 1991, p. 63; A. Prost, *Les Anciens Combattants et la Société Française*, Paris, 1977, p. 40.
5. R. Bessell, *Germany after the First World War*, Oxford, 1993, pp. 258–64.
6. Eksteins, *Rites of Spring*, p. 81.
7. Rosa Bracco has noted that Robert Graves could use both modes at different times: see R. M. Bracco, *Merchants of Hope: British Middlebrow Writers and the First World War*, Oxford, 1993, p. 7.

Bibliography

Archival Sources

Names in square brackets are those used as short titles in footnotes to the text.

Association of Northumberland Local History Societies
War Memorials Survey, WMST36.1.
Barnsley Archive [Barnsley]
Town Clerk's In Letters, File 35, Barnsley War Memorial.
Bethnal Green, Metropolitan Borough of
Minutes of Proceedings 1919.
Borthwick Institute of Historical Research, University of York
Atkinson Brierley Papers, Boxes 56, 104, 105, 108, and 109. (These papers were in the care of York City Archives when consulted, and full Borthwick references are not given.)
Cambridgeshire Record Office
R88/110, Burwell Parish Minutes.
Carlisle, City of
Proceedings of the Council and Committees, vol. XXXIII.
Clwyd Record Office, Hawarden [Clwyd]
P/45/1/379, Northop Church War Memorial Tablet.
Cumbria Record Office, Carlisle [Carlisle]
DX/5/59, Jackson Papers.
PR/102/81, Hayton War Memorial.
PR/5/186, Greystoke War Memorial Committee.
S/MB/Wo/1/3/863, Workington War Memorial, Papers.
Ca/C10/12/1, Carlisle Citizens League Minute Book No.2, 12 May 1915 - 23 Aug. 1923.
S/PC/38/43, Scaleby War Memorial Minute Book.
S/UD/M/1/2Z/6, Town's War Memorial Committee, Maryport.
Deptford, Metropolitan Borough of
Minutes of Proceedings, 1919 and 1921.
Durham County Record Office [Durham]
D/Br/E 45, Brancepeth Ecclesiastical Parish,
Correspondence and Papers Relating to Parish War Memorial.
D/Br/E 447 1-4, Brancepeth War Memorial Committee.

Enfield Archives
Edmonton United Services Club, Press Cuttings.
Gloucestershire Record Office [Gloucestershire]
P 348 VE 2/1, All Saints Viney Hill, Church Parochial Council.
Greater London Record Office
PC/CHA/3-5, London County Council War Charities Act Register, 788, Borough of Camberwell War Memorial.
Guildhall Library
20,374, James Budgett & Son, letters of appreciation for memorial tablet.
Hackney Archives Department [Hackney]
SN/W/1/1-25, Stoke Newington War Memorial Committee, Papers and Minutes.
Hampshire Record Office [Hampshire]
31 M 71/Z1, Steep War Memorial, Minutes of Meetings.
Hanley Public Library
S.I.850 A (6), Photograph, Stoke-on-Trent Cenotaph.
Harrogate Corporation
Minutes, 1920 and 1921.
Hull City Record Office [Hull]
City of Hull Great War Trust Scrapbook.
Imperial War Museum, Department of Printed Books
Box of Recruiting Leaflets.
Album of postcards, class 333.0.
Islington, Metropolitan Borough of
Minutes of Proceedings, 1918 and 1919.
Lambeth Palace Library
Davidson Papers, vol. 377.
Chronicle of Convocation, 1918.
Leeds City Libraries
LQ 940.465 L517, Leeds War Memorial: Cuttings and Papers.
Leeds University, Brotherton Library
Sadler Correspondence, Film 131, f.9.
Lincolnshire Archives Office [Lincolnshire]
SLUDC 11/6, Sleaford War Memorial Committee.
Scrivelsby with Dalderby par. 8/1, Parish Records.
National Library of Wales
Minor Deposit, 321 B, Llanbadern Fawr Parish War Memorial, Papers.
Minor Lists and Summaries 1052, Edward VII Welsh National Memorial Association.

Ms.102958, Solva Roads of Remembrance, Accounts.
Newcastle City Libraries
Press Cuttings.
Newcastle-upon-Tyne, City of
Proceedings of the Council, 1905.
Powys Archives [Powys]
R/UD/LW/234, Llandrindod Wells War Memorial.
Public Record Office
Cabinet Minutes, CAB 23.3, CAB 23.11, CAB 23.12, CAB 23.18.
Cabinet Papers, CAB 24.5, G202, Imperial War Memorial and Museum, Report of Lord Crawford's Committee; CAB 24.22: GT 1650 discussion paper by Sir Martin Conway; CAB 24.84, GT 7784, The Temporary Cenotaph in Whitehall; CAB 24.109, Memorandum on the Permanent Cenotaph.
HO 45/11557, file 392664, Observation of Armistice Day (Nov. 11th) Committee.
RAIL 1057/2868, London and North Western Railway, Papers Relating to the Unveiling of War Memorial, Euston.
RAIL 236/418/1 Great Northern Railway, War Memorial at King's Cross.
RAIL 258/447, Great Western Railway, Papers Relating to War Memorial at Paddington Station.
WORK 16/26 (8), War Shrine, Hyde Park (1918–1919).
WORK 20/30, Chilianwallah Monument, Chelsea Hospital.
WORK 20/139, Cenotaph, Erection of Permanent (1919-1932).
WORK 20/142, Guards Memorial, 1914–18 War (1919–1932).
Royal Artillery War Commemoration Fund [Royal Artillery]
Minutes.
Royal Society of British Sculptors
Minutes of Council, 1913–1917.
Scottish National War Memorial
Records, Bundles 1–47.
Sheffield Record Office [Sheffield]
CA 653 (1–19), War Memorial Sub-Committee.
Shropshire Record Office [Shropshire]
1919/1, Llanymynech War Memorial Minute Book.
Southwark Local Studies Library [Southwark]
Press Cuttings.

Stockport Archive Service [Stockport]
B/AA/4, Stockport War Memorial.
Strathclyde Regional Archives [Strathclyde]
G1/3/1, Lord Provost's File on the Establishment of War Memorials in Glasgow.
G4.1, Gladstone Memorial, Kelvin Memorial, Roberts Memorial and Glasgow War Memorial, Minutes.
Tower Hamlets Libraries [Tower Hamlets]
082.2, Memorials and Rolls of Honour, Poplar.
082.3, Memorials and Rolls of Honour, Bethnal Green.
LH 85/16, Photographs.
Tyne and Wear Archives Service [Tyne and Wear]
TWAS 52/80, Messrs Wood & Oakley, Letter Books, Jan. 1917 - Apr. 1924.
TWAS 142/17, Messrs Hedley, Order Book, 1900-1929.
University College of North Wales, Bangor [Bangor], Department of Manuscripts
Papers Relating to the North Wales Heroes' Memorial.
Wakefield Borough Council
Minutes, 1918.
Wakefield Library
Press Cuttings.
Westminster City Council
Minutes, 1923 and 1924.
West Yorkshire Archives, Bradford [Bradford]
BBC 1/57/25, City of Bradford, Special Committee re Peace Celebrations, 1919.
Bradford Corporation Finance and General Purposes Committee Minute Book 54.
BBC 1/56/4/6 Bradford Corporation Special Committees Minute Book No.4, 25 July 1919.
Wirral Archives Service [Wirral]
ZWO/16, Hoylake and West Kirby War Memorial Fund.

Contemporary Newspapers and Magazines

Architectural Review
Barnsley Chronicle
Birmingham Mail
Birmingham Post
Bradford Daily Telegraph

British Legion Journal
Builder
Carlisle Journal
Challenge
Church Family Newspaper
Church Times
Churchman's Family Magazine
City Press
Daily Herald
Daily Mail
Daily Mirror
Durham County Advertiser
East End News
East London Advertiser
Eastern Morning News
Enfield Gazette
Evening News
Finsbury Weekly News
Glasgow Herald
Graphic
Hackney and Kingsland Gazette
Hackney and Stoke Newington Recorder
Headway, The Journal of the League of Nations Union
Hoylake and West Kirby Advertiser
Illustrated London News
Islington Daily Gazette
Journal of the Royal Institute of British Architects
Keighley News
Kentish Mercury
Leeds Weekly Chronicle
Leicester Mercury
Lincolnshire Chronicle
Liverpool Echo
Liverpool Post and Mercury
London and North Western Railway Gazette
London County Council Staff Gazette
London Society Journal
Manchester Evening News
Manchester Guardian
Morning Post
Newcastle Evening Chronicle

News Chronicle
Palmers Green Gazette
Pembroke County Guardian
Progress (Lever Brothers)
Sheffield Mail
Shields Daily Gazette
Staffordshire Advertiser
Staffordshire Sentinel
Stockport Advertiser
The Times
Times Literary Supplement
Yorkshire Evening News
Yorkshire Evening Post
Yorkshire Herald
Yorkshire Observer
Yorkshire Post
Yorkshire Weekly Post

Published Works

Abercrombie, P., 'A Civic Society, an Outline of its Scope, Formation and Functions', *Town Planning Review*, vol. 8, no. 2 (1920), pp. 79-92.

—— 'The Place in General Education of Civic Survey and Town Planning', *Town Planning Review*, vol. 9, no. 2 (1921), pp. 105-10.

Able-Smith, B., *The Hospitals 1800–1948: A Study in Social Administration in England and Wales*, London, 1964.

Adshead, S., *Centres of Cities*, Burnley, 1918.

Aitken, W. F., 'Our War Memorials: 3 – In Town and Village', in J. A. Hammerton (ed.) *Wonderful Britain. Its Highways, Byways and Historic Places*, vol. 3, no. 24, London, 1928/29, pp. 1137–56.

Anderson, B., *Imagined Communities: Reflections on the Origin and Spread of Nationalism*, London, 1991.

Anderson, O., 'The Growth of Christian Militarism in mid-Victorian Britain', *English Historical Review*, vol. 86, (1971), pp. 46–72.

Armanski, G., *"und wenn wir sterben müssen": Die politische Ästhetik von Kriegerdenkmälern*, Hamburg, 1988.

Ashworth, T., *Trench Warfare 1914–1918: The Live and Let Live*

System, London, 1980.

Austin, J. L., *How To Do Things With Words*, Oxford, 1976.

Bach, M., *Studien zur Geschichte des deutschen Kriegerdenkmals in Westfalen und Lippe*, Frankfurt-am-Main, 1985.

Barman, C., 'Our War Memorials: 1 - The London Area', in J. A. Hammerton (ed.) *Wonderful Britain. Its Highways, Byways and Historic Places*, vol. 3, no. 22, London, 1928/29, pp. 1017-36.

Ben-Amos, A., 'The Sacred Centre of Power: Paris and Republican State Funerals', *Journal of Interdisciplinary History*, vol. 22, no. 1 (1991), pp. 27-48.

Benson, A. C., *Lest We Forget*, London, 1917.

Berger, U., '"Immer war die Plastik die Kunst nach dem Kriege": Zur Rolle der Bildhauerei bei der Kriegerdenkmalproduktion in der Zeit der Weimarer Republik', in R. Rother (ed.), *Die Letzten Tage der Menschheit: Bilder des Ersten Weltkrieges*, Berlin, 1994, pp. 423-34.

Bessell, R., *Germany after the First World War*, Oxford, 1993.

Birn, D. S., *The League of Nations Union*, Oxford, 1981.

Blomfield, R., *Memoirs of an Architect*, London, 1932.

Bodnar, J., *Remaking America: Public Memory, Commemoration, and Patriotism in the Twentieth Century*, Princeton, 1992.

Bogacz, T., 'War Neurosis and Cultural Change in England, 1914-1922: The Work of the War Office Committee of Enquiry into "Shell Shock"', *Journal of Contemporary History*, vol. 24, no. 2 (1989), pp. 227-56.

Boorman, D., *At the Going Down of the Sun: British First World War Memorials*, Dunnington Hall, 1988.

Borg, A., *War Memorials from Antiquity to the Present*, London, 1991.

Bracco, R. M., *Merchants of Hope: British Middlebrow Writers and the First World War*, Providence and Oxford, 1993.

Brittain, V., *Chronicle of Youth, Vera Brittain's War Diary, 1913-1917*, ed. A. Bishop, London, 1981.

Buitenhuis, P., *The Great War of Words: Literature as Propaganda 1914-1918 and After*, London, 1989.

Bushaway, B., 'Name Upon Name: The Great War and Remembrance', in R. Porter (ed.), *Myths of the English*, London, 1992, pp. 136-67.

Cannadine, D., 'War, Death, Grief and Mourning in Modern

Britain', in J. Whaley (ed.), *Mirrors of Mortality: Studies in the Social History of Death*, London, 1981, pp. 187–242.

—— 'The Context, Performance and Meaning of Ritual: The British Monarchy and the "Invention of Tradition", *c*. 1820–1977', in E. Hobsbawm and T. Ranger (eds) *The Invention of Tradition*, Cambridge, 1984, pp. 101–64.

Carr, A. C., 'Bereavement as a Relative Experience', in B. Schoenberg, I. Gerber, A. Wiener, A. H. Kutscher, D. Peretz and A. C. Carr, *Bereavement: Its Psychosocial Aspects*, New York, 1975, pp. 3–8.

Carrington, C., *Soldier from the Wars Returning*, London, 1964.

Central Committee for the Protection of Churches, *The Protection of Our English Churches: Report for 1923*, Oxford, 1923.

Churchill, W. S., *The World Crisis: The Aftermath*, London, 1929.

Clark, T. J., 'Preliminaries to a Possible Treatment of "Olympia" in 1865', *Screen*, vol. 21, no. 1 (1980), pp. 18–41.

—— 'A Note in Reply to Peter Wollen', *Screen*, vol. 21, no. 3 (1980), pp. 97–100.

Clarke, I. F., *Voices Prophesying War*, London, 1970.

Clutton-Brock, A., *On War Memorials*, London, 1917.

Colborne, J. and Brine, F., *Graves and Epitaphs of our Fallen Heroes in the Crimea and Scutari*, London, 1857.

Colley, L., 'The Apotheosis of George III', *Past and Present*, no. 102, (1984), pp. 94–129.

Collins, J., Barbican Art Gallery, *Eric Gill: Sculptures*, London, 1992.

Coppin, R., 'Remembrance Sunday', in *Theology*, vol. 68, no. 55 (1965), pp. 525–30.

Cox, J., *The English Churches in a Secular Society*, Oxford, 1982.

Crossing, W., *Old Stone Crosses of the Dartmoor Borders*, London, 1892.

Davis, S. G., *Parades and Power: Street Theatre in Nineteenth Century Philadelphia*, Berkeley and London, 1988.

Dyer, G., *The Missing of the Somme*, Harmondsworth, 1995.

Eksteins, M., *Rites of Spring: The Great War and the Modern Age*, London, 1989.

Englander, D., 'The National Union of Ex-Servicemen and the Labour Movement, 1918–1920', *History*, vol. 76, no. 246 (1991), pp. 24–42.

Epstein, J., 'Understanding the Cap of Liberty: Symbolic Practice and Social Conflict in Early Nineteenth-century England', *Past and Present*, no. 122, (1989), pp. 75–118.

ffoulkes, C., *Arms and the Tower*, London, 1939.

Fine Art Society, *Gilbert Ledward, RA, PRBS: Drawings for Sculpture, a Centenary Tribute*, London, 1988.

Fussell, P., *The Great War and Modern Memory*, Oxford, 1977.

Gaffin, J. and Thomas, D., *Caring and Sharing: The Centenary History of the Co-operative Women's Guild*, Manchester, 1983.

Gates, W. G. (ed.), *Portsmouth in the Great War*, Portsmouth, 1919.

Geertz, C., 'Ethos, World View, and the Analysis of Sacred Symbols', in Geertz, *The Interpretation of Cultures, Selected Essays*, New York, 1973, pp. 126–41.

—— 'Centers, Kings and Charisma', in J. Ben-David and T. Nichols Clark (eds), *Culture and its Creators, Essays in Honour of Edward Shils*, London, 1977, pp. 150–71.

Gibbs, P., *Realities of War*, London, 1920.

—— *Ten Years After: A Reminder*, London, 1924.

Gilbert, M., *The Roots of Appeasement*, London, 1966.

Giroud, J. and Michel, R., *Les Monuments aux Morts de la Vaucluse*, L'Isle sur Sorgue, 1991.

Glaves-Smith, J., 'The Primitive, Objectivity and Modernity: Some Issues in British Sculpture in the 1920s', in S. Nairne and N. Serota (eds), *British Sculpture in the Twentieth Century*, London, 1981, pp. 72–81.

—— 'Realism and Propaganda in the Work of Charles Sargeant Jagger and Their Relationship to Artistic Tradition', in A. Compton (ed.), *Charles Sargeant Jagger: War and Peace Sculpture*, London, 1985, pp. 51–78.

Goodman, A., *The Street Memorials of Saint Albans Abbey Parish*, St Albans, 1987.

Gorer, G., *Death, Grief and Mourning in Contemporary Britain*, London, 1965.

Greenberg, A., 'Lutyens' Cenotaph', *Journal of the Society of Architectural Historians*, vol. 48 (1989), pp. 5–23.

Gregory, A. M., *The Silence of Memory: Armistice Day 1919–1946*, Oxford, 1994.

Gruber, E., '". . . death is built into life." War Memorials and War Monuments in the Weimar Republic', *Daidalos*, no. 49 (1993), pp. 78–81.

Guy, J., *The British Avant-Garde: The Theory and Politics of Tradition*, London, 1991.

Halévy, E., *Halévy's History of the English People in the Nineteenth Century, Vol. 5: Imperialism and the Rise of Labour (1895–1905)*, London, 1961.

Hall, S., 'Variants of Liberalism', in J. Donald and S. Hall (eds), *Politics and Ideology*, Milton Keynes, 1985, pp. 34–69.

Hay, I., *Their Name Liveth: the Scottish National War Memorial*, London, 1931.

Hennock, E. P., *Fit and Proper Persons: Ideal and Reality in Nineteenth Century Local Government*, London, 1973.

Herbert, A. P., *The Secret Battle*, London, 1928.

Herzogenrath, W., 'Denkmäler wider das Vergessen', in R. Rother (ed.), *Die letzten Tage der Menschheit: Bilder des Ersten Weltkrieges*, Berlin, 1994, pp. 445–50.

Higgonet, M., Jensen, J., Michel, S., and Weitz, C. (eds), *Behind the Lines: Gender and the Two World Wars*, New Haven., 1987

Hobsbawm, E. J., *Nations and Nationalism since 1780: Programme, Myth and Reality*, Cambridge, 1990.

Holtby, W., *South Riding: An English Landscape*, London, 1988.

Homberger, E., 'The Story of the Cenotaph', *Times Literary Supplement*, 12 Nov. 1976, pp. 1429–30.

Horn, P., *Rural Life in England in the First World War*, New York, 1984.

Hughes, C., 'The New Armies', in I. Beckett and K. Simpson (eds), *A Nation in Arms: A Social History of the British Army in the First World War*, Manchester, 1985, pp. 98–125.

Hunt, L., *Politics, Culture and Class in the French Revolution*, London, 1984.

Hussey, C., *The Life of Sir Edwin Lutyens*, London, 1950.

Hynes, S., *A War Imagined. The First World War and English Culture*, London, 1990.

Inglis, F. C., *The Scottish National War Memorial*, Edinburgh, 1932.

Inglis, K. S., 'The Homecoming: The War Memorial Movement in Cambridge, England', *Journal of Contemporary History*, vol. 27, no. 4 (1992), pp. 583–605.

—— 'Entombing Unknown Soldiers: From London and Paris to Baghdad', *History and Memory*, no. 5 (1993), pp. 7–31.

—— and Phillips, J., 'War Memorials in Australia and New

Zealand: A Comparative Survey', in J. Rickard and P. Spearritt (eds), *Packaging the Past? Public Histories*, Melbourne, 1991 (*Australian Historical Studies*, special issue, vol. 24, no. 96), pp. 171-91.

Jack, G., *War Shrines*, Burnley, 1918.

Jones, B. and Howell, B., *Popular Arts of the First World War*, London, 1972.

Kedourie, E., *Nationalism*, London, 1966.

Keith-Lucas, B., *The English Local Government Franchise*, Oxford, 1952.

Kelly's Directory of Sheffield and Rotherham, London, 1928.

Kent, G. R., 'Sadler, Gill and the Money Changers', in University Gallery, Leeds, *Michael Sadler*, Leeds, 1989, pp. 34–8.

Kertzer, D. I., *Ritual, Politics and Power*, New Haven and London, 1988.

King, A., 'Acts and Monuments: National Celebrations in Britain from the Napoleonic to the Great War', in A. O'Day (ed.), *Government and Institutions in the Post-1832 United Kingdom*, Studies in British History, vol. 34, Lewiston and Lampeter, 1995, pp. 237–68.

Kyba, P., *Covenants without the Sword: Public Opinion and British Defence Policy 1931–1935*, Waterloo, Ontario, 1983.

Laffin, J. (ed.), *Letters from the Front: 1914–1918*, London, 1973.

Lamerton, R., *Care of the Dying*, Harmondsworth, 1980.

Laqueur, T. W., 'Memory and Naming in the Great War', in J. R. Gillis, *Commemorations: The Politics of National Identity*, Princeton, 1994, pp. 150–67.

Leed, E., *No Man's Land: Combat and Identity in World War I*, Cambridge, 1979.

Lincolnshire Incorporated Chamber of Commerce, *Annual Report*, 1915.

Lloyd, D. W., *Battlefield Tourism: Pilgrimage and the Commemoration of the Great War in Britain, Australia and Canada, 1919–1939*, Oxford, 1998.

Longford, E., *Victoria R.I.*, London, 1964.

Longworth, P., *The Unending Vigil: A History of the Commonwealth War Graves Commission 1917–1984*, London, 1985.

McIntyre, C., *Monuments of War: How to Read a War Memorial*, London, 1990.

Maclean, F. J. 'Our War Memorials: 2 - The Great Cities and Some Others', in J. A. Hammerton, (ed.), *Wonderful Britain. Its Highways, Byways and Historic Places*, vol. 3, no. 23, London, 1928/29, pp. 1083–1102.

Macmillan, H., *Winds of Change 1914–1939*, London, 1968.

Marrin, A., *The Last Crusade: The Church of England in the First World War*, Durham, North Carolina, 1974.

Mawson, T. H., *An Imperial Obligation*, London, 1917.

Middlemas, K. and Barnes, J., *Baldwin*, London, 1969.

Minogue, K. R., *Nationalism*, London, 1967.

Mitford, B. R., *Westwell, (Nr. Burford), Oxfordshire. A Short History of the Prehistoric Henge, Church, Manor and Village, BC 1700?–AD 1951. Largely compiled from the researches made in 1928–9 by the late General Bertram Revely Mitford, CB, CMG, DSO*, no place, 1952.

Moriarty, C., 'The Absent Dead and Figurative First World War Memorials', *Transactions of the Ancient Monuments Society*, vol. 39 (1995), pp. 8–40.

Morton, H. V., *In Search of England*, London, 1929.

Mosse, G. L., *Fallen Soldiers: Reshaping the Memory of the First World War*, Oxford, 1990.

Osborne, J. M., *The Voluntary Recruiting Movement in Britain, 1914–1916*, New York, 1982.

Parliamentary Debates, first series, vols. 21 and 37, 1815 and 1818.

——, third series, vol. 309, 1886.

——, fifth series, vol. 244, 1919.

Parliamentary Papers, *Reports from Commissioners*, 1921, vol. 6, Cmd.1335, Voluntary Hospitals Committee, Final Report, 13 Mar. 1921.

Penny, N., 'English Sculpture and the First World War', *Oxford Art Journal*, vol. 4, no. 2 (1981), pp. 36–42.

—— '"Amor Publicus Posuit": Monuments for the People and of the People', *Burlington Magazine*, vol. 109, no. 1017, Dec. 1987, pp. 793–800.

Pickering, P. A., 'Class Without Words: Symbolic Communication in the Chartist Movement', *Past and Present*, no. 112 (1986), pp. 144–62.

Pomeroy, L., 'The Making of a War Memorial', *Town Planning Review*, vol. 9, no. 4 (1921), pp. 213–15.

Pope, A., *Old Stone Crosses of Dorset*, London, 1906.

Poster, M., *Foucault, Marxism and History: Mode of Production versus Mode of Information*, Cambridge, 1984.

Price, R., *An Imperial War and the British Working Class, Working Class Reactions to the Boer War, 1899–1902*, London, 1972.

Prost, A., *Les Anciens Combattants et la Société Française*, Paris, 1977.

Quigley, H., *Passchendaele and the Somme: A Diary of 1917*, London, 1928.

Quinn, M., *The Swastika: Constructing the Symbol*, London, 1994.

Richardson, W., *History of the Parish of Wallsend*, Newcastle-upon-Tyne, 1923.

Rimmer, A., *Ancient Stone Crosses of England*, London, 1875.

Royal Academy of Art, *Annual Report*, 1918.

Royal Artillery War Commemoration Fund and Royal Artillery Association, *Report of the RA War Commemoration Fund and the Royal Artillery Association*, 1920.

Royal Society of British Sculptors, *Annual Report of Council and Accounts*, 1920 and 1921.

Ryan, M., 'The American Parade: Representations of the Nineteenth-century Social Order', in L. Hunt (ed.), *The New Cultural History*, London, 1989, pp. 131–53.

Sillars, S., *Art and Survival in First World War Britain*, London, 1982.

Silver, K., *Esprit de Corps: The Art of the Parisian Avant-garde and the First World War*, Princeton, 1989.

Smith, A. D., *Theories of Nationalism*, London, 1983.

Sperber, D., *Rethinking Symbolism*, Cambridge, 1975.

Summers, A., 'Militarism in Britain before the Great War', *History Workshop*, no. 2 (1976), pp. 104–23.

Swinton, G., 'Castles in the Air at Charing Cross', *Nineteenth Century and After*, vol. 80, Nov. 1916, pp. 966–80.

Tietz, J., 'Monumente des Gedenkens', in R. Rother (ed.), *Die letzten Tage der Menschheit: Bilder des Ersten Weltkrieges*, Berlin, 1994, pp. 397–408.

Trevelyan, G. M., *The Life of John Bright*, London, 1925.

Turner, E. S., *Dear Old Blighty*, London, 1980.

Valance, A., *Old Crosses and Lych Gates*, London, 1920.

Ward, S. R., 'Intelligence Surveillance of British Ex-Servicemen', *Historical Journal*, vol. 16, no. 1 (1973), pp. 178–88.

Warren, E., *War Memorials*, London, 1919.

Wayside Cross Society, *Wayside Crosses*, London, 1917.

Weintraub, S., *A Stillness Heard Round the World, The End of the Great War: November 1918*, Oxford, 1985.

White, E. M., 'The Purpose of Civics, and How it is Served in Recent English Text-Books', *Sociological Review*, vol. 15 (1923), pp. 206–7.

Wiener, A., Gerber, I., Battin, D., and Arkin, A. M., 'The Process and Phenomenology of Bereavement', in B. Schoenberg, I. Gerber, A. Wiener, A. H. Kutscher, D. Peretz, and A. C. Carr, *Bereavement: Its Psychosocial Aspects*, New York, 1975, pp. 53–65.

Wilkinson, A., *The Church of England and the First World War*, London, 1978.

Willemen, P., 'Notes on Subjectivity – On Reading Edward Branigan's "Subjectivity Under Siege"', *Screen*, vol. 19, no. 1 (1978), pp. 41–69.

Wilson, T., *The Myriad Faces of War: Britain and the Great War 1914–1918*, Cambridge, 1986.

Winter, D., *Death's Men: Soldiers of the Great War*, London, 1978.

Winter, J. M., *Sites of Memory, Sites of Mourning: The Great War in European Cultural History*, Cambridge, 1995.

Wootton, G., *The Official History of the British Legion*, London, 1956.

Yarrington, A., *The Commemoration of the Hero, 1800–1864, Monuments to the British Victors of the Napoleonic Wars*, London, 1988.

Unpublished Theses and Dissertations

Bell, G., '"Monuments to the Fallen": Scottish War Memorials of the Great War', Ph.D. thesis, University of Strathclyde, 1993.

Carus C., 'Walter Henry Brierley, 1862–1926, York Architect', Dissertation for Diploma in Conservation Studies, University of York, 1973.

Connelly, M., 'The Commemoration of the Great War in the City and East London', Ph.D. thesis, University of London, 1995.

Gaffney, A., '"Poppies on the Up Platform": Commemoration of the Great War in Wales', Ph.D. thesis, University College of Cardiff, 1996.

King, A., 'Urban Improvement and Public Pressure: The Civic Society Movement *c.*1902–1930', Dissertation for M.Sc. in History of Modern Architecture, University College London, 1987.

Moriarty, C., 'Narrative and the Absent Body: The Mechanics of Meaning in First World War Memorials', D.Phil. thesis, University of Sussex, 1995.

Index